AF564437

Corporate Accounting
Theory and Practice

Corporate Accounting
Theory and Practice

Joseph King

Corporate Accounting: Theory and Practice

ISBN 978-93-5111-444-4

Published in 2014 in India by

RANDOM PUBLICATIONS

4376-A/4B, Gali Murari Lal, Ansari Road
New Delhi-110 002
Phone : +91-11-43580356, +91-11-23289044
e-mail: randomexports@gmail.com, sales@randompublications.com, info@randompublications.com

Reprinted 2023

Type Setting by: Friends Media, Delhi-110089
Digitally Printed at: Replika Press Pvt. Ltd.

Preface

Corporate Accounting is comprised of two operating units including General Accounting and Accounts Payable, which service the campus, Office of the President (UCOP) and UC Merced in a variety of ways. The General Accounting department is responsible for maintaining the financial book of records for UCLA, UCOP and UCM, and supporting the financial systems. General Accounting is also responsible for protecting the University's financial assets, as well as preparing financial reports for UCLA. This includes maintaining the integrity of the general ledger and the data input from subsidiary systems, maintenance of the accounting structure including the establishment of account numbers, fund numbers under GA's control and object codes. The staff performs fund management procedures for general funds, gift, special state appropriations, plant, endowment, auxiliary, income producing and agency funds. Additional responsibilities include reconciliation and auditing of cash deposits and bank accounts, preparation of state claims, state sales and use tax filings, and the training for University accounting and general ledger applications.

Corporate Finance professionals manage an organization's money, including forecasting where it will come from, knowing where it is, and making recommendations for spending to ensure the greatest return. Activities may involve poring over spreadsheets detailing cash flow, profitability, and expenses, looking for ways to free up capital, increase profitability, and decrease expenses. Within corporations, any department wishing to make a large expenditure must typically run it by the Finance department to ensure funding. Opportunities for career progression can be in Treasury, Financial Planning and Analysis, Financial Reporting, Operations Accounting, etc. Day-to-day operations. Balance the books, track expenses and revenue, execute payroll, and pay the bills. Compile all the financial data needed to issue a company's financial statements in accordance with government regulations. General accountants are responsible for producing all of the financial records a corporation uses to track its progress internally and to meet government regulations. Such workers also gather all the information needed to compute a company's balance sheet, profit and loss statements, and income statements. They also track the corporate budget, cash flow, and pay all the bills. Usually, your first job in general accounting will be in accounts payable or accounts receivable. Success in accounting might lead you to a position as a controller, overseeing a larger group, aggregating information, or working on portions of the corporate budget.

The book will be of use to the students, researchers and general readers of this subject.

I thank all members of my team who have helped in the preparation of the book. My special thanks go to "Random Publications" who have published the book.

—Joseph King

Contents

1

Cost Accounting and the Generally Accepted Accounting Principles

The main purpose of financial accounting is to provide investors (such as shareholders) or creditors (e.g. banks) information about the company and the performance of the administration.

The financial information prepared for this purpose is governed by the Generally Accepted Accounting Principles (GAAP), which provide consistency in the accountancy data used for purposes of reporting from a company to another.

This means that the information of cost accounting used to calculate the cost of goods sold, inventory valuation, accounting and other financial information used for external reports should be prepared in accordance with GAAP.

In contrast to the cost information for financial reporting to shareholders, the cost information for managerial use (that is, between the organization) need not to agree with the PGCA.

The administration is free to set their own definitions for cost information. In fact, the accountancy data used for external reporting is most often inappropriate for making managerial decisions.

For example, management decisions deal with the future, then the future estimated costs have more value in making decisions than historical cost or current that are reported externally. Unless otherwise provided contrary, we assume that the cost information is developed for internal use by managers and do not have to agree with the PGCA.

This does not mean that there is a "correct" or "incorrect" of accounting costs. This means that the best or correct accounting of costs is through the method that provides relevant information for decision makers so that he or she makes the best decision.

Clients of Cost Accounting

Of all the participants in a business to whom the administration must consider, the most important is *the customer*. Without customers, the organization loses its ability and reason to exist; customers provide the approach to the organization. The cost information itself is a product with its own customers. Customers are managers. At the level of production, where products are assembled or services are performed, the information is needed to control and improve operations. This information is provided and is frequently used to monitor the efficiency of the activities performed. For example, if the average rate of defects is 1% in a manufacturing process and the information of cost accounting system indicates a default rate of 2% on the previous day, employees of production must use this information to identify what is causing the defect rate to increase and correct the problem.

In an average level of management, where managers supervise the work and decisions of operation, cost information is used to identify problems by seeing if some aspects of the operation are different from what was expected. At the executive level, the financial information is used to assess the overall performance of the company. This information is strategic in nature and is typically provided monthly, by quarter, or annually. The cost accountants must work with users (or clients) of the cost accounting information to provide the best possible information for management purposes.

The most serious problems with accounting systems occur when managers use accounting information that was developed for external reporting for decision-making. Decision-making requires information commonly different than that provided to shareholders in the financial statements. It is important that companies understand that the various uses of the accountancy data require different types of accounting information.

Cost Accounting and Ethics

The design of costing systems is ultimately about the allowance of costs to various activities, products, projects and corporate units, and people. The manner in which this is done affects prices, reimbursement and payment. As some already know, based on events, the cost accounting systems design has the potential to be misused and fraud to customers, employees or shareholders. As user or preparer of the cost information, you need to be aware of what it implies how the information is used. And most important, you need to be aware of when the system has the potential to be abused.

Uses of Cost Data

The cost information is used for two purposes in most organizations: 1) the cost accounting systems provide information to evaluate the performance of an organizational unit or his manager, and 2) also provide the means for estimating the unit cost of products or services that the organization can manufacture or provide to others.

a. *Performance measurement.* This measurement can be done by comparing current costs with those who were expected - *or standard costs budgeted cost* - to the degree of knowing which of them have been controlled. Deviations of expected with the current *-variances -* can be identified, evaluated and discussed by managers.

b. *Cost of goods and services.* In manufacturing companies, the costs of goods must be measured to determine the cost of items transferred from work in process inventory to finished products. To meet the demands for information, a cost system should measure all the costs of manufacturing process and allocate a portion of those costs to each unit of output. The costs to obtain, maintain and manage the manufacturing plant or building should be added to the cost of material and productive work that requires each unit. The first are called indirect costs and the two last are called direct costs.

c. *Profit analysis:* Information in costs is essential to analyse the profits obtained from a product or product line. The information on the cost of a product enables managers to assess the contribution margin - *the difference between the price and variable costs* - and the gross margin - *the difference between the price and the total cost of the product.*

d. *Product mix:* For the companies that offer more than one product or service the cost information is key to handle the mix of products or services offered to customers. With information on cost-profit, a manager can lead the effort in sales and advertising for products that generate greater value. The products that do not create any profit can be removed, have a price reassignation, or tied up with products that have greater utility.

e. *Price assignation:* Regardless of where prices are determined by the forces of market demand, product differentiation and advertising offer to many managers some sort of idea to assign prices to products or services. The costs of products and trends commonly offer signals to managers that prices should be changed. An example could be the change in the cost of a material or critical component which can give a signal to reassess the price of a product or service.

f. *Cost of service:* Many products require the seller to provide additional services to customers. In such cases, the information about the cost of service is so important for managers as the cost of production. The same for companies that offer services only, unless the cost of service is measured, there is no way to know whether providing the service is profitable or not, or whether changes in prices or advertising are needed.

Looked from another angle, the uses that the administration of a company can give to the costs can be grouped into 4 categories, specified below:

Cost of getting costs	It provides reports on profits and valuates the inventory.
Cost of planning	Set goals and select roads economic-financial, leading the company to its achievement, from where you are.
Cost of controlling	Allows know if the targets set are being reached and in turn, serves as a basis for taking corrective actions.
Cost of decision making	It provides information to select the best alternative.

The Cost of Anything Depends on the Purpose to Determine the Cost.

Cost of Getting Costs

As mentioned before, "cost of getting costs " means to provide reports on costs for measuring profits and valuate inventory.

Ilustration:

Cost of Planning

The "cost of planning" are used to define objectives and select roads economic-financial, leading the company to its achievement, from where you are.

Illustration:

PLANNING

DECIDE TODAY WHAT SHOULD BE DONE IN THE FUTURE

What?

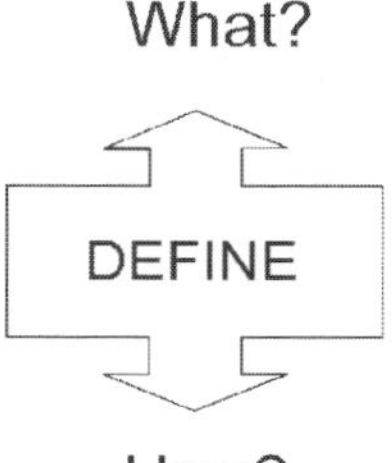

How?

General Classification of Costs

Classification		*Base to Identify*
Relevant Cost	Irrelevant Cost	Affected or unaffected by the decision
Opportunity Cost	Outlay Cost	Nature of sacrifice
Historical Cost	Future Cost	Degree of anticipation in its determination
Variable Cost	Fixed Cost	Relationship with the volume of activity
Identifiable Cost	Common Cost	Identification with an operation unit
Disbursement Cost	Virtual Cost	Relationship with an immediate cash flow
Incremental Cost	Inmerged Cost	Relationship with an increase in activity
Avoided Costs (Discretionary)	Commited Cost	Grade of control
Replacement Cost	Historical Cost	Moment of valuation

Classification of Costs According to Production Costs

According to the cost of production	Raw Material
	Direct Labor
	Overhead

Classification of Costs According to Volume of Activity

According to volume of activity	Fixed
	Variable

Different Costs for Different Purposes

Pricing	Price = Costs of the previous months / (1 - % Contribution Margin) Price = 2.65 / (1 - .4) = 4.16
Valuation of inventories (Methods)	Last purchase cost X Inventory amount = 2.65 X 100 = 265
Cost of sales	Units sold X Production costs per unit = 500 X 2.53 = 1,265
Cash disbursement budget. Purchases budget.	Amount of units to buy X Future costs = Future cash disbursement = 200 X 2.75 = 550
Performance evaluation	Expected cost = 2.25Real cost = 2.50Actual cost = 2.50Unfavorable variance = 0.25

Inventory Valuation

Inventories are considered by many companies as a very significant asset. The inventory accounting involves two major aspects: 1) the cost of inventory purchased or manufactured needs to be determined and 2) the cost is retained in the inventory accounts of the company until the product is sold.

Inventory Valuation Methods, Determine Cost of Sales

Specificidentification	Each item sold and each unit remaining in the inventory are individually identified
FIFO (First-in, first-out)	The actual physical flow is irrelevant, the important thing is that the flow of costs assumes that the first articlesin entering the inventory are the first to be sold (cost of sales) or consumed (cost of production). The final inventory is made up of the last articles that became part of inventories.
LIFO (Last-in, first-out)	The actual physical flow is irrelevant, the important thing is that the flow of costs assumes that the last articles that became part of the inventory are the first to be sold (cost of sales) or consumed (cost of production).The final inventory is comprised ofthe first articles that became part of inventories.
Weighted Average	This method requires calculating the average unit cost ofthe goods in the beggining inventory including the purchases made in the accounting period. Based on this average cost per unit is determined both the cost of sales (production) and the ending inventory of the period.

Examples of Inventory Valuation and Cost of Sales

METALS, INC.		COST FLOWS		
		FIFO	W. AVG.	LIFO
Brooches, Beggining Inventory 1-Jan-1999	29 @ $5.00	$145	$145	$145
Purchases, 1999		2,075	2,075	2,075
Goods available for sale, 1999		$2,220	$2,220	$2,220
Brooches, Ending Inventory 31-Dec-1999				
	50 @ $10.50 = $525 4 @ 9.00 = 36	$ 561		
	54 @ $7.96		$ 430	
	29 @ $5.00 = $145 25 @ 6.00 = 150			$ 295
Brooches, Cost of the Sales, 1999		$1,659	$1.790	$1,925

Cost Behavior

Knowing the behavior of costs is very useful in the management of a company for a variety of purposes. For example, know how costs behave, enables managers or administrators predict profits when sales volume and production changes. Knowing the behavior of costs is also useful for estimating costs. In turn, the estimated costs affect various decisions of the administration, like for example, if it should use machinery exceeded capacity to produce and sell a product at a reduced price. The behavior of a cost refers to the manner in which a cost changes at the time that a related activity changes. To understand the behavior of costs, the following two factors must be considered: First, the activities that is believed that cause the cost to be incurred mues be identified. These activities are called *activity* bases (or *activity drivers).* Second, the activity range on which changes in the cost are of interest must be specified. This activity range is called *relevant rank.*

Variable Costs Behavior

When the activity level is measured in units produced, direct material and labour costs are generally classified as direct variable costs. The *variable costs* are costs that vary in proportion to the total change in the level of activity.

For example, assume that the company Sound, Inc. produces sound systems under the brand name "Loud". The parts for the sound system are purchased from external suppliers for $10 USD per unit and are assembled at the plant Sound, Inc. in San Benito, USA. The direct materials costs for the model Loud-10 in a relevant range are from 5000 to 30000 units of production are shown below:

Units produced (Loud Model-10)	*Direct Materials Cost per unit*	*Total Direct Material Cost*
5,000	$10	$50,000
10,000	10	100,000
15,000	10	150,000
20,000	10	200,000
25,000	10	250,000
30,000	10	300,000

The variable cost per unit is the same, while the total variable cost changes in proportion to changes in the basis of activity. For model Loud-10, for example, the cost of direct materials for 10,000 units ($100,000) is twice the cost of direct materials for 5,000 units ($50,000).

The total cost of materials varies in direct proportion to the number of units produced because the direct cost of materials per unit ($10) is the same for all levels of production. Then, producing 20,000 additional units of product Loud-10 would increase the cost of direct materials by $200,000, to produce 25,000 additional units would increase the cost by $250000 and so on.

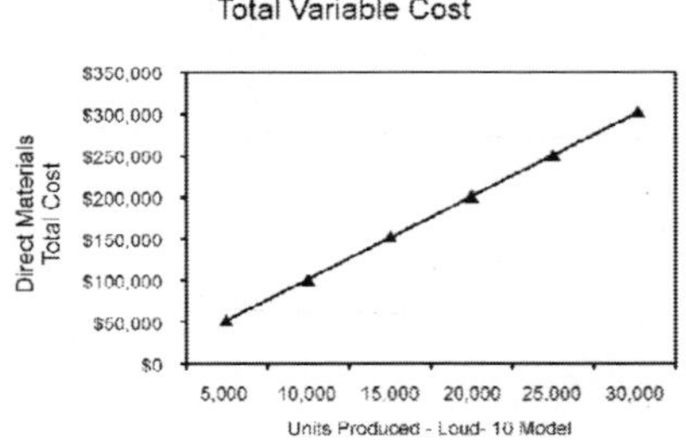

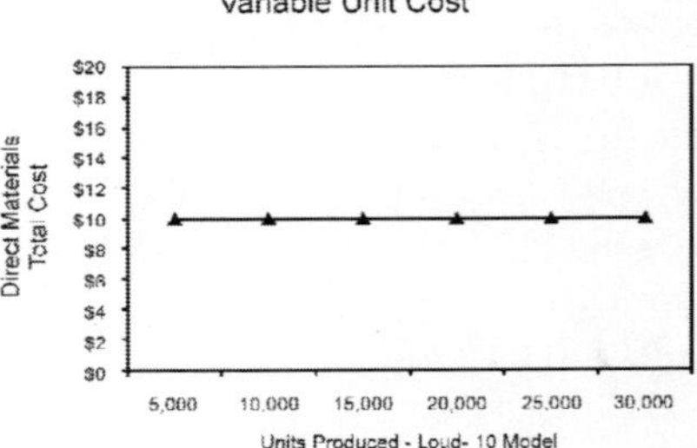

Fixed Costs Behavior

When units produced is a measure of activity, examples of fixed costs include the depreciation of equipment in a straight line of a factory, plant's machinery and equipment insurance, supervisors salaries, etcetera. The fixed costs are costs that continue the same in their total even if the level of activity changes.

As an example, assume that Hana Inc. produces and distributes cheese pies at its plant in Los Angeles, USA. The general production supervisor at the plant in Los Angeles is Vicente Fernandez, who is paid a salary of $ 75000 USD per year.

The relevant range of activity for a year is 50000 to 300000 cheese cakes. The salary of Vincent is a fixed cost that does not vary with the number of units produced. Regardless of the number of cakes produced between the range of 50000 to 300000, Vincent receives a salary of $ 75000. Even if the fixed cost remains unchanged when the number of cakes produced changes, the fixed cost by cake changes. The more cakes are produced, total fixed costs are distributed among more cakes, and then lowers the cost per cake. This relationship can be seen in the wage example of $75,000 of Vicente Fernandez shown below:

Cakes Produced	***V. Fernandez Total Salary***	***Salary per cake produced***
50,000	$75,000	$1.500
100,000	75,000	0.750
150,000	75,000	0.500
200,000	75,000	0.375
250,000	75,000	0.300
300,000	75,000	0.250

Seen in graphics would be as follows:

Total Fixed Cost

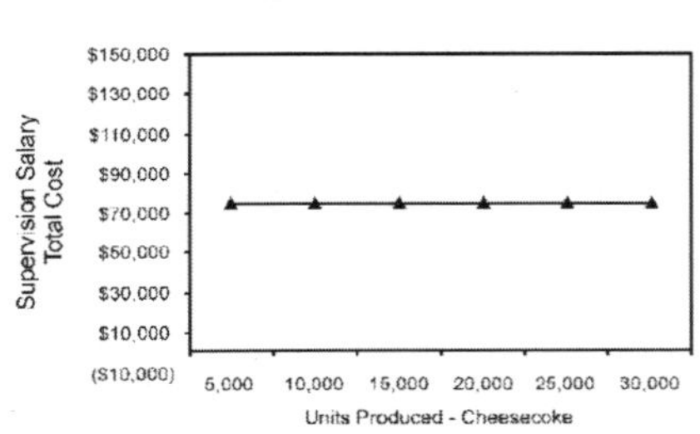

Fixed Unit Cost

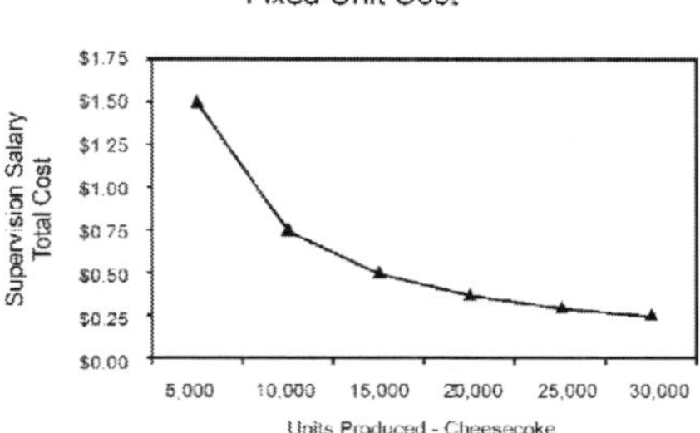

Cost Systems

The objective of a cost system or costing system is accumulate the costs of goods or services. The information on the cost of a product or service is used by managers to set the prices of the product, control operations, and develop financial statements. Also, the cost system improves control by providing information on the costs incurred by each department or manufacturing process.

Cost Systems Depending on how Costs of Production are Accumulated

Job Order Cost System

A job order cost system provides a separate record for the cost of each quantity of product passing through the factory. A quantity of each particular product is called *order*. A job order cost system fits better in the industries that develop products with that have different specifications most of the time or that have a wide variety of products in stock. Many service companies use this type of system for costing orders by accumulating the costs associated with providing services to their customers. Some characteristics of the job order cost systems are listed below:

- They accumulate in batches
- Production under specific orders
- Normally does not produces the same article
- Examples: Accounting firm, construction company, law practice, apparel manufacturing, movie studio.

Process Cost System

In a process cost system, costs are accumulated for each department or process in the factory. A process cost system fits more in companies manufacturing products which are not distinguishable with each other during a process of continuous production. Some characteristics of process cost systems are listed below:

- They accumulate costs by department
- Production continuous and homogeneous
- Examples: Oil Refinery, food processing, paper processing, soft drinks, medicines, buckets, toys, pants.

"When" should the cost of production be determined?

- Before we begin the process - Default costs (estimated or standard)
- After or at the same time of the process - Actual costs (current or historical).

Standard Costs and Variance Analysis

The standard costs are developed based on direct and indirect costs budgeted. The standard cost is a measure of how much should cost to produce or deliver a product or service. The standard cost of a product is made of the costs of the components required to produce that product. For example, the standard cost of a leather jacket includes:

- Cost of materials (leather, zipper, buttons, etc.)
- Direct labour cost (the time required to cut the design, sew it, etcetera, at the rate of production of employees who work in the process), and
- Indirect manufacturing costs related to the product (depreciation of the skin cutter machine, electricity, rent of the factory, etc.).

Once the standard cost is established, this provides the basis for decision-making, to analyse and control costs, and to measure the inventory and the cost of goods sold.

The standard costs serve as a benchmark against which actual costs are compared. The differences between current costs and standard costs are called *variances.*

The actual costs may differ from the standard costs due to differences in price, differences in quantity, errors, or other conditions. To determine the reasons for the variances a corrective action may be suggested or demonstrate that the products are currently costing more or less than the anticipated.

Direct Cost

The direct costs, such as materials and labour, are the costs that can be specifically assigned to a unit of products. The standard cost for the direct costs of a product involves two components: the price component and quantity component.

The standard cost for one unit of production is calculated by multiplying the standard quantity to be used by the price per standard unit.

Example: Assume that our leather jacket contains an average of 2 meters of skin at a cost of $16.00 per meter, a zipper at a cost of $5.00 per meter and two buttons at a cost of $0.50 each. Based on a time study recently made by the administration, a jacket requires an average of 5 hours of time spent by an employee to be produced. The production workers are paid on average $10 per hour of work, including benefits. The standard cost for the direct costs (the one for indirect costs will be seen later in this section) shall be as follows:

Materials	***Quantity X Price***	***= Standard Cost***
Skin	2 meters X $ 16.00	$32.00
Zipper	1 Zipper X $ 5.00	$5.00
Buttons	2 X buttons $ 0.50	$1.00
Materials Total Cost		$38.00
Direct Labour Cost	5 hours X $10.00	$50.00
Total Direct Cost		$88.00

Throughout the year, our leather jacket company will buy leather, zippers and buttons, and also recruit and pay to production employees. But what hill happened 1) if the company found skin at a lower price with a new supplier, which it is offering a discount, 2) a new machine has been acquired by the company to minimize the amount of material required by each jacket reducing the material scrap; 3) due to a very special order, the company had to ask their workers to work overtime, which must be paid on time and a half the normal rate, i.e. 150%; 4) the new machine to improved productivity, and now are used only 4.8 hours to produce a jacket. These differences will lead to variations between actual cost and standard costs budgeted as follows:

Materials	***Quantity X Price***	***= Standard Cost***
Skin	1.5 meters X $12.00	$18.00
Zipper	1 Zipper X $5.00	$5.00
Buttons	2 botones X $0.50 2 X buttons $ 0.50	$1.00
Materials Total Cost		$24.00
Direct Labour Cost	4.6 hours X $ 15.00	$69.00
Total Direct Cost		$93.00

Now it's easy to see how jackets cost $5.00 more than what was budgeted. To understand a variance or variation, it must be analysed and broken into its component parts. The analysis of variance in material would be:

Materials	***Quantity X Price***	***= Standard Cost***
Skin:		
Budget	2 meters X $16.00	$32.00
Actual	1.5 meters X $12.00	$18.00
Material Variance	$14.00 Favorable	
Price variance	($16.00 - $12.00) X 1.5 meters	$6.00 Favorable
Variance in quantity	(2.0 - 1.5) X $16.00	$8.00 Favorable
Material Variance		$14.00 Favorable

The analysis of variance in direct labour would be the following:

Direct Labour	***Quantity X Price = Standard Cost***	
DL:		
Budget	5 hours X $10.00	$50.00
Actual	4.6 meters X $15.00	$69.00
DL Variance		$ 19.00 Unfavorable
Price variance	($ 10.00 - $ 15.00) X 4.6 meters	$23.00 Unfavorable
Variance in quantity	(5.0 - 4.6) X $10.00	$4.00 Favorable
DL Variance		$19.00 Unfavorable

The variance is added as follows:

Standard Cost	$88.00
Actual Cost	$93.00
Total Variance	$5.00 Unfavorable
Material variance	$14.00 Favorable
DL Variance	$19.00 Unfavorable
Total Variance	$ 5.00 Unfavorable

The formulas to analyse variances can be expressed as follows:

Price Variance	(SP - AP) X AQ
Variance in quantity	(SQ - AQ) X SP
Total Variance	(SP X SQ) - (AP X AQ)
Where:	
SP = Standard Price	
AP = Current Price	
SQ = Standard Quantity	

Overhead or Indirect Costs

The direct costs vary in relation to the volume of units produced. Overhead or indirect costs or general expenses, however, are elements that vary directly with the volume (variable costs) and other elements that do not (fixed costs). Overhead Budgets. One way to budget the overhead is ignoring the indirect effects of volume. This approach is called fixed *costs budget.* Under this approach, the administration determines the amount of overhead that should be taken based on a desired or normal level of production. The total expenditure becomes the overhead budget against which performance is measured, regardless of the level of production currently achieved. An example of this would be as follows:

***Table:** Overhead Permitted (in thousands).*

Rent	$500
Machinery Depreciation	500
Supervision Salaries	1,000
Indirect Material	800
Electricity	800
Total	$3,600

The performance at the end of the year may be measured against the total $3'600,000. However, not taking into account the true nature of costs, may lead to a manager to take inaccurate conclusions about the performance. For example, lets assume that this budget is based on a "normal" level of production of leather jackets (160,000 units). Also assume that the costs of electricity, accounting in part for cutting machines and sewing, vary with the level of production. So, if 200,000 jackets are produced during the year, the cost of electricity will exceed $800,000, say that these were a total of $1'000,000. Comparing this with a fixed budget, the manager can say that the supervisor of the warehouse did his job poorly in terms of managing the costs of electricity, when in fact, excessive spending is due solely to 40,000 extra jackets that occurred. The other approach for budgeting overhead is called *flexible budget.* A flexible budget specifies a cost permissible at each possible level of production. Once the period is completed and the volume of production known, the standard budget is determined by reference to flexible budget for the current level of production. This is a parallel method to the way used to determine the budget for direct materials and manpower. Example of a simplified flexible budget:

Amounts in Thousands

A flexible budget allows us to analyse in a more intelligent way the variable overhead.

Overhead absorption: Now that our flexible budget is established, we need to establish how we are going to allocate indirect costs to our products. The total cost of a product should include all indirect costs that were generated to bring the product to its complete form. So apart from the direct labour and materials, the standard cost of a product includes indirect costs as well. But, manpower and materials are easy to measure and allocate their products. It is much more difficult to determine how much rent, indirect material, or depreciation was consumed by a particular product.

Utilization Capacity	40%	60%	70%	80% (Normal)	100%	
Direct Labor Cost (rate per piece)	$4,000	$6,000	$7,000	$8,000	$10,000	
Overhead Allowed						**Cost Behavior**
Rent	$500	$500	$500	$500	$500	No change or Fixed
Depreciation	500	500	500	500	500	No change or fixed
Supervision	500	1,000	1,000	1,000	1,500	Phased Cost
Indirect Material	400	600	700	800	1,000	Variable at 10% of Direct Labor
Electricity	600	700	750	800	900	Semivariable: $400 + 5% of DL
TOTAL	**$2,250**	**$3,300**	**$3,450**	**$3,600**	**$4,400**	

The accountants solve this problem by using an overhead allowance method. This is called *overhead absorption*. First indirect costs are collected in *sets of costs*. A group can include all the rent, other all the costs associated with the inspection, other the costs of supervision, etc. Now the sets of costs are allocated to products using a *driver of cost*. For simplicity, in the rest of this note we will assume that all indirect costs are added in a single set of cost for assignment.

In companies that produce a single product, the overall costs can be allocated based on units, using the units produced in the period as a driver of cost. The total budgeted indirect cost ($ 3.6 million using the example above) will be divided between the volume of production planned (assuming 200,000 jackets). Then for each jacket produced, $18.00 ($ 3.6 million between 200,000) shall apply as indirect costs. The standard cost per jacket under this method would be then:

Table: *Standard Cost.*

Materials	$38.00
Manpower (Direct labour)	$50.00
Overhead (Indirect cost)	$18.00
Total Standard Cost	$106.00

In multi-product firms, it is necessary to use a different method or cost driver than the number of units produced, so a more fair distribution of indirect cost between products can be made. For example, if our company makes leather gloves in addition to jackets and gloves can be manufactured in a quarter of the time it takes to produce a jacket, it would be unfair to charge each pair of gloves the same indirect cost that is charged to each jacket. Some other method of utilization of capacity must be used, as the labour hours, the amount paid by workforce in currency (either dollars, pesos, quarters, etc.) or machine hours. The choice for a business in particular should be based on which variable is the one that best measures the level of utilization of capacity for that business. For example, the overall costs of machinery depreciation can be allocated based on the number of machine hours per product as a cost driver. The entire cost of supervision can be distributed using the direct labour hours as a cost driver.

Since our production process of jackets is just more intense in direct labour, we will use the monetary cost of labour as a method of allocation (in this example we will use as currency the U.S. dollars). Using the direct labour dollars, the standard cost of overhead for a jacket would be $0.45 for each dollar of direct labour ($3.6 million of budgeted indirect cost divided by the total $8.0 million of budgeted manpower). Then, for a jacket $22.50 would be applied by indirect cost ($50.00 dollars per jacket multiplied by the $0.45 rate of indirect cost per DL dollar). The total standard cost for a leather jacket would be as follows:

Table: *Standard Cost*

Materials	$38.00
Manpower (Direct labour)	$50.00
Overhead (Indirect Cost)	$22.50
Total Standard Cost	$110.50

This would be the amount to be accumulated as inventory by each jacket produced. However, differences between the planned and actual volume will make a *volume variance* to emerge. The volume variance can be explain as follows:

	Plan	***Actual***
Direct Labour / jacket	$50.00	$50.00
Overhead rate	x $0.45	x $0.45
Overhead cost / Jacket	$22.50	$22.50
Jackets produced	160,000	140,000
Total Overhead Absorption	$3,600,000	$3,150,000

If the plan was to produce 160,000 jackets and currently there were only 140,000, and if we assume that the $3.6 million in indirect costs are fixed and that at the end of the year we only have $3.15 million of absorption by finished product; if the actual costs were $3.6 million, that compared with the absorption have led to a volume variance of $450,000.

Cost-volume-profit Analysis

The *cost-volume-profit analysis* is the systematic examination of the relationship between selling prices, sales, production volumes, costs, expenses and profits.

This analysis provides very useful information for decision-making in the management of a company. For example, the analysis can be used in establishing sales prices, in the product mix selection to sell, in the decision to choose marketing strategies, and in the analysis of the impact on profits by changes in costs. In the current environment of business, a business administration must act and take decisions in a fast and accurate manner. As a result, the importance of *cost-volume-profit* is still increasing as time passes.

Contribution Margin

A relationship between the cost, volume and profit is the *contribution margin*. El margen de contribucion es el exceso de ingresos por ventas sobre los costos variables. The contribution margin is the revenue excess from sales over variable costs. The concept of contribution margin is particularly useful in the planning of business because it gives an insight into the potential profits that can generate a business. The following chart includes the income statement of the company Fusion, Inc. which has been prepared to show its contribution margin:

Sales	$1,000,000
(-) Variable Costs	600,000
= Contribution margin	$400,000
(-) Fixed Costs	300,000
= Income from Operations	$ 100,000 $ 100.000

Contribution Margin Ratio

The margin contribution can also be expressed as a percentage. The *contribution margin ratio,* which is sometimes called the profit-volume ratio, indicates the percentage of each sales dollar available to cover fixed costs and to provide operating revenue. For the company Fusion, Inc. the contribution margin ratio is 40%, which is computed as follows:

	Sales -
Variable Costs	Contribution margin
ratio =	------------------------
	Sales

Contribution margin ratio = ($1,000,000 - $600,000) / $1,000,000 = 40%

The contribution margin ratio measures the effect on operating income of an increase or a decrease in sales volume. For example, assume that the management of Fusion, Inc. is studying the effect of adding $80,000 in sales orders.

Multiplying the contribution margin ratio (40%) by the change in sales volume ($80,000) indicates that operating income will increase $32,000 if additional orders are obtained. To validate this analysis the table below shows the income statement of the company including additional orders:

Sales	$1,080,000
(-) Variable Costs ($1,080,000 X 60%)	648,000
Contribution margin ($1,080,000 X 40%)	$432,000
(-) Fixed Costs	300,000
Income from Operations	$132,000

Variable costs as a percentage of sales are equal to 100% minus the contribution margin ratio. Thus, in the above income statement, the variable costs are 60% (100% - 40%) of sales, or $648,000 ($1'080,000 X 60%). The total contribution margin $432,000, can also be computed directly by multiplying the sales by the contribution margin ratio ($1'080,000 X 40%).

Unit Contribution Margin

The unit contribution margin is also useful to analize the profit potential of proposed projects.

The *unit contribution margin* is the dollars from each unit of sales available to cover the fixed costs of operation and provide operating profits. For example, if Fusion, Inc.'sunit selling price is $20 and its unit variable cost is $12, the unit contribution margin is $8 ($20 - $12).

The *contribution margin percentage* is most useful when the increase or decrease in sales volume is measured in sales dollars. To illustrate, assume that the company Fusion, Inc. sold 50,000 units. Its operating income is $100,000, as shown in the following contribution margin income statement:

Sales (50.000 units X $20)	$1,000,000
(-) Variable Costs (50,000 X $12)	600,000
Contribution Margin (50,000 units X $8)	$ 400,000
(-) Fixed Costs	300,000
Income from operations	$100,000

If sales of the company Fusion, Inc. could be increased by 15,000 units from 50,000 to 65,000 units, its operating income would increased by $120,000 (15000 units X $8), as shown below:

Sales (65,000 units X $20)	$1,300,000
(-) Variable Costs (65,000 units X $12)	780,000
Contribution margin (65,000 X $8)	$520,000
(-) Fixed Costs	300,000
Income from operations	$220,000

Base Costing

Activity Based Costing (ABC) is a two-stage product costing method that assigns costs first to activities and then to the products based on each product's use of activities. An activity is any discrete task that an organization undertakes to make or deliver a product or service. Activity-based costing is based on the concept that products consume activities and activities consume resources.

Activity-based costing involves the following four steps:

1. Identify the activities -such as processing orders- that consume resources and assign costs to them.
2. Identify the cost driver(s) associated with each activity. A cost driver causes, or "drives" an activity's costs. For the order-processing activity, the cost driver could be the number of orders.
3. Compute a cost rate per cost driver unit or transaction. The cost driver rate could be the cost per order, for example.
4. Assign costs to products by multiplying the cost driver rate by the volume of cost driver units consumed by the product. For example, the cost per order multiplied by the number of orders processed for a particular song during the month of March measures the cost of the order processing activity for that song during March.

Identifying activities that use resources: Often the most interesting and challenging part of the exercise is identifying activities that use resources because doing so requires understanding all activities required to make a product. In fact, much of the value of activity-based costing comes from this exercise even without changing the way product costs are computed. When managers step back and analize the processes (activities) they follow to produce a good or service, they often uncover many nonvalue-added steps, which they can eliminate.

Choosing cost driver: The following table shows several examples of the types of cost drivers that companies use. Most are related either to the volume of production or to the complexity of the production or marketing process.

Machine-hours used	Computer time used
Labour-hours or labour cost incurred	Number pf items produced or sold
Pounds of material handled	Customers served
Pages typed	Flight hours completed
Machine setups	Surgeries performed
Purchased orders completed	Scrap/rework orders completed
Quality inspections performed	Hours of testing time spent
Number of parts installed in a product	Number of different customers served

Miles Driven

The best cost driver is one that is causally related to the cost being allocated. Finding an allocation base that is causally related to the cost is often not possible.

With an ABC system, the selection of an allocation base, or cost driver, is often easier because we can use a measure of the activity volume.

For example, a reasonable allocation base for machine set-up costs is machine set-up hours. Notice that many of the cost drivers in the previous table refer to an activity.

Computing a Cost Rate per Cost Driver. In general, predetermined rates for allocating indirect costs to products are computed as follows:

Predetermined rate = Estimated indirect cost / Estimated volume of allocation base.

This formula applied to any indirect cost, wheter manufacturing overhead or administrative, distribution, selling, or any other indirect costs. Workers and machines perform activities on each product as it is produced.

Costs are allocated to a product by multiplying each activity's predetermined rate by the volume of activity used in making it.

In the two-stage cost system, the first stage consists of activities, not departments. Instead of a department rate, activity-based costing computes a cost driver rate for each activity center.

This means that each activity has an associated cost pool. If the cost driver for material handling is the number of production runs, for example, the company must be able to estimate the costs of material handling before the period and, ideally, track the actual cost of material handling as it is incurred during the period. Assigning costs to products. The final step in the activity-based costing system is to assign the activity costs to products.

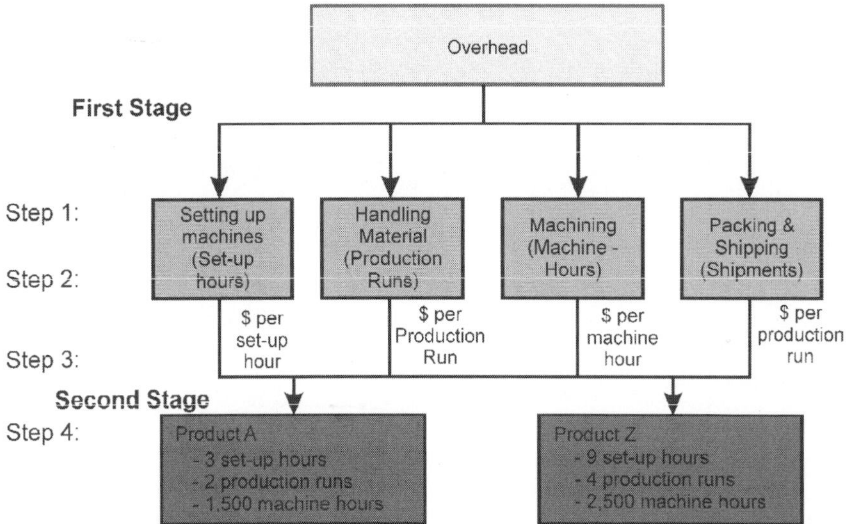

We do this just as we have done for the other product costing systems we have considered. We multiply the cost driver rates by the number of units of the cost driver in each product. The following table shows a cost flow diagram with the four steps of developing activity-based costs graphically.

Cost Overrun

A cost overrun, also known as a cost increase or budget overrun, is an unexpected cost incurred in excess of a budgeted amount due to an under-estimation of the actual cost during budgeting. Cost overrun should be distinguished from cost escalation, which is used to express an *anticipated* growth in a budgeted cost due to factors such as inflation.

Cost overrun is common in infrastructure, building, and technology projects. A comprehensive study of cost overrun published in the Journal of the American Planning Association in 2002 found that 9 out of ten construction projects had underestimated costs. Overruns of 50 to one hundred percent were common. Cost underestimation was found in each of 20 nations and five continents covered by the study, and cost underestimation had not decreased in the 70 years for which data were available.

For IT projects, an industry study by the Standish Group found that the average cost overrun was 43 percent; 71 percent of projects were over budget, exceeded time estimates, and had estimated too narrow a scope; and total waste was estimated at $55 billion per year in the US alone.

Many major construction projects have incurred cost overruns. The Suez Canal cost 20 times as much as the earliest estimates; even the cost estimate produced the year before construction began underestimated the project's actual costs by a factor of three.

The Sydney Opera House cost 15 times more than was originally projected, and the Concorde supersonic aeroplane cost 12 times more than predicted.[1] When Boston's "Big Dig" tunnel construction project was completed, the project was 275 percent ($11 billion) over budget. The Channel Tunnel between the UK and France had a construction cost overrun of 80 percent, and a 140-percent financing cost overrun.

Causes

Three types of explanation for cost overrun exist: technical, psychological, and political-economic. Technical explanations account for cost overrun in terms of imperfect forecasting techniques, inadequate data, etc. Psychological explanations account for overrun in terms of optimism bias with forecasters.

Scope creep, where the requirements or targets rises during the project, is common. Finally, political-economic explanations see overrun as the result of strategic misre-presentation of scope or budgets.

All three explanations can be considered forms of risk. A project's budgeted costs should always include cost contingency funds to cover risks (other than scope changes imposed on the project).

As has been shown in cost engineering research, poor risk analysis and contingency estimating practices account for many project cost overruns.

Numerous studies have found that the greatest cause of cost growth was poorly-defined scope at the time that the budget was established. The *cost growth*, or overrun of the budget before cost contingency is added, can be predicted by rating the extent of scope definition, even on complex projects with new technology.

Professor Bent Flyvbjerg of Oxford University and Martin Wachs of University of California, Los Angeles have shown that big public-works projects often have cost overruns due to strategic misrepresentation—"that is, lying", as Flyvbjerg defines the term.

Cost overrun is typically calculated in one of two ways: either as a percentage, namely actual cost minus budgeted cost, in percent of budgeted cost; or as a ratio of actual cost divided by budgeted cost. For example, if the budget for building a new bridge was $100 million, and the actual cost was $150 million, then the cost overrun may be expressed by the ratio 1.5, or as 50 percent.

2

Financial Statements and the Framework of Accounting

Financial Accounting

Accounting provides an account – an explanation or report in financial terms – about the transactions of an organisation. Accounting enables managers to satisfy the stakeholders in the organisation (owners, government, financiers, suppliers, customers, employees etc.) that they have acted in the best interests of stakeholders rather than themselves.

These explanations are provided to stakeholders through financial statements or reports, often referred to as the company's 'accounts'. The main financial reports are the Profit and Loss account, the Balance Sheet and the Cash Flow statement.

There is a legal requirement for the financial statements of companies (other than very small ones) to be audited.

Auditors are professionally qualified accountants who have to conduct an audit – an independent examination of the financial statements – and form an opinion as to whether the financial statements form a true and fair view and have been prepared in accordance with the Companies Act.

Although the requirement for a true and fair view is subjective and has never been tested at law, it takes precedence over accounting standards.

Accounting standards are principles to which accounting reports should conform. They are aimed at:

- Achieving comparability between companies, through reducing the variety of accounting practice;
- Providing full disclosure of material (i.e. significant) factors through the judgements made by the preparers of those financial reports; and
- Ensuring that the information provided is meaningful for the users of financial reports.

However, a criticism of the standards is that they are set by the preparers (professional accountants) rather than the users (shareholders and financiers) of financial reports. Financial Reporting Standards (FRSs) are issued by the Accounting Standards Board (ASB) and Statements of Standard Accounting Practice (SSAPs) were issued by the Accounting Standards Committee, which preceded the ASB. FRSs and SSAPs govern many aspects of the presentation of financial statements and the disclosure of information.

A Financial Reporting Review Panel has the power to seek revision of a company's accounts where those accounts do not comply with the standards and if necessary to seek a court order to ensure compliance. Interestingly, the US equivalent of the true and fair view is for financial statements to be presented fairly and in accordance with Generally Accepted Accounting Principles (or GAAP).

There is a move towards the harmonization of accounting standards between countries through the work of the International Accounting Standards Board (IASB). This has been a consequence of the globalization of capital markets, with the consequent need for accounting rules that can be understood by international investors.

The dominance of multinational corporations and the desire of companies to be listed on several stock exchanges have led to the need to rationalize different reporting practices in different countries. In Europe, all listed companies of member states of the European Union have to comply with IASB standards by 2005.

Reporting Profitability

Businesses exist to make a profit. Thus, the basic accounting concept is that:

$$\text{profit} = \text{income} - \text{expenses}$$

However, business profitability is determined by the matching principle – matching income earned with the expenses incurred in earning that income. Income is the value of sales of goods or services produced by the business. Expenses are all the costs incurred in buying, making or providing those goods or services and all the marketing and selling, production, logistics, human resource, IT, financing, administration and management costs involved in operating the business. The profit (or loss) of a business for a financial period is reported in a Profit and Loss account.

The turnover is the business income or sales of goods and services. The cost of sales is either:

- The cost of providing a service; or
- The cost of buying goods sold by a retailer; or
- The cost of raw materials and production costs for a product manufacturer.

However, not all the goods bought by a retailer or used in production will have been sold in the same period as the sales are made. The matching principle requires that the business adjusts for increases or decreases in inventory – the stock of goods bought or produced for resale but not yet sold.

Therefore, the cost of sales in the accounts is more properly described as the cost of goods sold, not the cost of goods produced. Because the production and sale of services are simultaneous, the cost of services produced always equals the cost of services sold (there is no such thing as an inventory of services).

The distinction between cost of sales and expenses leads to two types of profit being reported: gross profit and operating profit. Gross profit is the difference between the selling price and the purchase (or production) cost of the goods or services sold. Using a simple example, a retailer selling baked beans may buy each tin for 5p and sell it for 9p. The gross profit is 4p per tin.

gross profit = sales – cost of sales

Expenses will include all the other (selling, administration, finance etc.) costs of the business, that is those not directly concerned with buying, making or providing goods or services, but supporting that activity. The same retailer may treat the rent of the store, salaries of employees, distribution and computer costs and so on as expenses in order to determine the operating profit.

operating profit = gross profit – expenses

The operating profit is one of the most significant figures because it represents the profit generated from the ordinary operations of the business. It is also called net profit, profit before interest and taxes (PBIT) or earnings before interest and taxes (EBIT).

The distinction between cost of sales and expenses can vary between industries and organisations. A single store may treat only the product cost as the cost of sales and salaries and rent as expenses. A large retail chain may include the salaries of staff and the store rental as cost of sales with expenses covering the head office, corporate costs. For any particular business, it is important to determine the demarcation between cost of sales and expenses. From operating profit, a company must pay interest to its lenders, income tax to the government and a dividend to shareholders (for their share of the profits as they – unlike lenders – do not receive an interest rate for their investment). The remaining profit is retained by the business as part of its capital.

Reporting Financial Position

Not all business transactions appear in the Profit and Loss account. The second financial statement is the Balance Sheet. This shows the financial position of the business – its assets, liabilities and capital – at the end of a financial period. Some business payments are to acquire assets.

Fixed assets are things that the business owns and uses as part of its infrastructure. There are two types of fixed assets: tangible and intangible. Tangible fixed assets comprise those physical assets that can be seen and touched, such as buildings, machinery, vehicles, computers etc. Intangible fixed assets comprise non-physical assets such as the customer goodwill of a business or its intellectual property, e.g. its ownership of patents and trademarks.

Current assets include money in the bank, debtors (the sales to customers on credit, but unpaid) and inventory (the stock of goods bought or manufactured, but unsold). The word current in accounting means 12 months, so current assets are those that will change their form during the next year.

Sometimes assets are acquired or expenses incurred without paying for them immediately. In doing so, the business incurs liabilities. Liabilities are debts that the business owes. Liabilities – called creditors in the Balance Sheet – may be current liabilities such as bank overdrafts, trade creditors (purchases of goods on credit, but unpaid) and amounts due for taxes etc. As for assets, the word current means that the liabilities will be repaid within 12 months. Current liabilities also form part of working capital.

Long-term liabilities or creditors due after more than one year cover loans to finance the business that are repayable after 12 months and certain kinds of provisions. Capital is a particular kind of liability, as it is the money invested by the owners in the business. As mentioned above, capital is increased by the retained profits of the business (the profit after paying interest, tax and dividends).

In the Balance Sheet, the assets must agree with the total of liabilities and capital, because what the business owns is represented by what it owes to outsiders (liabilities) and to the owners (capital). This is called the accounting equation:

assets = liabilities + capital

or

assets – liabilities = capital

However, the capital of the business does not represent the value of the business – it is the result of the application of a number of accounting principles. In addition to the Financial Reporting Standards and Statements of Standard Accounting Practice referred to earlier, there are some basic accounting principles that are generally accepted by the accounting profession as being important in preparing accounting reports. However, an important principle that is particularly relevant to the interpretation of accounting reports is the matching principle.

The matching (or accruals) principle recognizes income when it is earned and recognizes expenses when they are incurred (accrual accounting), not when money is received or paid out (cash accounting). While cash is very important in business, the accruals method provides a more meaningful picture of the financial performance of a business from year to year.

Accruals Accounting

Unlike a system of cash accounting, where receipts are treated as income and payments as expenses (which is common in not-for-profit organisations), the matching principle requires a system of accrual accounting, which takes account of the timing differences between receipts and payments and when those cash flows are treated as income earned and expenses incurred for the calculation of profit. Accruals accounting makes adjustments for:

- Prepayments;
- Accruals; and
- Provisions.

The matching principle requires that certain cash payments made in advance are treated as prepayments, i.e. made in advance of when they are treated as an expense for profit purposes. Other expenses are accrued, i.e. treated as expenses for profit purposes even though no cash payment has yet been made.

A good example of a prepayment is insurance, which is paid 12 months in advance. Assume that a business which has a financial year ending 31 March pays its 12 months insurance premium of £12,000 in advance on 1 January. At its year end, the business will only treat £3,000 (3/12 of £12,000) as an expense and will treat the remaining £9,000 as a prepayment (a current asset in the Balance Sheet).

A good example of an accrual is electricity, which like most utilities is paid (often quarterly) in arrears. If the same business usually receives its electricity bill in May (covering the period March to May) it will need to accrue an expense for the month of March, even if the bill has not yet been received.

If the prior year's bill was £2,400 for the same quarter (allowing for seasonal fluctuations in usage) then the business will accrue £800 (1/3 of £2,400).

A further example of the matching principle is in the creation of provisions. Provisions are estimates of possible liabilities that may arise. An example of a possible future liability is a provision for warranty claims that may be payable on sales of products. The estimate will be based on the likely costs to be incurred in the future.

Other types of provisions cover reductions in asset values. The main examples are:

- *Doubtful debts:* customers may experience difficulty in paying their accounts and a provision may be made based on experience that a proportion of debtors will never pay.
- *Inventory:* some stock may be obsolete but still held in the store. A provision reduces the value of the obsolete stock to its sale or scrap value (if any).
- *Depreciation:* this is a charge against profits, intended to write off the value of each fixed asset over its useful life.

Provisions for likely future liabilities are shown in the Balance Sheet as liabilities, while provisions that reduce asset values are shown as deductions from the cost of the asset. The most important provision, because it typically involves a large amount of money, is for depreciation.

Depreciation

Fixed assets are capitalized in the Balance Sheet so that the purchase of fixed assets does not affect profit. However, depreciation is an expense that spreads the cost of the asset over its useful life. The following example illustrates the matching principle in relation to depreciation. An asset costs £100,000. It is expected to have a life of four years and have a resale value of £20,000 at the end of that time.

It is important to recognize that the cash outflow of £100,000 occurs when the asset is bought. The depreciation charge of £20,000 per annum is a non-cash expense each year.

If the asset is then sold, any profit or loss on sale is treated as a separate item in the Profit and Loss account. Alternatively, the asset can be depreciated to a nil value in the Balance Sheet even though it is still in use. A type of depreciation used for certain assets, such as goodwill or leasehold property improvements, is called amortization, which has the same meaning and is calculated in the same way as depreciation. In reporting profits, some companies show the profit before depreciation (or amortization) is deducted, because it can be a substantial cost, but one that does not result in any cash flow. A variation of EBIT is EBITDA: earnings before interest, taxes, depreciation and amortization. Reporting cash flow The third financial statement is the cash flow. The Cash Flow statement shows the movement in cash for the business during a financial period. It includes:

- Cash flow from operations;
- Interest receipts and payments;
- Income taxes paid;
- Capital expenditure (i.e. the purchase of new fixed assets);
- Dividends paid to shareholders;
- New borrowings or repayment of borrowings.

The cash flow from operations differs from the operating profit because of:

- Depreciation, which as a non-cash expense is added back to profit (since operating profit is the result after depreciation is deducted);
- Increases (or decreases) in working capital (e.g. debtors, inventory, prepayments, creditors and accruals), which reduce (or increase) available cash.

The management of working capital is a crucial element of cash management.

Working Capital

Working capital is the difference between current assets and current liabilities (or creditors). In practical terms, we are primarily concerned with stock and debtors, although prepayments are a further element of current assets. Current liabilities comprise creditors and accruals. The other element of working capital is bank, representing either surplus cash (a current asset) or short-term borrowing through a bank overdraft facility (a creditor).

Money tied up in debtors and stock puts pressure on the firm, either to reduce the level of that investment or to seek additional borrowings. Alternatively, cash surpluses can be invested to generate additional income through interest earned.

Managing working capital is essential for success, as the ability to avoid a cash crisis and pay debts as they fall due depends on:

- Managing debtors through effective credit approval, invoicing and collection activity;
- Managing stock through effective ordering, storage and identification of stock;
- Managing trade creditors by negotiation of trade terms and through taking advantage of settlement discounts; and
- Managing cash by effective forecasting, short-term borrowing and/or investment of surplus cash where possible.

Managing Debtors

The main measure of how effectively debtors are managed is the number of days' sales outstanding.

The target number of days' sales outstanding will be a function of the industry, the credit terms offered by the firm and its efficiency in both credit approval and collection activity. Management of debtors will aim to reduce days' sales outstanding over time and minimize bad debts. Acceptance policies will aim to determine the creditworthiness of new customers before sales are made. This can be achieved by checking trade and bank references, searching company accounts and consulting a credit bureau for any adverse reports. Credit limits can be set for each customer.

Collection policy should ensure that invoices and statements are issued quickly and accurately, that any queries are investigated as soon as they are identified and that continual follow-up (by telephone and post) of late-paying customers should take place. Discounts may be offered for settlement within credit terms. Bad debts may occur because a customer's business fails. For this reason, firms establish a provision to cover the likelihood of customers not being able to pay their debts.

Managing Stock

Sound management of stock requires an accurate and up-to-date stock control system. Often in stock control the Pareto principle (also called the 80/20 rule) applies. This recognizes that a small proportion (often about 20 per cent) of the number of stock items accounts for a relatively large proportion (say 80 per cent) of the total value. In stock control, ABC analysis takes the approach that, rather than attempt to manage all stock items equally, efforts should be made to prioritize the 'A' items that account for most value, then 'B' items and only if time permits the many smaller-value 'C' items. Some businesses adopt just-in-time (JIT) methods to minimize stockholding, treating any stock as a wasted resource. JIT requires sophisticated production planning, inventory control and supply chain management so that stock is only received as it is required for production or sale. Stock may be written off because of stock losses, obsolescence or damage. For this reason, firms establish a provision to cover the likelihood of writing off part of the value of stock.

Managing Creditors

Just as it is important to collect debts from customers, it is also essential to ensure that suppliers are paid within their credit terms. As for debtors, the main measure of how effectively creditors are managed is the number of days' purchases outstanding.

The number of days' purchases outstanding will reflect credit terms offered by the supplier, any discounts that may be obtained for prompt payment and the collection action taken by the supplier. Failure to pay creditors may result in the loss or stoppage of supply, which can then affect the ability of a business to satisfy its customers' orders.

A Theoretical Perspective on Financial Statements

A necessary ingredient for shareholder value, given the separation of ownership from control in most large business organisations, is the control of what managers actually do. Control is considered in the rational-economic paradigm through the notion of contract, in which the role of control is to measure and reward performance such that there will be greater goal congruence, i.e. that individuals pursuing their own self-interest will also pursue the collective interest. There are two main versions of contractual theory: agency theory and transaction cost economics. Agency theory sees the economy as a network of interlocking contracts. The transaction cost approach sees the economy as a mixture of markets and hierarchies.

Agency Theory

Agency theory is concerned with contractual relationships within the firm, between a principal and an agent, whose rights and duties are specified by a contract of employment. This model recognizes the behaviour of an agent (the manager), whose actions the management accounting and control system seeks to influence and control. Both are assumed to be rational-economic persons motivated solely by self-interest, although they may differ with respect to their preferences, beliefs and information.

The principal wishes to influence what the agent does, but delegates tasks to the agent in an uncertain environment. The agent expends effort in the performance of these tasks.

The outcome depends on both environmental factors and the effort expended by the agent. Under the sharing rule, the agent usually receives a reward, being a share of the outcome. The reward will depend on the information system used to measure the outcome. Consequently, financial reports play an important role in regulating the actions of agents.

The assumption of agency theory is that the agent obtains utility (a benefit) from the reward but disutility from expending effort. Both principal and agent are assumed to be risk averse and utility maximizers.

The agency model involves seeking an employment contract that specifies the sharing rule and the information system. An accounting system can provide output measures from which an agent's efforts can be inferred, but the measures may not accurately reflect the effort expended. This leads to uncertainty about the relationship between the accounting measure and the agent's effort. If the principal cannot observe the agent's effort, or infer it from measured output, the agent may have an incentive to act in a manner different to the employment contract – this is called moral hazard. A principal who can observe the agent's effort but does not have access to all the information held by the agent does not know whether the effort expended has been based on the agent's information or whether the agent has 'shirked'.

This is called adverse selection. Moral hazard and adverse selection are a consequence of information asymmetry. This happens because principal and agent have different amounts of information. A function of accounting under agency theory is to improve efficiency by minimizing the losses caused through moral hazard and adverse selection.

Seal gives the example of renting a holiday home that is used by the owner only a few weeks of the year. The owner (the principal) may appoint a local agent to let out the home. The agency problem is how to motivate and monitor the agent in return for the commission earned by the agent. The owner will expect regular accounts of income and expenditure. Agency theorists use this reasoning to explain the development of financial accounting and auditing in more complex agency relationships. There are problems with agency theory, however. It ignores the effect of capital markets by assuming a single owner rather than a group of owners. The model focuses on single-period behaviour; many individuals violate the assumptions of rational self-interested behaviour and the agency perspective is narrow because there is no regard given to power, trust, ethical issues or equity, all of which may affect behaviour.

Interpreting Financial Statements and Alternative Theoretical Perspectives

Interpreting Financial Statements

Financial statements are an important part of a company's Annual Report, which is required for all companies listed on the Stock Exchange. For companies not listed, the Companies Act requires the preparation of financial statements. The process of interpreting financial statements begins with a consideration of the wider context: economic conditions; changes in the industry (e.g. regulation, technology); and the competitive advantage (e.g. marketing, operations, distribution etc.) held by the business. Within this context, often gained through the financial press and trade periodicals, the Annual Report itself can be considered. The Annual Report for a listed company typically contains:

1. A financial summary – the key financial information.
2. The chairman's or directors' report. This provides a useful summary of the key factors affecting the company's performance over the past year and its prospects for the future. It is important to read this information as it provides a background to the financial statements, in particular the company's products and

major market segments. It is important to 'read between the lines' in this report, since the intention of the Annual Report is to paint a 'glossy' picture of the business. However, as competitors will also read the Annual Report, the company takes care not to disclose more than is necessary.

3. The statutory reports (i.e. those required by the Companies Act) by the directors and auditors. These will help to identify any key issues that may be found in the accounts themselves.
4. The financial statements: Profit and Loss account, Balance Sheet and Cash Flow statement. The consolidated figures should be used, as these are the total figures for the group of companies that comprise the whole business.
5. Notes to the accounts, which provide detailed figures and explanations to the accounts. These often run to many pages.
6. A five-year summary of key financial information.

The Accounting Standards Board recommends that listed companies include an operating and financial review that provides 'a framework for the directors to discuss and analyse the business's performance and the factors underlying its results and financial position, in order to assist users to assess for themselves the future potential of the business'.

The operating and financial review would replace much of the information contained in the chairman's or directors' reports (item 2 above).

The Profit and Loss account, Balance Sheet and Cash Flow statement can be studied using ratios. Ratios are typically two numbers, with one being expressed as a percentage of the other. Ratio analysis can be used to help interpret trends in performance year on year and by benchmarking to industry averages or to the performance of individual competitors. Ratio analysis can be used to interpret performance against five criteria:

- The rate of profitability;
- Liquidity, i.e. cash flow;
- Gearing, i.e. the proportion of borrowings to shareholders' investment;
- How efficiently assets are utilized; and
- The returns to shareholders.

Ratio Analysis

There are different definitions that can be used for each ratio. However, it is important that whatever ratios are used, they are meaningful to the business and applied consistently. The most common ratios follow.

Profitability

Each of the profitability ratios provides a different method of interpreting profitability. Satisfactory business performance requires an adequate return on shareholders' funds and total capital employed in the business (the total of the investment by shareholders and lenders). Profit must also be achieved as a percentage of sales, which must itself grow year on year. The operating profit and gross profit margins emphasize different elements of business performance.

A business that has an acid test of less than 100 per cent may experience difficulty in paying its debts as they fall due. On the other hand, a company with too high a working capital ratio may not be utilizing its assets effectively. The higher the gearing, the higher the risk of repaying debt and interest. The lower the interest cover, the more pressure there is on profits to fund interest charges. However, because external funds are being used, the rate of profit earned by shareholders is higher where external funds are used. The relationship between risk and return is an important feature of interpreting business performance.

While in the above example the return on capital employed is a constant 20 per cent (an operating profit of £20,000 on capital employed of £100,000), the return on shareholders' funds increases as debt replaces equity.

This improvement to the return to shareholders carries a risk, which increases as the proportion of profits taken by the interest charge increases (and is reflected in the interest cover ratio). If profits turn down, there are substantially more risks carried by the highly geared business. This is a measure of how efficiently assets are utilized to generate sales. Investment in assets has as its principal purpose the generation of sales. Three other efficiency ratios are those concerning debtors' collections, stock turnover and creditors' payments.

The shareholder ratios are measures of returns to shareholders on their investment in the business. The dividend and earnings ratios reflect the annual return to shareholders, while the P/E ratio measures the number of years over which the investment in shares will be recovered through earnings.

Interpreting Financial Information using Ratios

The interpretation of any ratio depends on the industry. In particular, the ratio needs to be interpreted as a trend over time, or by comparison to industry averages of competitor ratios. These comparisons help determine whether performance is improving and where improvement maybe necessary. Based on the understanding of the business context and competitive conditions and the information provided by ratio analysis, users of financial statements can make judgements about the pattern of past performance and prospects for a company and its financial strength. Broadly speaking, businesses seek:

- Increasing rates of profit on shareholders' funds, capital employed and sales;
- Adequate liquidity (a ratio of current assets to liabilities of not less than 100 per cent) to ensure that debts can be paid as they fall due, but not an excessive rate to suggest that funds are inefficiently used;
- A level of debt commensurate with the business risk taken;
- High efficiency as a result of maximizing sales from the business's investments; and
- A satisfactory return on the investment made by shareholders.

When considering the movement in a ratio over two or more years, it is important to look at possible causes for the movement. These can be gained by understanding that either the numerator (top number in the ratio) or denominator (bottom number in the ratio) or both can influence the change. Some of the possible explanations behind changes in ratios are described below.

Profitability

Improvements in the returns on shareholders' funds (ROI) and capital employed (ROCE) may either be because profits have increased and/or because the capital used to generate those profits has altered. When businesses are taken over by others, one way of improving ROI or ROCE is to increase profits by reducing costs (often as a result of economies of scale), but another is to maintain profits while reducing assets and repaying debt. Improvements in operating profitability as a proportion of sales (PBIT or EBIT) are the result of profitability growing at a faster rate than sales growth, a result either of a higher gross margin or lower expenses. Note that sales growth may result in a higher profit but not necessarily in a higher rate of profit as a percentage of sales. Improvement in the rate of gross profit may be the result of higher selling prices, lower cost of sales, or changes in the mix of product/services sold or different market segments in which they are sold, which may reflect differential profitability. Naturally, the opposite explanations hold true for deterioration in profitability.

Liquidity

Improvements in the working capital and acid test ratios are the result of changing the balance between current assets and current liabilities. Money changes form between debtors, stock, bank and creditors. Borrowing over the long term in order to fund current assets will improve this ratio, as will profits that generate cash flow. By contrast, using liquid funds to repay long-term loans or incurring losses will reduce the working capital used to repay creditors.

Gearing

The gearing ratio reflects the balance between long-term debt and shareholders' equity. It changes as a result of changes in either shareholders' funds (more shares may be issued), raising new borrowings or repayments of debt. As debt increases in proportion to shareholders' funds, the gearing ratio will increase. Interest cover may increase as a result of higher profits or lower borrowings (and reduce as a result of lower profits or higher borrowings), but even with constant borrowings changes in the interest rate paid will also influence this ratio.

Activity/efficiency

Asset turnover improves either because sales increase or the total assets used reduce, a similar situation to that described above for ROCE. The efficiency with which debtors are collected, inventory is managed and creditors paid is also an important measure.

Shareholder Return

Decisions made by directors influence both the dividend per share and the dividend payout ratio. Dividends are a decision made by directors on the basis of the proportion of profits they want to distribute and the capital needed to be retained in the business to fund growth. Often, shareholder value considerations will dictate the level of dividends, which businesses do not like to reduce on a per share basis. This is sometimes at the cost of retaining fewer profits and then having to borrow additional funds to support growth strategies.

However, the number of shares issued also affects this ratio, as share issues will result in a lower dividend per share unless the total dividend is increased. As companies have little influence over their share price, which is a result of market expectations as much as past performance, dividend yield, while influenced by the dividend paid per share, is more readily influenced by changes in the market price of the shares. Earnings per share is influenced, as for profitability, by the profit but also (like dividends) by the number of shares issued. As for the dividend yield, the price/earnings (P/E) ratio is often more a result of changes in the share price than in the profits reflected in the earnings per share.

Social and Environmental Reporting

The concern with stakeholders rather than shareholders began in the 1970s and is generally associated with the publication in 1975 of The Corporate Report, a publication by the Accounting Standards Steering Committee. Accounting academics began to question profit as the sole measure of business performance and suggested a wider social responsibility for business and social accounting. Concepts of corporate social accounting and socially responsible accounting – most recently corporate social and environmental reporting (CSR) – attempt to highlight the impact of organisations on society.

Jones suggested three reasons for this:

1. A moral imperative that business organisations were insufficiently aware of the social consequences of their activities.
2. External pressure from government and pressure groups and the demand by some institutional investors for ethical investments. This was linked to the role of accounting in demonstrating how well organisations were fulfilling their social contract, the implied contract between an organisation and society.
3. Internal change taking place within organisations as a result of education etc. However, there has been little support for broader social accounting because accountants and managers have generally seen themselves as the agents of owners. Social reporting could be seen as undermining the power of shareholders and the foundation of the capitalist economic system. There are also technical difficulties associated with social reporting and a dominant belief among business leaders that government and not business had the responsibility to determine what was reported.

During the 1980s and 1990s environmental accounting focused on responsibility for the natural environment and in particular on sustainability as a result of concerns about ozone depletion, the greenhouse effect and global warming.

These concerns were associated with the growth of pressure groups such as Greenpeace and Friends of the Earth. Part of the appeal of environmental accounting was that issues of energy efficiency, recycling and reductions in packaging had cost-saving potential and therefore profits and social responsibility came to be seen as not necessarily mutually exclusive.

Zadek argued that social and ethical accounting, auditing and reporting together provide one of the few practical mechanisms for companies to integrate new patterns of civil accountability and governance with a business success model focused on stakeholders and core non-financial as well as financial values.

Socially responsible businesses: find the spaces in the pipeline between investors and consumers where some choice in behaviour is possible... [and] a far more ambitious agenda of shifting the basic boundaries by raising public awareness towards social and environmental agendas and supporting the emergence of new forms of investors that take non-financial criteria into account.

A further example of how the boundaries of accounting are set in arguably inappropriate ways by the rational-economic paradigm is in the exclusion of intellectual capital from financial statements.

Intellectual Capital

Edvinsson and Malone defined intellectual capital as 'the hidden dynamic factors that underlie the visible company'. Stewart defined intellectual capital as 'formalized, captured and leveraged knowledge'. Intellectual capital is of particular interest to accountants in increasingly knowledge-based economies in which the limitations of traditional financial statements erode their value as a tool supporting meaningful decision-making.

Three dimensions of intellectual capital have been identified in the literature: human (developing and leveraging individual knowledge and skills); organisational (internal structures, systems and procedures); and customer (loyalty, brand, image etc.). The disclosure of information about intellectual capital as an extension to financial reporting has been proposed by various accounting academics. The most publicized example is the Skandia Navigator.

While most businesses espouse a commitment to employees and the value of their knowledge, as well as to some form of social or environmental responsibility, this is often merely rhetoric, a facade to appease the interest groups of stakeholders. The institutional setting of organisations provides another perspective from which to view accounting and reporting.

Institutional Theory

Institutional theory is valuable because it locates the organisation within its historical and contextual setting. It is predicated on the need for legitimation and on isomorphic processes. Scott describes legitimation as the result of organisations being dependent, to a greater or lesser extent, on support from the environment for their survival and continued operation. Organisations need the support of governmental institutions where their operations are regulated (and few organisations are not regulated in some form or other). Organisations are also dependent on the acquisition of resources (labour, finance, technology etc.) for their purposes. If an organisation is not legitimated, it may incur sanctions of a legal, economic or social nature.

The second significant aspect of institutional power is the operation of isomorphism, the tendency for different organisations to adopt similar characteristics. DiMaggio and Powell identified three forms of isomorphism: coercive, as a result of political influence and the need to gain legitimacy; mimetic, following from standard responses to uncertainty; and normative, associated with professionalization. They held that isomorphic tendencies between organisations were a result of wider belief systems and cultural frames of reference.

Processes of education, inter-organisational movement of personnel and professionalization emphasize these belief systems and cultural values at an institutional level and facilitate the mimetic processes that result in organisations imitating each other. Isomorphic tendencies exist because 'organisations compete not just for resources and customers, but for political power and institutional legitimacy, for social as well as economic fitness'.

These legitimating and isomorphic processes become taken for granted by organisations as they strive to satisfy the demands of external regulators, resource suppliers and professional groups. These taken-for-granted processes themselves become institutionalized in the systems and processes – including accounting and reporting – adopted by organisations. Meyer argued that accounting arises 'in response to the demands made by powerful elements in the environment on which organisations are dependent'. Each of these theoretical perspectives provides a different view of the role of preparers and the needs of users of financial statements. This perspective also follows through to the users of management accounting information. However, as we have suggested earlier accounting is not without its limitations.

Creative Accounting and Ethics

Accounting choices, according to Francis, are moral choices:

Accounting is important precisely to the extent the accountant can transform the world, can influence the lived experience of others in ways which cause that experience to differ from what it would be in the absence of accounting, or in the presence of an alternative kind of accounting.

Creative accounting practices have been justified by managers for reasons of income smoothing, to bring profits closer to forecasts; changing accounting policies to distract attention from poor performance; or maintaining or boosting share prices. Despite the role of accounting standards and other regulations, creative accounting has always played a part in the efforts made by a few companies to present their performance in a better light.

Griffiths commented on the power of financial analysts and investment advisers in the City (of London) and the aim of company directors to present the business as having steady growth in income and profits.

This desire for a smoothing effect can be achieved by practices such as accruals, stock valuation, creating or reducing provisions, capitalizing or expensing costs and off-Balance Sheet financing (which was the main factor in Enron's downfall in the United States). While creative accounting has been frowned on, earnings management has not.

Under earnings management, directors aim to satisfy the market expectations influenced by stock analysts. Smith described the techniques adopted by companies and claimed that 'much of the apparent growth in profits which had occurred in the 1980s was the result of accounting sleight of hand rather than genuine economic growth'.

However, although accounting standards continually improve, there are always loopholes that accountants seem to find as quickly as standards are produced. Richardson and Richardson emphasized the role of accountants in organisations. They occupy special positions that privilege them to information that has the potential to reveal deviant top management behaviour, which can lead to social and emotional costs for innocent stakeholders and to corporate failures. As these conflicts are unlikely to be resolved internally, the authors argue for the ability to 'blow the whistle'.

However, as things stand, it is more likely that the accountant will simply leave the organisation. The problem with whistle blowing, the authors comment, is that to some it is an act of subversion, while to others it is an act of citizenship. To the organisation, it is an act of disloyalty.

3

Financial Capital vs. Real Capital

Financial capital or just capital in finance and accounting, refers to the funds provided by lenders (and investors) to businesses to purchase real capital equipment for producing goods/services.

Real Capital or Economic Capital comprises physical goods that assist in the production of other goods and services, e.g. shovels for gravediggers, sewing machines for tailors, or machinery and tooling for factories.

Financial capital generally refers to saved-up financial wealth, especially that used to start or maintain a business. A financial concept of capital is adopted by most entities in preparing their financial reports.

Under a financial concept of capital, such as invested money or invested purchasing power, capital is synonymous with the net assets or equity of the entity. Under a physical concept of capital, such as operating capability, capital is regarded as the productive capacity of the entity based on, for example, units of output per day. Financial capital maintenance can be measured in either nominal monetary units or units of constant purchasing power.

There are thus three concepts of capital maintenance in terms of International Financial Reporting Standards (IFRS): (1) Physical capital maintenance (2) Financial capital maintenance in nominal monetary units (3) Financial capital maintenance in units of constant purchasing power. Financial capital is provided by lenders for a price: interest. Also see time value of money for a more detailed description of how financial capital may be analysed.

Furthermore, financial capital, is any liquid medium or mechanism that represents wealth, or other styles of capital. It is, however, usually purchasing power in the form of money available for the production or purchasing of goods, etcetera. Capital can also be obtained by producing more than what is immediately required and saving the surplus. Financial capital has been subcategorised by some academics as economic or "productive capital" necessary for operations, signalling capital which signals a company's financial strength to shareholders, and regulatory capital which fulfills capital requirements.

Sources of Capital

- Long term - usually above 7 years
  - Share Capital
  - Mortgage loan
  - Retained Profit
  - Venture Capital
  - Debenture
  - Project Finance
- Medium term - usually between 2 and 7 years
  - Term Loans
  - Leasing
  - Hire Purchase
- Short term - usually under 2 years
  - Bank Overdraft
  - Trade Credit
  - Deferred Expenses
  - Factoring.

Capital Market

- Long-term funds are bought and sold:
  - Shares
  - Debentures
  - Long-term loans, often with a mortgage bond as security
  - Reserve funds
  - Euro Bonds
  - Law Firms.

Money Market

- Financial institutions can use short-term savings to lend out in the form of short-term loans:
- Credit on open account
- Bank overdraft
- Short-term loans
- Bills of exchange
- Factoring of debtors.

Differences between Shares and Debentures

- Shareholders are effectively owners; debenture-holders are creditors.
- Shareholders may vote at AGMs and be elected as directors; debenture-holders may not vote at AGMs or be elected as directors.
- Shareholders receive profit in the form of dividends; debenture-holders receive a fixed rate of interest.
- If there is no profit, the shareholder does not receive a dividend; interest is paid to debenture-holders regardless of whether or not a profit has been made.
- In case of dissolution of firms debenture holders are paid first as compared to shareholder.

Fixed Capital

This is money which is used to purchase assets that will remain permanently in the business and help it to make a profit.

Factors Determining Fixed Capital Requirements

- Nature of business
- Size of business
- Stage of development
- Capital invested by the owners
- location of that area

Working Capital

Working capital is that part of capital invested which is used for running the business such like money which is used to buy stock, pay expenses and finance credit.

Factors determining working capital requirements:

- Size of business
- Stage of development
- Time of production
- Rate of stock turnover ratio
- Buying and selling terms
- Seasonal consumption
- Seasonal product
- Profit level
- Growth and expansion
- Production cycle
- General nature of business
- Business cycle business policies.

Instruments

A contract regarding any combination of capital assets is called a financial instrument, and may serve as a

- Medium of exchange,
- Standard of deferred payment,
- Unit of account, or
- Store of value.

Most indigenous forms of money (wampum, shells, tally sticks and such) and the modern fiat money is only a "symbolic" storage of value and not a real storage of value like commodity money.

Own and Borrowed Capital

Capital contributed by the owner or entrepreneur of a business, and obtained, for example, by means of savings or inheritance, is known as own capital or equity, whereas that which is granted by another person or institution is called borrowed capital, and this must usually be paid back with interest. The ratio between debt and equity is named leverage. It has to be optimised as a high leverage can bring a higher profit but create solvency risk.

Borrowed Capital

This is capital which the business borrows from institutions or people, and includes debentures:

- Redeemable debentures
- Irredeemable debentures
- Debentures to bearer
- Ordinary debentures.

Own Capital

This is capital that owners of a business (shareholders and partners, for example) provide:

- Preference shares/hybrid source of finance
    * Ordinary preference shares
    * Cumulative preference shares
    * Participating preference shares
- Ordinary shares
- Bonus shares
- Founders' shares.

These have preference over the equity shares. This means the payments made to the shareholders are first paid to the preference shareholder(s) and then to the equity shareholders.

Issuing and Trading

Like money, financial instruments may be "backed" by state military fiat, credit (i.e. social capital held by banks and their depositors), or commodity resources.

Governments generally closely control the supply of it and usually require some "reserve" be held by institutions granting credit. Trading between various national currency instruments is conducted on a money market. Such trading reveals differences in probability of debt collection or store of value function of that currency, as assigned by traders.

When in forms other than money, financial capital may be traded on bond markets or reinsurance markets with varying degrees of trust in the social capital (not just credits) of bond-issuers, insurers, and others who issue and trade in financial instruments.

When payment is deferred on any such instrument, typically an interest rate is higher than the standard interest rates paid by banks, or charged by the central bank on its money. Often such instruments are called fixed-income instruments if they have reliable payment schedules associated with the uniform rate of interest. A variable-rate instrument, such as many consumer mortgages, will reflect the standard rate for deferred payment set by the central bank prime rate, increasing it by some fixed percentage. Other instruments, such as citizen entitlements, e.g. "U.S. Social Security", or other pensions, may be indexed to the rate of inflation, to provide a reliable value stream.

Trading in stock markets or commodity markets is actually trade in underlying assets which are not wholly financial in themselves, although they often move up and down in value in direct response to the trading in more purely financial derivatives.

Typically commodity markets depend on politics that affect international trade, e.g. boycotts and embargoes, or factors that influence natural capital, e.g. weather that affects food crops.

Meanwhile, stock markets are more influenced by trust in corporate leaders, i.e. individual capital, by consumers, i.e. social capital or "brand capital" (in some analyses), and internal organisational efficiency, i.e. instructional capital and infrastructural capital. Some enterprises issue instruments to specifically track one limited division or brand. "Financial futures", "Short selling" and "financial options" apply to these markets, and are typically pure financial bets on outcomes, rather than being a direct representation of any underlying asset.

Broadening the Notion

The relationship between financial capital, money, and all other styles of capital, especially human capital or labour, is assumed in central bank policy and regulations regarding instruments as above. Such relationships and policies are characterised by a political economy - feudalist, socialist, capitalist, green, anarchist or otherwise.

In effect, the means of money supply and other regulations on financial capital represent the economic sense of the value system of the society itself, as they determine the allocation of labour in that society. So, for instance, rules for increasing or reducing the money supply based on perceived inflation, or on measuring well-being, reflect some such values, reflect the importance of using (all forms of) financial capital as a stable store of value.

If this is very important, inflation control is key - any amount of money inflation reduces the value of financial capital with respect to all other types. If, however, the medium of exchange function is more critical, new money may be more freely issued regardless of impact on either inflation or well-being.

Marxian Perspectives

It is common in Marxist theory to refer to the role of "Finance Capital" as the determining and ruling class interest in capitalist society, particularly in the latter stages.

Valuation

Normally, a financial instrument is priced accordingly to the perception by capital market players of its expected return and risk.

Unit of account functions may come into question if valuations of complex financial instruments vary drastically based on timing. The "book value", "mark-to-market" and "mark-to-future" conventions are three different approaches to reconciling financial capital value units of account.

Economic Role

Socialism, capitalism, feudalism, anarchism, other civic theories take markedly different views of the role of financial capital in social life, and propose various political restrictions to deal with that.

Finance capitalism is the production of profit from the manipulation of financial capital. It is held in contrast to industrial capitalism, where profit is made from the manufacture of goods.

Historical Costs

In accounting, historical costs is the original monetary value of an economic item. Historical cost is based on the stable measuring unit assumption. In some circumstances, assets and liabilities may be shown at their historical cost, as if there had been no change in value since the date of acquisition.

The balance sheet value of the item may therefore differ from the "true" value. While historical cost is criticized for its inaccuracy (deviation from "true" value), it remains in use in most accounting systems. Various corrections to historical cost are used, many of which require the use of management judgment and may be difficult to implement or verify.

The trend in most accounting standards is a move to more accurate reflection of the fair or market value, although the historical cost principle remains in use, particularly for assets of little importance. Depreciation affects the carrying value of an asset on the balance sheet. The historical cost will equal the carrying value if there has been no change recorded in the value of the asset since acquisition. Improvements may be added to the cost basis of an asset.

Historical cost does not generally reflect current market valuation. Alternative measurement bases to the historical cost measurement basis, which may be applied for some types of assets for which market values are readily available, require that the carrying value of an asset (or liability) be updated to the market price (mark-to-market valuation) or some other estimate of value that better approximates the real value. Accounting standards may also have different methods required or allowed (even for different types of balance sheet variable real value non-monetary assets or liabilities) as to how the resultant change in value of an asset or liability is recorded, as a part of income or as a direct change to shareholders' equity. The Constant Item Purchasing Power Accounting model is an International Accounting Standards Board approved alternative basic accounting model to the traditional Historical Cost Accounting model.

Historical Cost Basis (Original Cost)

Under the historical cost basis of accounting, assets and liabilities are recorded at their values when first acquired. They are not then generally restated for changes in values. Costs recorded in the Income Statement are based on the historical cost of items sold or used, rather than their replacement costs.

For example –

- A company acquires an asset in year 1 for $100;
- The asset is still held at the end of year 1, when its market value is $120;
- The company sells the asset in year 2 for $115.

At the end year 1 the asset is recorded in the balance sheet at cost of $100. No account is taken of the increase in value from $100 to $120 in year 1. In year 2 the company records a sale of $115. The cost of sales is $100, being the historical cost of the asset. This gives rise to a profit of $15 which is wholly recognised in year 2.

Measurement under the Historical Cost Basis

Inventory

It is standard under the historical cost basis to write down the value of inventory (stock) to a lower cost and net realisable value. As a result:-

- A downward movement in the realisable value of inventory below cost is recognised immediately
- An upward movement in the realisable value of inventory is not recognised until the inventory is sold.

Property, Plant and Equipment

Property, plant and equipment is recorded at cost under the historical cost basis. Cost includes:

- Purchase price, including import duties and non-refundable purchase taxes, after deducting trade discounts and rebates;
- Any costs directly attributable to bringing the asset to the location and condition necessary for it to be capable of operating. These can include site preparation, delivery and handling costs, installation, assembly, testing, professional fees and the costs of employees directly involved in these activities.

In IFRS, cost also includes the initial estimate of the costs of dismantling and removing the item and restoring it. Cost may include the cost of borrowing to finance construction if this policy is consistently adopted.

Cost is then subject to depreciation with to write off the cost of the asset over its estimated useful life down to the recoverable amount. In most cases the method is "straight line", with the same depreciation charge from the date when an asset is brought into use until it is expected to be sold or no further economic benefits obtained from it, but other patterns of depreciation are used if assets are used proportionately more in some periods than others.

Assets and Liabilities Denominated in Foreign Currency

Monetary items such as cash balances, receivables and payables which are denominated in foreign currency are reported using the closing exchange rate under IFRS.

Exceptions to the Historical Cost Basis of Accounting

Revaluation of Property, Plant and Equipment

Under IFRS it is acceptable, but not required, to restate the values of property, plant and equipment to fair value. 'Fair value' is the amount for which an asset could be exchanged, or a liability settled, between knowledgeable, willing parties in an arm's length transaction.

Such a policy must be applied to all assets of a particular class. It would therefore be acceptable for an entity to revalue freehold properties every three years. The revaluations must be made with sufficient regularity to ensure that the carrying value does not differ materially from market value in subsequent years. A surplus on revaluation would be recorded as a reserve movement, not as income.

Derivative Financial Instruments

Under IFRS and US GAAP derivative financial instruments are stated at fair value ("mark to market") with movements recorded in the income statement.

Financial Reporting in Hyperinflationary Economies

IFRS requires a separate method of accounting in currencies deemed to be hyperinflationary. The characteristics of a hyperinflation include the population keeping its wealth in nonmonetary assets or relatively stable foreign currencies, prices quoted in foreign currencies or widespread indexation of prices. This might arise if cumulative inflation reaches or exceeds 100% over three years. An entity operating in a hyperinflationary economy:

- Records a gain or loss on its 'net monetary position' in its income statement.
- Records nonmonetary items (for example, property, plant & equipment) in the balance sheet by applying indexation to their historical cost.

Management Accounting Techniques

In management accounting there are a number of techniques used as alternatives to historical cost accounting including:-

- Measuring profit on sale of inventory by reference to its replacement cost. If inventory with a historical cost of $100 is sold for $115 when it costs $110 to replace it, the profit recorded would be $5 only based on replacement cost, not $15;
- Charging economic rent for assets, particularly property. If a business uses a 20-year old property which it owns, depreciation on a historical cost basis might be insignificant. However, the management accounts could show a notional rent payable, being perhaps opportunity cost - the amount the business could receive if it let the property to a third party.

IASB Approved Alternative to Historical Cost Accounting

The IASB's Framework introduced Constant Item Purchasing Power Accounting as an alternative to Historical Cost Accounting in 1989 in Par. 104 (a) where it states that financial capital maintenance - not variable real value nonmonetary items, e.g. property, plant, equipment, inventory, intangible assets, etc., - can be measured in either nominal monetary units - the traditional HCA model - or in units of constant purchasing power: the CIPPA model. The specific choice of measuring financial capital maintenance in units of constant purchasing power (the CIPPA model) at all levels of inflation and deflation as contained in the Framework for the Preparation and Presentation of Financial Statements, was approved by the International Accounting Standards Board's predecessor body, the International Accounting Standards Committee Board, in April 1989 for publication in July 1989 and adopted by the IASB in April 2001.

"In the absence of a Standard or an Interpretation that specifically applies to a transaction, management must use its judgement in developing and applying an accounting policy that results in information that is relevant and reliable.

In making that judgement, IAS 8.11 requires management to consider the definitions, recognition criteria, and measurement concepts for assets, liabilities, income, and expenses in the Framework. This elevation of the importance of the Framework was added in the 2003 revisions to IAS 8."

IAS8, 11:

> *"In making the judgement, management shall refer to, and consider the applicability of, the following sources in descending order: (a) the requirements and guidance in Standards and Interpretations dealing with similar and related issues; and (b) the definitions, recognition criteria and measurement concepts for assets, liabilities, income and expenses in the Framework."*

There is no applicable International Financial Reporting Standard or Interpretation regarding the valuation of constant real value nonmonetary items, e.g. issued share capital, retained earnings, capital reserves, all other items in Shareholders Equity, trade debtors, trade creditors, deferred tax assets and liabilities, taxes payable and receivable, all other nonmonetary receivables and payables, Profit and Loss account items such as salaries, wages, rents, etc. The Framework is thus applicable.

The CIPPA model is chosen by hardly any accountant in non-hyperinflationary economies even though it would maintain the real values of constant real value nonmonetary items - e.g. issued share capital, retained income, other shareholder equity items, trade debtors, trade creditors, etc. for an unlimited period of time. This is because the CIPPA model is generally viewed by accountants as a 1970's failed inflation accounting model that requires all nonmonetary items - variable real value nonmonetary items and constant real value nonmonetary items - to be inflation-adjusted by means of the Consumer Price Index.

The IASB did not approve CIPPA in 1989 as an inflation accounting model. CIPPA by measuring financial capital maintenance in units of constant purchasing power incorporates an alternative capital concept, financial capital maintenance concept and profit determination concept to the Historical Cost capital concept, financial capital maintenance concept and profit determination concept.

CIPPA only requires all constant real value nonmonetary items, e.g. issued share capital, retained income, all other items in Shareholders Equity, trade debtors, trade creditors, deferred tax assets and liabilities, taxes payable and receivable, all items in the profit and loss account, etc. to be valued in units of constant purchasing power.

Variable real value nonmonetary items, e.g. property, plant, equipment, listed and unlisted shares, inventory, etc. are valued in terms of IFRS and are not required in terms of the Framework, Par. 104 (a) to be valued in units of constant purchasing power.

The IASB requires entities to implement IAS 29 which is a Constant Purchasing Power Accounting model during hyperinflation.

Advantages and Disadvantages of Historical Cost Accounting

Advantages

- Historical cost accounts are straightforward to produce
- Historical cost accounts do not record gains until they are realised
- Historical cost accounts are still used in most accounting systems.

Disadvantages

- Historical cost accounts give no indication of current values of the assets of a business
- Historical cost accounts do not record the opportunity costs of the use of older assets, particularly property which may be recorded at a value based on costs incurred many years ago
- Historical cost accounts do not measure the loss of value of monetary assets as a result of inflation.

Constant-purchasing-power accounting (CPPA) is: A consistent method of indexing accounts by means of a general index which reflects changes in the purchasing power of money. It therefore attempts to deal with the inflation problem in the sense in which this is popularly understood, as a decline in the value of the currency. It attempts to deal with this problem by converting *all* of the currency unit measurement in accounts into units at a common date by means of the index."

International Accounting Standard IAS 29 Financial Reporting in Hyperinflationary Economies is the International Accounting Standards Board´s inflation accounting model under which all nonmonetary items (variable and constant real value nonmonetary items) in historical cost or current cost period-end financial statements are restated in terms of the period-end consumer price index (CPI) only during hyperinflation which the IASB describes as an exceptional circumstance. IAS 29 does not require valuation of nonmonetary items in units of constant purchasing power on a daily basis during the accounting period. IAS 29 does not require consistent daily indexing by means of a general index which reflects daily or even hourly changes in the purchasing power of money during hyperinflation. It simply requires restatement of HC and CC period-end financial statements.

Mark-to-market

Mark-to-market or fair value accounting refers to accounting for the fair value of an asset or liability based on the current market price of the asset or liability, or for similar assets and liabilities, or based on another objectively assessed "fair" value. Fair value accounting has been a part of Generally Accepted Accounting Principles (GAAP) in the United States since the early 1990s, and has been used increasingly since then.

Mark-to-market accounting can change values on the balance sheet frequently, as market conditions change. In contrast, historical cost accounting, based on the past transactions, is simpler, more stable, and easier to perform, but does not reflect current fair value at all. It summarizes past transactions instead. Mark-to-market accounting can become inaccurate if market prices change unpredictably. Buyers and sellers may claim a number of specific instances when this is the case, including inability to both accurately and collectively value the future income and expenses, often due to unreliable information, over-optimistic, and over-pessimistic expectations.

History and Development

The practice of *mark to market* as an accounting device first developed among traders on futures exchanges in the 20th century. It was not until the 1980s that the practice spread to big banks and corporations far from the traditional exchange trading pits, and beginning in the 1990s, mark-to-market accounting began to give rise to scandals.

To understand the original practice, consider that a futures trader, when taking a position, deposits money with the exchange, called a "margin". This is intended to protect the exchange against loss. At the end of every trading day, the contract is marked to its present market value.

If the trader is on the winning side of a deal, his contract has increased in value that day, and the exchange pays this profit into his account. On the other hand, if the market price of his contract has declined, the exchange charges his account that holds the deposited margin.

If the balance of this accounts falls below the deposit required to maintain the position, the trader must immediately pay additional margin into the account to maintain his position (a "margin call"). As an example, the Chicago Mercantile Exchange, taking the process one step further, marks positions to market *twice* a day, at 10:00 am and 2:00 pm.

Over-the-counter (OTC) derivatives on the other hand are formula-based financial contracts between buyers and sellers, and are not traded on exchanges, so their market prices are not established by any active, regulated market trading.

Market values are, therefore, not objectively determined or readily available (purchasers of derivative contracts are customarily furnished by computer programs which compute market values based upon data input from the active markets and the provided formulas). During their early development, OTC derivatives such as interest rate swaps were not marked to market frequently. Deals were monitored on a quarterly or annual basis, when gains or losses would be acknowledged or payments exchanged.

As the practice of marking to market caught on in corporations and banks, some of them seem to have discovered that this was a tempting way to commit accounting fraud, especially when the market price could not be objectively determined (because there was no real day-to-day market available or the asset value was derived from other traded commodities, such as crude oil futures), so assets were being 'marked to model' in a hypothetical or synthetic manner using estimated valuations derived from financial modelling, and sometimes marked in a manipulative way to achieve spurious valuations.

Internal Revenue Code Section 475 contains the mark to market accounting method rule for taxation.

Section 475 provides that qualified securities dealers that elect mark to market treatment shall recognize gain or loss as if the property were sold for its fair market value on the last business day of the year, and any gain or loss shall be taken into account in that year.

The section also provides that dealers in commodities can elect mark to market treatment for any commodity (or their derivatives) which is actively traded (i.e., for which there is an established financial market that provides a reasonable basis to determine fair market value by disseminating price quotes from broker/dealers or actual prices from recent transactions).

FAS 115

Accounting for Certain Investments in Debt and Equity Securities (Issued May 1993):

This statement addresses the accounting and reporting for investments in equity securities that have readily determinable fair values and for all investments in debt securities. Those investments are to be classified in three categories and accounted for as follows:

- Debt securities that the enterprise has the positive intent and ability to hold to maturity are classified as "held-to-maturity" securities and reported at amortized cost less impairment. (amortization refers to spreading payments over multiple periods)
- Debt and equity securities that are bought and held principally for the purpose of selling them in the near term are classified as "trading" securities and reported at fair value, with unrealised gains and losses included in earnings.
- Debt and equity securities not classified as either held-to-maturity securities or trading securities are classified as "available-for-sale" securities and reported at fair value, with unrealised gains and losses excluded from earnings and reported in a separate component of shareholders' equity (Other Comprehensive Income).

FAS 157

Statements of Financial Accounting Standards No. 157, *Fair Value Measurements*, commonly known as "FAS 157", is an accounting standard issued in September 2006 by the Financial Accounting Standards Board (FASB) which became effective for entities with fiscal years beginning after November 15, 2007.

FAS Statement 157 includes the following:

- Clarity on the definition of fair value;
- A fair value hierarchy used to classify the source of information used in fair value measurements (i.e., market-based or non-market based);
- Expanded disclosure requirements for assets and liabilities measured at fair value; and
- A modification of the long-standing accounting presumption that a measurement date-specific *transaction price* of an asset or liability equals its same measurement date-specific *fair value*.
- Clarification that changes in credit risk (both that of the counterparty and the company's own credit rating) must be included in the valuation.

FAS 157 defines "fair value" as: "The price that would be received to sell an asset or paid to transfer a liability in an orderly transaction between market participants at the measurement date."

FAS 157 only applies when another accounting rule requires or permits a fair value measure for that item. While FAS 157 does not introduce any new requirements mandating the use of fair value, the definition as outlined does introduce certain key differences.

First, it is based on the exit price (for an asset, the price at which it would be sold (bid price)) rather than an entry price (for an asset, the price at which it would be bought (ask price)), regardless of whether the entity plans to hold the asset for investment or resell it later.

Second, FAS 157 emphasizes that fair value is market-based rather than entity-specific. Thus, the optimism that often characterizes an asset acquirer must be replaced with the skepticism that typically characterizes a dispassionate, risk-averse buyer.

FAS 157's fair value hierarchy underpins the concepts of the standard. The hierarchy ranks the quality and reliability of information used to determine fair values, with level 1 inputs being the most reliable and level 3 inputs being the least reliable. Information based on direct observations of transactions (e.g., quoted prices) involving the same assets and liabilities, not assumptions, offers superior reliability; whereas, inputs based on unobservable data or a reporting entity's own assumptions about the assumptions market participants would use are the least reliable. A typical example of the latter is shares of a privately held company whose value is based on projected cash flows.

Problems can arise when the market-based measurement does not accurately reflect the underlying asset's true value. This can occur when a company is forced to calculate the selling price of these assets or liabilities during unfavourable or volatile times, such as a financial crisis. For example, if the liquidity is low or investors are fearful, the current selling price of a bank's assets could be much lower than the value under normal liquidity conditions.

The result would be a lowered shareholders' equity. This issue was seen during the financial crisis of 2008/09 where many securities held on banks' balance sheets could not be valued efficiently as the markets had disappeared from them. In April 2009, however, the Financial Accounting Standards Board (FASB) voted on and approved new guidelines that would allow for the valuation to be based on a price that would be received in an orderly market rather than a forced liquidation, starting in the first quarter of 2009.

Although FAS 157 does not require fair value to be used on any new classes of assets, it does apply to assets and liabilities that are carried at fair value in accordance with other applicable rules. The accounting rules for which assets and liabilities are held at fair value are complex.

Mutual funds and securities firms have carried their assets and some liabilities at fair value for decades in accordance with securities regulations and other accounting guidance. For commercial banks and other types of financial services firms, some asset classes are required to be carried at fair value, such as derivatives and marketable equity securities.

For other types of assets, such as loan receivables and debt securities, it depends on whether the assets are held for trading (active buying and selling) or for investment. All trading assets are carried at fair value. Loans and debt securities that are held for investment or to maturity are carried at amortised cost, unless they are deemed to be impaired (in which case, a loss is recognised). However, if they are available for sale or held for sale, they are required to be carried at fair value or the lower of cost or fair value, respectively. (FAS 65 and FAS 114 cover the accounting for loans, and FAS 115 covers the accounting for securities.) Notwithstanding the above, companies are permitted to account for almost any financial instrument at fair value, which they might elect to do in lieu of historical cost accounting.

Thus, FAS 157 applies in the cases above where a company is required or elects to carry an asset or liability at fair value.

The rule requires a mark to "market," rather than to some theoretical price calculated by a computer — a system often criticized as "mark to make-believe." (Occasionally, for certain types of assets, the rule allows for using a model).

Sometimes, there is a thin market for assets, which trade relatively infrequently - often during an economic crisis. In these periods, there are few, if any buyers for such products.

This complicates the marking process. In the absence of market information, an entity is allowed to use its own assumptions, but the objective is still the same: what would be the current value in a sale to a willing buyer. In developing its own assumptions, the entity can not ignore any available market data, such as interest rates, default rates, prepayment speeds, etc.

FAS 157 makes no distinction between non cash-generating assets, i.e., broken equipment, which can theoretically have zero value if nobody will buy them in the market – and cash-generating assets, like securities, which are still worth something for as long as they earn some income from their underlying assets. The latter cannot be marked down indefinitely, or at some point, can create incentives for company insiders to buy them out from the company at the under-valued prices. Insiders are in the best position to determine the creditworthiness of such securities going forward. In theory, this price pressure should balance market prices to accurately reflect the "fair value" of a particular asset. Purchasers of distressed assets should step in to buy undervalued securities, thus moving prices higher, allowing other Companies to consequently mark up their similar holdings.

Also new in FAS 157 is the idea of nonperformance risk. FAS 157 requires that in valuing a liability, an entity should consider the nonperformance risk. If FAS 157 simply required that fair value be recorded as an exit price, then nonperformance risk would be extinguished upon exit. However, FAS 157 defines fair value as the price at which you would transfer a liability. In other words, the nonperformance that must be valued should incorporate the correct discount rate for an ongoing contract. An example would be to apply higher discount rate to the future cash flows to account for the credit risk above the stated interest rate. The Basis for Conclusions section has an extensive explanation of what was intended by the original statement with regards to nonperformance risk (paragraphs C40-C49).

In response to the rapid developments of the financial crisis of 2007–2008, the FASB is fast tracking the issuance of the proposed FAS 157-d, Determining the Fair Value of a Financial Asset in a Market That Is Not Active.

Simple Example

Example: If an investor owns 10 shares of a stock purchased for $4 per share, and that stock now trades at $6, the "mark-to-market" value of the shares is equal to (10 shares * $6), or $60, whereas the book value might (depending on the accounting principles used) only equal $40.

Similarly, if the stock falls to $3, the mark-to-market value is $30 and the investor has lost $10 of the original investment. If the stock was purchased on margin, this might trigger a margin call and the investor would have to come up with an amount sufficient to meet the margin requirements for his account.

Marking-to-market a Derivatives Position

In marking-to-market a derivatives position, at predetermined periodic intervals, each counterparty exchanges the change in the market value of their position in cash.

For OTC derivatives, when one counterparty defaults, the sequence of events that follows is governed by an ISDA contract. When using models to calculate the ongoing exposure, FAS 157 requires that the entity consider the default risk ("nonperformance risk") of the counterparty and make a necessary adjustment to its calculations.

For exchange traded derivatives, if one of the counterparties defaults in this periodic exchange, that counterparty's position is immediately closed by the exchange and the clearing house is substituted for that counterparty's position. Marking-to-market virtually eliminates credit risk, but it requires the use of monitoring systems that usually only large institutions can afford.

Use by Brokers

Stock brokers allow their clients to access credit via margin accounts. These accounts allow clients to borrow funds to buy securities. Therefore, the amount of funds available is more than the value of cash (or equivalents).

The credit is provided by charging a rate of interest, in a similar way as banks provide loans. Even though the value of securities (stocks or other financial instruments such as options) fluctuates in the market, the value of accounts is not calculated in real time. Marking-to-market is performed typically at the end of the trading day, and if the account value falls below a given threshold, (typically a predefined ratio by the broker), the broker issues a margin call that requires the client to deposit more funds or liquidate his account.

Effect on Subprime Crisis and Emergency Economic Stabilisation Act of 2008

Former Federal Deposit Insurance Corporation Chair William Isaac placed much of the blame for the subprime mortgage crisis on the Securities and Exchange Commission and its fair-value accounting rules, especially the requirement for banks to mark their assets to market, particularly mortgage-backed securities. Whether or not this is true has been the subject of ongoing debate.

The debate arises because this accounting rule requires companies to adjust the value of marketable securities (such as the mortgage-backed securities (MBS) at the centre of the crisis) to their market value. The intent of the standard is to help investors understand the value of these assets at a point in time, rather than just their historical purchase price. Because the market for these assets is distressed, it is difficult to sell many MBS at other than prices which may (or may not) be reflective of market stresses, which may be below the value that the mortgage cash flow related to the MBS would merit. As initially interpreted by companies and their auditors, the typically lower sale value was used as the market value rather than the cash flow value. Many large financial institutions recognised significant losses during 2007 and 2008 as a result of marking-down MBS asset prices to market value.

For some institutions, this also triggered a margin call, where lenders that had provided the funds using the MBS as collateral had contractual rights to get their money back. This resulted in further forced sales of MBS and emergency efforts to obtain cash (liquidity) to pay off the margin call. Markdowns may also reduce the value of bank regulatory capital, requiring additional capital raising and creating uncertainty regarding the health of the bank.

It is the combination of the extensive use of financial leverage (i.e., borrowing to invest, leaving limited room in the event of a downturn), margin calls and large reported losses that may have exacerbated the crisis. If cash flow-derived value — which excludes market judgment as to default risk but may also more accurately reflect 'actual' value if the market is sufficiently distressed — is used (rather than sale value), the size of market-value adjustments under the accounting standard would typically be reduced.

One might question why banks or government-sponsored enterprises (Fannie Mae and Freddie Mac) are allowed to use high-risk, difficult-to-value assets like MBS or deferred tax assets as part of their regulatory capital base. Whether a margin call is involved is not part of the accounting standard itself; it is part of the contracts negotiated between lender and borrower.

Critics charge that claims that this had happened are akin to claiming "the problem, in short, is not that the banks acted irresponsibly in creating financial instruments that blew up, or in making loans that could never be repaid. It is that someone is forcing them to fess up. If only the banks could pretend the assets were valuable, then the system would be safe."

On September 30, 2008, the SEC and the FASB issued a joint clarification regarding the implementation of fair value accounting in cases where a market is disorderly or inactive. This guidance clarifies that forced liquidations are not indicative of fair value, as this is not an "orderly" transaction. Further, it clarifies that estimates of fair value can be made using the expected cash flows from such instruments, provided that the estimates reflect adjustments that a willing buyer would make, such as adjustments for default and liquidity risks.

Section 132 of the Emergency Economic Stabilisation Act of 2008, titled "Authority to Suspend Mark-to-Market Accounting" restates the Securities and Exchange Commission's authority to suspend the application of FAS 157 if the SEC determines that it is in the public interest and protects investors.

Section 133 of the Act, titled "Study on Mark-to-Market Accounting," requires the SEC, in consultation with the Federal Reserve Board and the Department of the Treasury, to conduct a study on mark-to-market accounting standards as provided in FAS 157, including its effects on balance sheets, impact on the quality of financial information, and other matters, and to report to Congress within 90 days on its findings. The *Emergency Economic Stabilisation Act of 2008* was passed and signed into law on October 3, 2008. On October 7, 2008, the SEC began to conduct a study on "mark-to-market" accounting, as authorised by Sec. 133 of the Emergency Economic Stabilisation Act of 2008.

On October 10, 2008, the FASB issued further guidance to provide an example of how to estimate fair value in cases where the market for that asset is not active at a reporting date.

On December 30, 2008, the SEC issued its report under Sec. 133 and decided not to suspend mark-to-market accounting.

On March 9, 2009, In remarks made in the Council on Foreign Relations in Washington, Federal Reserve Chairman Ben Bernanke said, "We should review regulatory policies and accounting rules to ensure that they do not induce excessive (swings in the financial system and economy)".

Although he doesn't support the full suspension of basic proposition of Mark to Market principles, he is open to improving it and provide "guidance" on reasonable ways to value assets to reduce their pro-cyclical effects.

On March 16, 2009, FASB proposed allowing companies to use more leeway in valuing their assets under "mark-to-market" accounting, a move that could ease balance-sheet pressures many companies say they are feeling during the economic crisis.

On April 2, 2009, after a 15-day public comment period, FASB eased the mark-to-market rules. Financial institutions are still required by the rules to mark transactions to market prices but more so in a steady market and less so when the market is inactive. To proponents of the rules, this removes the unnecessary "positive feedback loop" that can result in a deeply weakened economy.

On April 9, 2009, FASB issued the official update to FAS 157 that eases the mark-to-market rules when the market is unsteady or inactive. Early adopters were allowed to apply the ruling as of March 15, 2009, and the rest as of June 15, 2009. It was anticipated that these changes could significantly boost banks' statements of earnings and allow them to defer reporting losses. The changes, however, affected accounting standards applicable to a broad range of derivatives, not just banks holding mortgage-backed securities.

Opponents argue that the implications for investors are that the valuation of assets underlying such securities will be increasingly difficult to analyse, not less so. An example would be determining a company's actual assets, equity and earnings, which will be overstated if the assets are not allowed to be marked down appropriately.

In January 2010, Adair Turner, Chairman of the UK's Financial Services Authority, said that marking to market had been a cause of inflated bankers' bonuses. This is because it produces a self-reinforcing cycle during a rising market that feeds into banks' profit estimates.

4

Cash Flow Statement

In financial accounting, a cash flow statement, also known as *statement of cash flows* or *funds flow statement*, is a financial statement that shows how changes in balance sheet accounts and income affect cash and cash equivalents, and breaks the analysis down to operating, investing, and financing activities. Essentially, the cash flow statement is concerned with the flow of cash in and cash out of the business.

The statement captures both the current operating results and the accompanying changes in the balance sheet.

As an analytical tool, the statement of cash flows is useful in determining the short-term viability of a company, particularly its ability to pay bills.

International Accounting Standard 7 (IAS 7), is the International Accounting Standard that deals with cash flow statements.

People and groups interested in cash flow statements include:

- Accounting personnel, who need to know whether the organisation will be able to cover payroll and other immediate expenses
- Potential lenders or creditors, who want a clear picture of a company's ability to repay
- Potential investors, who need to judge whether the company is financially sound
- Potential employees or contractors, who need to know whether the company will be able to afford compensation
- Shareholders of the business.

Purpose

***Table** : Statement of Cash Flow - Simple Example* for the period 01/01/2006 to 12/31/2006

Cash flow from operations	$4,000
Cash flow from investing	($1,000)
Cash flow from financing	($2,000)
Net cash flow	$1,000

Parentheses indicate negative values

The cash flow statement was previously known as the flow of Cash statement. The cash flow statement reflects a firm's liquidity. The balance sheet is a snapshot of a firm's financial resources and obligations at a single point in time, and the income statement summarizes a firm's financial transactions over an interval of time. These two financial statements reflect the accrual basis accounting used by firms to match revenues with the expenses associated with generating those revenues.

The cash flow statement includes only inflows and outflows of cash and cash equivalents; it excludes transactions that do not directly affect cash receipts and payments. These non-cash transactions include depreciation or write-offs on bad debts or credit losses to name a few. The cash flow statement is a cash basis report on three types of financial activities: operating activities, investing activities, and financing activities. Non-cash activities are usually reported in footnotes.

The cash flow statement is intended to

1. provide information on a firm's liquidity and solvency and its ability to change cash flows in future circumstances
2. provide additional information for evaluating changes in assets, liabilities and equity
3. improve the comparability of different firms' operating performance by eliminating the effects of different accounting methods
4. indicate the amount, timing and probability of future cash flows

The cash flow statement has been adopted as a standard financial statement because it eliminates allocations, which might be derived from different accounting methods, such as various timeframes for depreciating fixed assets.

History & Variations

Cash basis financial statements were very common before accrual basis financial statements. The "flow of funds" statements of the past were cash flow statements. In 1863, the Dowlais Iron Company had recovered from a business slump, but had no cash to invest for a new blast furnace, despite having made a profit. To explain why there were no funds to invest, the manager made a new financial statement that was called a *comparison balance sheet*, which showed that the company was holding too much inventory. This new financial statement was the genesis of Cash Flow Statement that is used today.

In the United States in 1971, the Financial Accounting Standards Board (FASB) defined rules that made it mandatory under Generally Accepted Accounting Principles (US GAAP) to report sources and uses of funds, but the definition of "funds" was not clear." Net working capital" might be cash or might be the difference between current assets and current liabilities.

From the late 1970 to the mid-1980s, the FASB discussed the usefulness of predicting future cash flows. In 1987, FASB Statement No. 95 (FAS 95) mandated that firms provide cash flow statements. In 1992, the International Accounting Standards Board issued International Accounting Standard 7 (IAS 7), *Cash Flow Statements*, which became effective in 1994, mandating that firms provide cash flow statements.

US GAAP and IAS 7 rules for cash flow statements are similar, but some of the differences are:

- IAS 7 requires that the cash flow statement include changes in both cash and cash equivalents. US GAAP permits using cash alone or cash and cash equivalents.
- IAS 7 permits bank borrowings (overdraft) in certain countries to be included in cash equivalents rather than being considered a part of financing activities.
- IAS 7 allows interest paid to be included in operating activities or financing activities. US GAAP requires that interest paid be included in operating activities.
- US GAAP (FAS 95) requires that when the direct method is used to present the operating activities of the cash flow statement, a supplemental schedule must also present a cash flow statement using the indirect method. The IASC strongly recommends the direct method but allows either method. The

IASC considers the indirect method less clear to users of financial statements. Cash flow statements are most commonly prepared using the indirect method, which is not especially useful in projecting future cash flows.

Cash Flow Activities

The cash flow statement is partitioned into three segments, namely: 1) cash flow resulting from operating activities; 2) cash flow resulting from investing activities; and 3) cash flow resulting from financing activities.

The money coming into the business is called cash inflow, and money going out from the business is called cash outflow.

Operating Activities

Operating activities include the production, sales and delivery of the company's product as well as collecting payment from its customers. This could include purchasing raw materials, building inventory, advertising, and shipping the product.

Under IAS 7, operating cash flows include:

- Receipts from the sale of goods or services
- Receipts for the sale of loans, debt or equity instruments in a trading portfolio
- Interest received on loans
- Dividends received on equity securities
- Payments to suppliers for goods and services
- Payments to employees or on behalf of employees
- Interest payments (alternatively, this can be reported under financing activities in IAS 7, and US GAAP).

Items which are added back to [or subtracted from, as appropriate] the net income figure (which is found on the Income Statement) to arrive at cash flows from operations generally include:

- Depreciation (loss of tangible asset value over time)
- Deferred tax
- Amortization (loss of intangible asset value over time)
- Any gains or losses associated with the sale of a non-current asset, because associated cash flows do not belong in the operating section. (unrealised gains/losses are also added back from the income statement).

Investing Activities

Examples of Investing activities are;

- Purchase or Sale of an asset (assets can be land, building, equipment, marketable securities, etc.)
- Loans made to suppliers or received from customers
- Payments related to mergers and acquisitions.

Financing Activities

Financing activities include the inflow of cash from investors such as banks and shareholders, as well as the outflow of cash to shareholders as dividends as the company generates income. Other activities which impact the long-term liabilities and equity of the company are also listed in the financing activities section of the cash flow statement.

Under IAS 7,

- Proceeds from issuing short-term or long-term debt
- Payments of dividends
- Payments for repurchase of company shares
- Repayment of debt principal, including capital leases
- For non-profit organisations, receipts of donor-restricted cash that is limited to long-term purposes.

Items under the financing activities section include:

- Dividends paid
- Sale or repurchase of the company's stock
- Net borrowings
- Payment of dividend tax.

Disclosure of Non-cash Activities

Under IAS 7, non-cash investing and financing activities are disclosed in footnotes to the financial statements. Under US General Accepted Accounting Principles (GAAP), non-cash activities may be disclosed in a footnote or within the cash flow statement itself. Non-cash financing activities may include

- Leasing to purchase an asset
- Converting debt to equity
- Exchanging non-cash assets or liabilities for other non-cash assets or liabilities
- Issuing shares in exchange for assets.

Preparation Methods

The direct method of preparing a cash flow statement results in a more easily understood report. The indirect method is almost universally used, because FAS 95 requires a supplementary report similar to the indirect method if a company chooses to use the direct method.

Direct Method

The direct method for creating a cash flow statement reports major classes of gross cash receipts and payments. Under IAS 7, dividends received may be reported under operating activities or under investing activities.

If taxes paid are directly linked to operating activities, they are reported under operating activities; if the taxes are directly linked to investing activities or financing activities, they are reported under investing or financing activities. *Sample cash flow statement using the direct method.*

***Table** : Cash flows from (used in) operating activities*

Cash receipts from customers	9,500
Cash paid to suppliers and employees	(2,000)
Cash generated from operations (sum)	7,500
Interest paid	(2,000)
Income taxes paid	(3,000)
Net cash flows from operating activities	2,500
Cash flows from (used in) investing activities	
Proceeds from the sale of equipment	7,500
Dividends received	3,000
Net cash flows from investing activities	10,500
Cash flows from (used in) financing activities	
Dividends paid	(2,500)
Net cash flows used in financing activities	(2,500)
Net increase in cash and cash equivalents	10,500
Cash and cash equivalents, beginning of year	1,000
Cash and cash equivalents, end of year	$11,500

Indirect Method

The indirect method uses net-income as a starting point, makes adjustments for all transactions for non-cash items, then adjusts from all cash-based transactions. An increase in an asset account is subtracted from net income, and an increase in a liability account is added back to net income. This method converts accrual-basis net income (or loss) into cash flow by using a series of additions and deductions.

Rules (Operating Activities)

Table: *To Find Cash Flows* from Operating Activities *using the Balance Sheet and Net Income*

For Increases in	***Net Inc Adj***
Current Assets (Non-Cash)	Decrease
Current Liabilities	Increase
For All Non-Cash...	
**Expenses* (Decreases in Fixed Assets)	Increase

**Non-cash expenses must be added back to NI. Such expenses may be represented on the balance sheet as decreases in long term asset accounts. Thus decreases in fixed assets increase NI.*

The following rules can be followed to calculate Cash Flows from Operating Activities when given only a two year comparative balance sheet and the Net Income figure.

Cash Flows from Operating Activities can be found by adjusting Net Income relative to the change in beginning and ending balances of Current Assets, Current Liabilities, and sometimes Long Term Assets. When comparing the change in long term assets over a year, the accountant must be certain that these changes were caused entirely by their devaluation rather than purchases or sales (i.e. they must be operating items not providing or using cash) or if they are nonoperating items.

- Decrease in non-cash current assets are added to net income
- Increase in non-cash current asset are subtracted from net income
- Increase in current liabilities are added to net income
- Decrease in current liabilities are subtracted from net income
- Expenses with no cash outflows are added back to net income (depreciation and/or amortization expense are the only operating items that have no effect on cash flows in the period)
- Revenues with no cash inflows are subtracted from net income
- Non operating losses are added back to net income
- Non operating gains are subtracted from net income

The intricacies of this procedure might be seen as,

Net Cash Flows from Operating Activities = Net Income + Rule Items

For example, consider a company that has a net income of $100 this year, and its A/R increased by $25 since the beginning of the year. If the balances of all other current assets, long term assets and current liabilities did not change over the year, the cash flows could be determined by the rules above as $100 – $25 = Cash Flows from Operating Activities = $75.

The logic is that, if the company made $100 that year (net income), and they are using the accrual accounting system (not cash based) then any income they generated that year which has not yet been paid for in cash should be subtracted from the net income figure in order to find cash flows from operating activities. And the increase in A/R meant that $25 of sales occurred on credit and have not yet been paid for in cash. In the case of finding Cash Flows when there is a change in a fixed asset account, say the Buildings and Equipment account decreases, the change is subtracted from Net Income. The reasoning behind this is that because Net Income is calculated by, Net Income = Rev - Cogs - Depreciation Exp - Other Exp then the Net Income figure will be decreased by the building's depreciation that year. This depreciation is not associated with an exchange of cash, therefore the depreciation is added back into net income to remove the non-cash activity.

Rules (Financing Activities)

Finding the Cash Flows from Financing Activities is much more intuitive and needs little explanation. Generally, the things to account for are financing activities:

- Include as outflows, reductions of long term notes payable (as would represent the cash repayment of debt on the balance sheet)
- Or as inflows, the issuance of new notes payable
- Include as outflows, all dividends paid by the entity to outside parties
- Or as inflows, dividend payments received from outside parties
- Include as outflows, the purchase of notes stocks or bonds
- Or as inflows, the receipt of payments on such financing vehicles.

In the case of more advanced accounting situations, such as when dealing with subsidiaries, the accountant must:

- Exclude intra-company dividend payments.
- Exclude intra-company bond interest.

A traditional equation for this might look something like,

Net Cash Flows from Financing Activities =

$$[\textit{Divs received from 3rd parties}] - [\textit{Divs paid to 3rd parties}] - \{\textit{Divs paid to NCI but not intracompany div payments}\}$$

Example: cash flow of XYZ:

Table : *XYZ co. Ltd. Cash Flow Statement(all numbers in millions of Rs.)*

Period ending	03/31/2010	03/31/2009	03/31/2008
Net income	21,538	24,589	17,046
Operating activities, cash flows provided by or used in:			
Depreciation and amortization	2,790	2,592	2,747
Adjustments to net income	4,617	621	2,910
Decrease (increase) in accounts receivable	12,503	17,236	—
Increase (decrease) in liabilities (A/P, taxes payable)	131,622	19,822	37,856
Decrease (increase) in inventories	—	—	—
Increase (decrease) in other operating activities	(173,057)	(33,061)	(62,963)
Net cash flow from operating activities	13	31,799	(2,404)
Investing activities, cash flows provided by or used in:			
Capital expenditures	(4,035)	(3,724)	(3,011)
Investments	(201,777)	(71,710)	(75,649)
Other cash flows from investing activities	1,606	17,009	(571)
Net cash flows from investing activities	(204,206)	(58,425)	(79,231)
Financing activities, cash flows provided by or used in:			
Dividends paid	(9,826)	(9,188)	(8,375)
Sale (repurchase) of stock	(5,327)	(12,090)	133
Increase (decrease) in debt	101,122	26,651	21,204
Other cash flows from financing activities	120,461	27,910	70,349
Net cash flows from financing activities	206,430	33,283	83,311
Effect of exchange rate changes	645	(1,840)	731
Net increase (decrease) in cash and cash equivalents	2,882	4,817	2,407

Statement of Retained Earnings

The Statement of Retained Earnings (and similarly the *Equity Statement*, *Statement of Owner's Equity* for a single proprietorship, *Statement of Partner's Equity* for partnership, and Statement of Retained Earnings and Stockholders' Equity for corporation) are basic financial statements.

The statements explain the changes in a company's retained earnings over the reporting period. They break down changes in the owners' interest in the organisation, and in the application of retained profit or surplus from one accounting period to the next. Line items typically include profits or losses from operations, dividends paid, issue or redemption of stock, and any other items charged or credited to retained earnings. The statements are expected by Generally Accepted Accounting Principles and explain the owners' equity and retained earnings shown on the balance sheet, where:

Owners' Equity = Assets – Liabilities.

Requirements of the U.S. GAAP

A retained earnings statement is required by the U.S. Generally Accepted Accounting Principles (U.S. GAAP) whenever comparative balance sheets and income statements are presented. It may appear in the balance sheet, in a combined income statement and changes in retained earnings statement, or as a separate schedule.

Therefore, the statement of retained earnings uses information from the income statement and provides information to the balance sheet. Retained earnings are part of the balance sheet (another basic financial statement) under "stockholders equity (shareholders' equity)" and is mostly affected by net income earned during a period of time by the company less any dividends paid to the company's owners/ stockholders. The retained earnings account on the balance sheet is said to represent an "accumulation of earnings" since net profits and losses are added/subtracted from the account from period to period. Retained Earnings are part of the Statement of Changes in Equity. The general equation can be expressed as following:

Ending Retained Earnings = *Beginning* Retained Earnings – Dividends Paid + Net Income

This equation is necessary to use to find the Profit Before Tax to use in the Cash Flow Statement under Operating Actvities when using the indirect method. This is used whenever a comprehensive income statement is not given but only the balance sheet is given.

Requirements of IFRS

IAS 1 requires a business entity to present a separate Statement of Changes in Equity (SOCE) as one of the components of financial statements.

The statement shall show: (IAS1.106):

1. total comprehensive income for the period, showing separately amounts attributable to owners of the parent and to non-controlling interests
2. the effects of retrospective application, when applicable, for each component
3. reconciliations between the carrying amounts at the *beginning* and the *end* of the period for each component of equity, separately disclosing:
   - profit or loss
   - each item of other comprehensive income
   - transactions with owners, showing separately contributions by and distributions to owners and changes in ownership *control.*

However, the amount of dividends recognised as distributions, and the related amount per share, *may* be presented in the notes instead of presenting in the statement of changes in equity. (IAS1.107).

For Small and Medium-size Enterprises (SMEs), the Statement of Changes in Equity should show all changes in equity including:

- total comprehensive income
- owners' investments
- dividends
- owners' withdrawals of capital
- treasury share transactions.

They can omit the statement of changes in equity if the entity has no owner investments or withdrawals other than dividends, and elects to present a combined statement of comprehensive income and retained earnings.

Income Statement

Income statement (also referred to as *profit and loss statement (P&L), statement of financial performance, earnings statement, operating statement* or *statement of operations*) is a company's financial statement that indicates how the revenue (money received from the sale of products and services before expenses are taken out, also known as the "top line") is transformed into the net income (the result after all revenues and expenses have been accounted for, also known as the "bottom line").

It displays the revenues recognised for a specific period, and the cost and expenses charged against these revenues, including write-offs (e.g., depreciation and amortization of various assets) and taxes. The purpose of the income statement is to show managers and investors whether the company made or lost money during the period being reported. The important thing to remember about an income statement is that it represents a period of time. This contrasts with the balance sheet, which represents a single moment in time.

Charitable organisations that are required to publish financial statements do not produce an income statement. Instead, they produce a similar statement that reflects funding sources compared against program expenses, administrative costs, and other operating commitments. This statement is commonly referred to as the statement of activities. Revenues and expenses are further categorised in the statement of activities by the donor restrictions on the funds received and expended. The income statement can be prepared in one of two methods. The Single Step income statement takes a simpler approach, totalling revenues and subtracting expenses to find the bottom line. The more complex Multi-Step income statement (as the name implies) takes several steps to find the bottom line, starting with the gross profit.

It then calculates operating expenses and, when deducted from the gross profit, yields income from operations. Adding to income from operations is the difference of other revenues and other expenses. When combined with income from operations, this yields income before taxes. The final step is to deduct taxes, which finally produces the net income for the period measured.

Usefulness and Limitations of Income Statement

Income statements should help investors and creditors determine the past financial performance of the enterprise, predict future performance, and assess the capability of generating future cash flows through report of the income and expenses. However, information of an income statement has several limitations:

- Items that might be relevant but cannot be reliably measured are not reported (*e.g.* brand recognition and loyalty).

- Some numbers depend on accounting methods used (*e.g.* using FIFO or LIFO accounting to measure inventory level).
- Some numbers depend on judgments and estimates (*e.g.* depreciation expense depends on estimated useful life and salvage value).

INCOME STATEMENT GREENHARBOR LLC

For the year ended DECEMBER 31 2010

Debit	Credit
Revenues	
GROSS REVENUES (including INTEREST income)	296,397
Expenses:	
ADVERTISING	6,300
BANK & CREDIT CARD FEES	144
BOOKKEEPING	2,350
SUBCONTRACTORS	88,000
ENTERTAINMENT	5,550
INSURANCE	750
LEGAL & PROFESSIONAL SERVICES	1,575
LICENSES	632
PRINTING, POSTAGE & STATIONERY	320
RENT	13,000
MATERIALS	74,400
TELEPHONE	1,000
UTILITIES	1,491
TOTAL EXPENSES	(195,512)
NET INCOME	100,885

Guidelines for statements of comprehensive income and income statements of business entities are formulated by the International Accounting Standards Board and numerous country-specific organisations, for example the FASB in the U.S.. Names and usage of different accounts in the income statement depend on the type of organisation, industry practices and the requirements of different jurisdictions. If applicable to the business, summary values for the following items should be included in the income statement:

Operating Section

- Revenue - Cash inflows or other enhancements of assets of an entity during a period from delivering or producing goods, rendering services, or other activities that constitute the entity's ongoing major operations. It is usually presented as sales minus sales discounts, returns, and allowances. Every time a business sells a product or performs a service, it obtains revenue. This often is referred to as gross revenue or sales revenue.

- Expenses - Cash outflows or other using-up of assets or incurrence of liabilities during a period from delivering or producing goods, rendering services, or carrying out other activities that constitute the entity's ongoing major operations.
- Cost of Goods Sold (COGS)/ Cost of Sales - represents the direct costs attributable to goods produced and sold by a business (manufacturing or merchandizing). It includes *material costs, direct labour*, and *overhead costs* (as inabsorption costing), and excludes operating costs (period costs) such as selling, administrative, advertising or R&D, etc.
- Selling, General and Administrative expenses (SG&A or SGA) - consist of the combined payroll costs. SGA is usually understood as a major portion of non-production related costs, in contrast to production costs such as direct labour.
- Selling expenses - represent expenses needed to sell products (e.g. *salaries of sales people, commissions and travel expenses, advertising, freight, shipping, depreciation of sales store buildings and equipment*, etc.).
- General and Administrative (G&A) expenses - represent expenses to manage the business (*salaries of officers/executives, legal and professional fees, utilities, insurance, depreciation of office building and equipment, office rents, office supplies*, etc.).
- Depreciation / Amortization - the charge with respect to fixed assets / intangible assets that have been capitalised on the balance sheet for a specific (accounting) period. It is a systematic and rational allocation of cost rather than the recognition of market value decrement.
- Research & Development (R&D) expenses - represent expenses included in research and development.

Expenses recognised in the income statement should be analysed either by nature (raw materials, transport costs, staffing costs, depreciation, employee benefit etc.) or by function (cost of sales, selling, administrative, etc.). (IAS 1.99) If an entity categorises by function, then additional information on the nature of expenses, at least, – depreciation, amortisation and employee benefits expense –

must be disclosed. (IAS 1.104) The major exclusive of costs of goods sold, are classified as operating expenses.

These represent the resources expended, except for inventory purchases, in generating the revenue for the period. Expenses often are divided into two broad sub classicifications selling expenses and administrative expenses.

Non-operating Section

- Other revenues or gains - revenues and gains from other than primary business activities (e.g. *rent, income from patents*). It also includes unusual gains that are either unusual or infrequent, but not both (e.g. *gain from sale of securities* or *gain from disposal of fixed assets*)
- Other expenses or losses - expenses or losses not related to primary business operations, (e.g. *foreign exchange loss*).
- Finance costs - costs of borrowing from various creditors (e.g. *interest expenses, bank charges*).
- Income tax expense - sum of the amount of tax payable to tax authorities in the current reporting period (current tax liabilities/tax payable) and the amount of deferred tax liabilities (or assets).

Irregular Items

They are reported separately because this way users can better predict future cash flows - irregular items most likely will not recur. These are reported *net of taxes.*

- Discontinued operations is the most common type of irregular items. Shifting business location(s), stopping production temporarily, or changes due to technological improvement do not qualify as discontinued operations. Discontinued operations *must* be shown separately.

Cumulative effect of changes in accounting policies (principles) is the difference between the book value of the affected assets (or liabilities) under the old policy (principle) and what the book value would have been if the new principle had been applied in the prior periods. For example, valuation of inventories using LIFO instead of weighted average method. The changes should be applied retrospectively and shown as adjustments to the *beginning* balance of affected components in Equity. All comparative financial statements should be restated. (IAS 8)

However, *changes in estimates* (e.g. estimated useful life of a fixed asset) only requires prospective changes. (IAS 8) No items may be presented in the income statement as extraordinary items.

(IAS 1.87) *Extraordinary items* are both unusual (abnormal) and infrequent, for example, unexpected natural disaster, expropriation, prohibitions under new regulations. Additional items may be needed to fairly present the entity's results of operations. (IAS 1.85)

Disclosures

Certain items must be disclosed separately in the notes (or the statement of comprehensive income), if material, including: (IAS 1.98)

- Write-downs of inventories to net realisable value or of property, plant and equipment to recoverable amount, as well as *reversals* of such write-downs
- Restructurings of the activities of an entity and *reversals* of any provisions for the costs of restructuring
- Disposals of items of property, plant and equipment
- Disposals of investments
- Discontinued operations
- Litigation settlements
- Other reversals of provisions.

Earnings Per Share

Because of its importance, earnings per share (EPS) are required to be disclosed on the face of the income statement. A company which reports any of the irregular items must also report EPS for these items either in the statement or in the notes.

$$\text{Earnings per share} = \frac{\text{Net income} - \text{Preferred stock dividends}}{\text{Weighted average of common stock shares outstanding}}$$

There are two forms of EPS reported:

- Basic: in this case "weighted average of shares outstanding" includes only actual stocks outstanding.
- Diluted: in this case "weighted average of shares outstanding" is calculated as if all stock options, warrants, convertible bonds, and other securities that could be transformed into shares *are* transformed. This increases the number of shares and so EPS decreases. Diluted EPS is considered to be a more reliable way to measure EPS.

Accumulated other Comprehensive Income

In 1997 the United States Financial Accounting Standards Board issued Statement on Financial Accounting Standards No. 130 entitled "Reporting Comprehensive Income". This statement required all income statement items to be reported either as a regular item in the income statement or a special item as other comprehensive income. It is commonly referred to as FAS130.

Comprehensive Income

Comprehensive income is the total non-owner change in equity for a reporting period. This change encompasses all changes in equity other than transactions from owners. Most of these changes appear in the income statement. A few special types of gains and losses are not shown in the income statement but as special items in shareholder equity section of the balance sheet.

Since these comprehensive income items are not closed to retained earnings each period they accumulate as shareholder equity items and thus are entitled "Accumulated Other Comprehensive Income" and is sometimes referred to as "AOCI". Accumulated other comprehensive income is a subsection in equity where "other comprehensive income" is accumulated (summed or "aggregated"). The balance of AOCI is presented in the Equity section of the Balance Sheet as is the Retained Earnings balance, which aggregates past and current Earnings, and past and current Dividends.

Other Comprehensive Income

Other comprehensive income is the difference between net income as in the Income Statement (Profit or Loss Account) and comprehensive income, and represents the certain gains and losses of the enterprise not recognised in the P&L Account. It is commonly referred to as "OCI".

In practice, it comprises the following items:

1. Unrealised gains and losses on available for sale securities [IAS 39/ *"FAS 115" - "Accounting for Certain Investments in Debt and Equity Securities"*]
2. Gains and losses on derivatives held as cash flow hedges (only for effective portions) [IAS 39/ *"FAS 133" - "Accounting for Derivative Instruments and Hedging Activities"*]
3. Gains and losses resulting from translating the financial statements of foreign subsidiaries (from foreign currency to

the presentation currency) [IAS 21/ *"FAS 52" - "Foreign Currency Translation"*],

4. Actuarial gains and losses on defined benefit plans recognised (Minimum pension liability adjustments) [IAS 19/ *"FAS 158" - "Employers' Accounting For Defined Benefit Pension And Other Postretirement Plans"*]
5. Changes in the revaluation surplus [IAS 16 and IAS 38].

While the AOCI balance is presented in Equity section of the balance sheet, the annual accounting entries, as flows, are presented sometimes in a Statement of Comprehensive Income. This statement expands the traditional Income Statement beyond Earnings to include OCI in order to present Comprehensive Income.

Under the revised IAS 1, all non-owner changes in equity (comprehensive income) must be presented *either* in one Statement of comprehensive income or in two statements (a separate income statement and a statement of comprehensive income).

Reclassification to Profit or Loss (P&L)

Flows presented initially in OCI sometimes are reclassified into Earnings (Profit or Loss) when certain conditions are met. For the five types of OCI described above, the triggers for reclassification are presented in the accounting standard that gives rise to the OCI flow.

Alterations to Definition of OCI

In the United States further alterations to this OCI definition occur when a new standard (including a revision of a previously issued accounting standard) identifies an item that can be measured, should be measured in the financial statements, represents a "flow" variable rather than a stock, or snapshot, variable, and does not represent a flow variable that should be presented in the Income Statement as a component of Earnings. The flow variable that is both measurable and should be recognised is then added to the list above of items that a reporting entity would include in AOCI.

In the third quarter of 2008 the United States Securities and Exchange Commission received several proposals to allow the recognition in AOCI of certain fair value changes on financial instruments. This proposal was initially well received by representatives of the banking community who felt that Earnings recognition of these fair value changes during the concurrent "credit meltdown of 2008" would be inappropriate. The effect of this proposal, on balance, would be to remove sizeable losses from Earnings and thus

Retained Earnings of banks, and assist them in preserving their regulatory capital. The regulatory capital of banks in the US and generally worldwide includes contributed equity capital and retained earnings but excludes AOCI, even though it is reported as a component of the Equity section of the Balance Sheet.

Why is Hedge Accounting Necessary?

Many financial institutions and corporate businesses (entities) use derivative financial instruments to hedge their exposure to different risks (for example interest rate risk, foreign exchange risk, commodity risk, etc.). Accounting for derivative financial instruments under International Accounting Standards is covered by IAS39 (Financial Instrument: Recognition and Measurement).

IAS39 requires that all derivatives are marked-to-market with changes in the mark-to-market being taken to the profit and loss account. For many entities this would result in a significant amount of profit and loss volatility arising from the use of derivatives. An entity can mitigate the profit and loss effect arising from derivatives used for hedging, through an optional part of IAS39 relating to hedge accounting.

What Hedge Accounting Options are Available to an Entity?

All economic hedges aim to manage foreign currency exposure, meaning they are undertaken for the economic aim of reducing potential loss from fluctuations in foreign exchange rates. However, not all hedges are designated for special accounting treatment. Accounting standards enable hedge accounting for three different designated forex hedges:

- A cash flow hedge may be designated for a highly probable forecasted transaction, a firm commitment (not recorded on the balance sheet), foreign currency cash flows of a recognised asset or liability, or a forecasted intercompany transaction.
- A fair value hedge may be designated for a firm commitment (not recorded) or foreign currency cash flows of a recognised asset or liability.
- A net investment hedge may be designated for the net investment in a foreign operation.

The aim of hedge accounting is to provide an offset to the mark-to-market movement of the derivative in the profit and loss account. For a fair value hedge this is achieved either by marking-to-market an asset or a liability which offsets the P&L movement of the derivative.

For a cashflow hedge some of the derivative volatility into a separate component of the entity's equity called the cash flow hedge reserve. Where a hedge relationship is effective (meets the 80%–125% rule), most of the mark-to-market derivative volatility will be offset in the profit and loss account. To achieve hedge accounting requires a large amount of compliance work involving documenting the hedge relationship and both prospectively and retrospectively proving that the hedge relationship is effective.

Simple Procedure of Hedge Accounting

To know simple procedure of hedge accounting, we should divide hedge into two parts. One is fair value hedge and other is cash flow hedge. When we have risk of decreasing the share prices, we take the contract of fair value hedge. We give option to other at current prices. If anybody accepts and if in future, prices of share decreases, we will get gain from option and will record like general income record.

In cash flow hedge accounting, we do hedge for reducing the risk of increasing the prices. If prices will increases, we will have to paid same but we will receive the cash profit from future contract. We also record the payment and gaining amount from such transactions.

XBRL (eXtensible Business Reporting Language)

XBRL (eXtensible Business Reporting Language) is a freely available, market-driven, open, and global standard for exchanging business information. XBRL allows information modelling and the expression of semantic meaning commonly required in business reporting. XBRL is XML-based. It uses the XML syntax and related XML technologies such as XML Schema, XLink, XPath, and Namespaces to articulate this semantic meaning. One use of XBRL is to define and exchange financial information, such as a financial statement. The XBRL Specification is developed and published by XBRL International, Inc. (XII). XBRL is a standards-based way to communicate and exchange business information between business systems.

These communications are defined by metadata set out in XBRL taxonomies, which capture the definition of individual reporting concepts as well as the relationships between concepts and other semantic meaning. Information being communicated or exchanged is provided within an XBRL instance. Early users of XBRL included regulators such as the U.S. Federal Deposit Insurance Corporation and the Committee of European Banking Supervisors (CEBS). Common functions in many countries that make use of XBRL include regulators of stock exchanges and securities, banking regulators, business registrars, revenue reporting and tax-filing agencies, and national statistical agencies. A wiki repository of XBRL projects is available to be freely explored and updated. An XBRL Adoption Survey is available as well. According to the FT "the Securities and Exchange Commission (SEC) in the US, the UK's HM Revenue & Customs (HMRC), and Companies House in Singapore have begun to require companies to use it, and other regulators are following suit."

Specification

The current (2008) version of XBRL is 2.1, with errata corrections. The normative version of all the XML Schemas is provided in the specification documents, not in separate files. A conformance suite is available to test processors of XBRL documents.

XBRL Document Structure

In typical usage, XBRL consists of an *XBRL instance'*, containing primarily the business facts being reported, and a collection of taxonomies (called a Discoverable Taxonomy Set (DTS)), which define metadata about these facts, such as what the facts mean and how they relate to one another. XBRL uses XML Schema, XLink, and X Pointer standards.

XBRL Instance

The XBRL instance begins with the <xbrl> root element. There may be more than one XBRL instance embedded in a larger XML document. The XBRL instance itself holds the following information:

- *Business Facts* – facts can be divided into two categories
- *Items* are facts holding a single value. They are represented by a single XML element with the value as its content.
- *Tuples* are facts holding multiple values. They are represented by a single XML element containing nested Items or Tuples.

In the design of XBRL, all Item facts must be assigned a context.

- *Contexts* define the entity (e.g. company or individual) to which the fact applies, the period of time the fact is relevant, and an optional scenario. Date and time information appearing in the period element must conform to ISO 8601. Scenarios provide further contextual information about the facts, such as whether the business values reported are actual, projected, or budgeted.
- *Units* define the units used by numeric or fractional facts within the document, such as USD, shares. XBRL allows more

complex units to be defined if necessary. Facts of a monetary nature must use a unit from the ISO 4217 namespace.

- *Footnotes* use XLink to associate one or more facts with some content.
- *References* to XBRL taxonomies, typically through schema references. It is also possible to link directly to a linkbase.

This is an example of a fictitious Dutch company's International Financial Reporting Standards (IFRS) statement instance file :

```
<?xml version="1.0" encoding="UTF-8"?>
<xbrli:xbrl
xmlns:ifrs-gp="http://xbrl.iasb.org/int/fr/ifrs/gp/2005-05-15"
xmlns:iso4217="http://www.xbrl.org/2003/iso4217"
xmlns:xbrli="http://www.xbrl.org/2003/instance"
xmlns:xbrll="http://www.xbrl.org/2003/linkbase"
xmlns:xlink="http://www.w3.org/1999/xlink">

       <xbrll:schemaRef xbrll:href="http://www.org.com/xbrl/
taxonomy" xlink:type="simple"/>

       <ifrs-gp:OtherOperatingIncomeTotalFinancialInstitutions
contextRef="J2004" decimals="0" unitRef="EUR">38679000000</ifrs-
gp:OtherOperatingIncomeTotalFinancialInstitutions>

       <ifrs-gp:OtherAdministrativeExpenses contextRef="J2004"
decimals="0"        unitRef="EUR">35996000000</ifrs-
gp:OtherAdministrativeExpenses>

       <ifrs-gp:OtherOperatingExpenses contextRef="J2004"
decimals="0"        unitRef="EUR">870000000</ifrs-
gp:OtherOperatingExpenses>

      ...

      <ifrs-gp:OtherOperatingIncomeTotalByNature
contextRef="J2004" decimals="0" unitRe="EUR">10430000000</
ifrs-gp:OtherOperatingIncomeTotalByNature>

      <xbrli:context id="BJ2004">

           <xbrli:entity>

                  <xbrli:identifier scheme="www.iqinfo.com/
xbrl">ACME</xbrli:identifier>

           </xbrli:entity>

           <xbrli:period>

                <xbrli:instant>2004-01-01</xbrli:instant>

           </xbrli:period>

      </xbrli:context>
```

```
    <xbrli:context id="EJ2004">
        <xbrli:entity>
            <xbrli:identifier scheme="www.iqinfo.com/
xbrl">ACME</xbrli:identifier>
        </xbrli:entity>
        <xbrli:period>
            <xbrli:instant>2004-12-31</xbrli:instant>
        </xbrli:period>
    </xbrli:context>
    <xbrli:context id="J2004">
        <xbrli:entity>
            <xbrli:identifier scheme="www.iqinfo.com/
xbrl">ACME</xbrli:identifier>
        </xbrli:entity>
        <xbrli:period>
            <xbrli:startDate>2004-01-01</xbrli:startDate>
            <xbrli:endDate>2004-12-31</xbrli:endDate>
        </xbrli:period>
    </xbrli:context>
    <xbrli:unit id="EUR">
        <xbrli:measure>iso4217:EUR</xbrli:measure>
    </xbrli:unit>
</xbrli:xbrl>
```

XBRL Taxonomy

An XBRL Taxonomy is a collection of taxonomy schemas and linkbases. A taxonomy schema is an XML schema document (file). Linkbases are XML documents (file) which follow the XLink specification. The schema must ultimately extend the XBRL instance schema document and typically extend other published XBRL schemas on the xbrl.org website.

- *Taxonomy schemas* define Item and Tuple "concepts" using <xsd:element> elements. Concepts provide names for the fact and indicate whether or not it's a tuple or an item, the data type (such as monetary, numeric, fractional, or textual), and potentially more metadata. Items and Tuples can be regarded as "implementations" of concepts, or specific instances of a concept. A good analogy for those familiar with object oriented programming would be that Concepts are the classes and

Items and Tuples are Object instances of those classes. This is the source of the use of the "XBRL instance" terminology. In addition to defining concepts, taxonomy schemas reference linkbase documents. Tuples instances are 1..n relationships with their parents; their metadata is simply the collection of their attributes.

- *Linkbases* are a collection of Links, which themselves are a collection of locators, arcs, and potentially resources. Locators are elements that essentially reference a concept and provide an arbitrary label for it. In turn, arcs are elements indicating that a concept links to another concept by referencing the labels defined by the locators. Some arcs link concepts to other concepts. Other arcs link concepts to resources, the most common of which are human-readable labels for the concepts. The XBRL 2.1 specification defines five different kinds of linkbases.
- Label Linkbase – This linkbase provides human readable strings for concepts. Using the label linkbase, multiple languages can be supported, as well as multiple strings within each language.
- Reference Linkbase – This linkbase associates concepts with citations of some body of authoritative literature.
- Calculation Linkbase – This linkbase associates concepts with other concepts so that values appearing in an instance document may be checked for consistency.
- Definition Linkbase – This linkbase associates concepts with other concepts using a variety of arc roles to express relations such as is-a, whole-part, etc.
- Presentation Linkbase – This linkbase associates concepts with other concepts so that the resulting relations can guide the creation of a user interface, rendering, or visualisation.

This is the taxonomy schema of the above shown instance file:

```
<?xml version="1.0" encoding="utf-8"?>
<schema
xmlns="http://www.w3.org/2001/XMLSchema"
xmlns:xbrli="http://www.xbrl.org/2003/instance"
xmlns:link="http://www.xbrl.org/2003/linkbase"
xmlns:xlink="http://www.w3.rg/1999/xlink"
xmlns:ifrs-gp="http://xbrl.iasb.org/int/fr/ifrs/gp/2005-05-15"
xmlns:ifrs-gp-rol="http://xbrl.iasb.org/int/fr/ifrs/gp/2005-05-15/
```

```
roles"
xmlns:samp="http://www.iqinfo.com/xbrl/taxonomy"
targetNamespace="http://www.iqinfo.com/xbrl/taxonomy"
elementFormDefault="qualified"
attributeFormDefault="unqualified">

      <annotation>
            <appinfo>
                  <link:linkbaseRef  xlink:type='simple'
                  xlink:href='http://xbrl.iasb.org/int/fr/ifrs/
gp/2005-05-15/ifrs-gp-pre-bs-liquidity-2005-05-15.xml'
                     xlink:role='http://www.xbrl.org/2003/role/
presentationLinkbaseRef'
                   xlink:arcrole='http://www.w3.org/1999/xlink/
properties/linkbase'  />

                  <link:linkbaseRef  xlink:type='simple'
                  xlink:href='http://xbrl.iasb.org/int/fr/ifrs/
gp/2005-05-15/ifrs-gp-pre-is-byNature-2005-05-15.xml'
                     xlink:role='http://www.xbrl.org/2003/role/
presentationLinkbaseRef'
                   xlink:arcrole='http://www.w3.org/1999/xlink/
properties/linkbase'  />

                  <link:linkbaseRef  xlink:type='simple'
                  xlink:href='http://xbrl.iasb.org/int/fr/ifrs/
gp/2005-05-15/ifrs-gp-cal-bs-liquidity-2005-05-15.xml'
                     xlink:role='http://www.xbrl.org/2003/role/
calculationLinkbaseRef'
                   xlink:arcrole='http://www.w3.org/1999/xlink/
properties/linkbase'  />

                  <link:linkbaseRef  xlink:type='simple'
                  xlink:href='http://xbrl.iasb.org/int/fr/ifrs/
gp/2005-05-15/ifrs-gp-cal-is-byNature-2005-05-15.xml'
                     xlink:role='http://www.xbrl.org/2003/role/
calculationLinkbaseRef'
        xlink:arcrole='http://www.w3.org/1999/xlink/properties/
linkbase'  />
         </appinfo>
      </annotation>
       <import  namespace="http://www.xbrl.org/2003/instance"
```

```
    schemaLocation="http://www.xbrl.org/2003/xbrl-instance-2003-12-
31.xsd" />
     <import namespace="http://xbrl.iasb.org/int/fr/ifrs/gp/2005-
05-15"
     schemaLocation="http://xbrl.iasb.org/int/fr/ifrs/gp/2005-05-
15/ifrs-gp-2005-05-15.xsd" />
</schema>
```

XBRL's Global Ledger Framework (XBRL GL) is the only set of taxonomies that is developed and recommended by XII.

XBRL Modules

XBRL International has issued and reissued a stability pledge in relation to the core XBRL 2.1 specification. In addition to the core XBRL 2.1 specification, work continues on the development of XBRL modules that define new, compatible functionality.

- XBRL Dimensions 1.0 – This module has achieved Public Recommendation status in 2005. A new edition of the Dimensions 1.0 Specification with errata corrections was issued on 7 September 2009. The Dimension 1.0 Specification is an optional extension to the XBRL 2.1 Specification that enriches the rules and procedures for constructing dimensional taxonomies and instance documents.

  It supports the use of XBRL taxonomy linkbases to define additional, structured contextual information for business facts. Each piece of contextual information is referred to as a "dimension." The base XBRL specification essentially defines three dimensions: reporting period, reporting entity (i.e.; a company or a division thereof), and a loosely-defined reporting scenario, originally intended to distinguish between actual vs. projected facts. Taxonomies using XBRL Dimensions can define new dimensions, specify the valid values ("domains") for dimensions, designate which dimensions apply to which business concepts through mechanisms called "hypercubes", and relate other taxonomy metadata (labels, presentation information, etc.) to dimensions.

- XBRL Formula 1.0 – This module achieved Public Recommendation status 22 June 2009. The Formula Specification 1.0 supports the creation of expressions (using XPath) that can be applied to XBRL instances to validate its information or to calculate new XBRL facts in a new instance.

- XBRL Rendering – This module achieved Public Recommendation status 20 April 2010. The Inline XBRL (Rendering) Specification has two deliverables. One is "Inline XBRL", a specification for embedding XBRL inside XHTML. The other is a Specified Transformations registry. The registry will leverage the label and presentation linkbases to provide a facility for more comprehensive report definition. For example, the label linkbase can tell you that the English name for the ifrs-gp:assets concept is "Assets", and the presentation linkbase can tell you that ifrs-gp:assets is the first concept in the hierarchy named "Balance Sheet". The Rendering Linkbase would add the metadata that the "Balance Sheet" usually runs with the labels (in presentation order) down the former leftmost column, and then shows it with the two most recent periods within the next columns, in a particularly defined, structured order.
- XBRL Versioning – This module will support the creation of a standard versioning report, which will document the differences between two versions of the same taxonomy. Many large taxonomies (such as the IFRS taxonomy) change every year.

Extensibility

Besides the creation of additional modules, XBRL International supports several methods for continuing expansion of shared XBRL functionality.

- Link Role Registry – This registry, hosted at xbrl.org, collects link roles and arc roles to promote reuse across taxonomies.
- Functions Registry – This registry collects XPath functions for reuse in formula linkbases.
- Format Registry – This registry collects common numeric formats for reuse in Inline XBRL applications.
- Best Practice RFCs – These documents will share common practices among community members to improve interoperability of design.

iXBRL

iXBRL (in-line Extensible Business Reporting Language) is a development of XBRL in which the XBRL tags are embedded in the formal document, e.g. a published report and accounts. It requires the formal document to be in XHTML format so that the BRL tags can be invisible when the document is viewed in a web browser or printed yet be present when the electronic file is processed or viewed in an XML editor.

There are two main ways of producing iXBRL documents:

1. a program can generate the iXBRL file from source data;
2. a version of a word processing package can be used which has been enhanced to handle the XBRL tags.

However, neither of these produces a native iXBRL document which is designed as a web page and marked up with XBRL tags. A good example of this is the IASC 2007 Annual Report. In the UK, HM Revenue and Customs requires businesses to submit their report and accounts and tax computations in iXBRL format when making their Corporation Tax return. Businesses and their agents can use HMRC's Online Filing software to prepare their report and accounts and tax computations in iXBRL format or they can prepare the iXBRL files themselves and submit them to HMRC.

HMRC's Online Filing software is an example of a program which generates iXBRL from source data. This uses a series of forms in which the key data (which will appear in XBRL tags) are entered in data entry fields. Additional data (the rest ofthe report and accounts) are entered in text boxes. The program generates the iXBRL report and accounts in a standard sequence of sections and a standard format. All other formatting of material is lost. While the resulting report and accounts meets HMRC's requirements, it is not an attractive document to view or read. The word processing package which has been enhanced for iXBRL most widely is Microsoft Word. This allows "round-tripping" between its own format for the precise layout of documents and HTML through the use of nonstandard extensions to HTML.

The iXBRL tags are typically held as comments within the document. One difference between XBRL and iXBRL is that in iXBRL a data item (e.g. profit) may appear repeatedly and is marked up as an XML tag each time it appears. With large and complex accounts, the resulting file may be too large for a web browser to handle. This happens more often when, as in the UK, the company report, which may contain many graphics, is combined with the accounts in a single iXBRL document. The iXBRL specification allows for a set of iXBRL documents to be treated as a single iXBRL document set ("IXDS").

History

XBRL's beginning can be traced to the initial efforts of one person, Charles Hoffman, a certified public accountant from Tacoma,

Washington. The American Institute of Certified Public Accountants (AICPA) was also instrumental in pulling together what eventually became XBRL International. The specification has gone through several versions, all of which are still available.

- 1.0 – This version was based on DTDs. It expressed the difference between data exchange in instance documents and metadata exchange in taxonomy documents. Taxonomies were expressed as XML Schema files, but these were not used for instance validation.
- 2.0 – This version introduced use of XML Schema substitution groups as a way of allowing schema validation of instances. Concept relations were broken out into separate XLink based linkbases. Context data in the instance was collected into a separate element.
- 2.1 – This version tightened the definition of terms significantly, allowing for the introduction of a conformance suite.
- SBR – In 2003 the Dutch government started the Netherlands Taxonomy Project (NTP) to create a multi agency taxonomy and communication infrastructure. The Dutch government now collaborates with Australia, New Zealand and Singapore in Standard Business Reporting (SBR) programs. The key objectives of SBR include reduced time and effort spent preparing and filing reports for government by businesses. SBR can be considered an application profile of XBRL.
- XBRLS – In 2008 Charlie Hoffman and Rene van Egmond proposed a simplified, user-friendly XBRL application profile of XBRL that makes using XBRL easier for most business users, improves the potential for interoperability, and improves the potential for comparability needed by most business users, business communities, regulators and independent software vendors.

Lack of Accuracy

In April 2009 a study of the North Carolina State University Department of Accounting College of Management evaluated the accuracy of XBRL filings for 22 companies participating in the SEC's voluntary filing program in 2006. Results of a comparison of XBRL filings to Forms 10-K revealed multiple errors in signage, amounts, labelling, and classification. The study considers that these errors are serious since XBRL data is computer-readable and users will not visually recognize the errors, especially when using XBRL analysis software.

Auditor's Report

The auditor's report is a formal opinion, or disclaimer thereof, issued by either an internal auditor or an independent external auditor as a result of an internal or external audit or evaluation performed on a legal entity or subdivision thereof (called an "auditee").

The report is subsequently provided to a "user" (such as an individual, a group of persons, a company, a government, or even the general public, among others) as an assurance service in order for the user to make decisions based on the results of the audit. An auditor' report is considered an essential tool when reporting financial information to users, particularly in business.

Since many third-party users prefer, or even require financial information to be certified by an independent external auditor, many auditee rely on auditor reports to certify their information in order to attract investors, obtain loans, and improve public appearance. Some have even stated that financial information without an auditor's report is "essentially worthless" for investing purposes.

Auditor's Report on Financial Statements

It is mportant to note that auditor's reports on financial statements are neither evaluations nor any other simila determination used to evaluate entities in order to make a decision. The report is only an opinion on whether the information presented is correct and free from material misstatements, whereas all other determinations are left for the user to decide. There are four common types of auditor's reports, each one presenting a different situation encountered during the auditor's work. The four reports are as follows:

Unqualified Opinion

An opinion is said to be unqualified when the Auditor concludes that the Financial Statements give a true and fair view in accordance with the financial reporting framework used for the preparation and presentation of the Financial Statements. An Auditor gives a Clean opinion of Unqualified Opinion when he or she does not have any significant reservation in respect of matters contained in the Financial Statements.

The most frequent type of report is referred to as the Unqualified Opinion, and is regarded by many as the equivalentof a "clean bill of health" to a patient, which hasled many to call it the Clean Opinion, but in reality it is not a clean bill of health. This type of report is issued by an auditor when the financial statements presented are free of material misstatements and are represented fairly in accordance with the Generally Accepted Accounting Principles (GAAP), which in other words means that the company's financial condition, position, and operations are fairly presented in the financial statements. It is the best type of report an auditee may receive from an external auditor.

An Unqualified Opinion indicates the following —

(1) The Financial Statements have been prepared using the Generally Accepted Accounting Principles which have been consistently applied;

(2) The Financial Statements comply with relevant statutory requirements and regulations;

(3) There is adequate disclosure of all material matters relevant to the proper presentation of the financial information subject to statutory requirements, where applicable;

(4) Any changes in the accounting principles or in the method of their application and the effects thereof have been properly determined and disclosed in the Financial Statements.

The report consists of a title and header, a main body, the auditor's signature and address, and the report's issuance date. US auditing standards require that the title includes "independent" to convey to the user that the report was unbiased in all respects. Traditionally, the main body of the unqualified report consists of three main paragraphs, each with distinct standard wording and individual purpose, however certain auditors (including PricewaterhouseCoopers) have since modified the arrangement of the main body (but not the wording) in order to differentiate themselves from other audit firms.

The first paragraph (commonly referred to as the introductory paragraph) states the audit work performed and identifies the responsibilities of the auditor and the auditee in relation to the financial statements. The second paragraph (commonly referred to as the scope paragraph) details the scope of audit work, provides a general description of the nature of the work, examples of procedures performed, and any limitations the audit faced based on the nature of the work. This paragraph also states that the audit was performed in accordance with the country's prevailing generally accepted auditing standards and regulations. The third paragraph (commonly referred to as the opinion paragraph) simply states the auditor's opinion on the financial statements and whether they are in accordance with generally accepted accounting principles.

The following is an example of a standard unqualified auditor's report on financial statements as it is used in most countries, using the name ABC Company as an auditee's name:

Qualified Opinion Report

A Qualified Opinion report is issued when the auditor encountered one of two types of situations which do not comply with generally accepted accounting principles, however the rest of the financial statements are fairly presented.

This type of opinion is very similar to an unqualified or "clean opinion", but the report states that the financial statements are fairly presented with a certain exception which is otherwise misstated. The two types of situations which would cause an auditor to issue this opinion over the Unqualified opinion are:

- Single deviation from GAAP – this type of qualification occurs when one or more areas of the financial statements do not conform with GAAP (e.g. are misstated), but do not affect the rest of the financial statements from being fairly presented when taken as a whole. Examples of this include a company dedicated to a retail business that did not correctly calculate the depreciation expense of its building. Even if this expense is considered material, since the rest of the financial statements do conform with GAAP, then the auditor qualifies the opinion by describing the depreciation misstatement in the report and continues to issue a clean opinion on the rest of the financial statements.
- Limitation of scope - this type of qualification occurs when the auditor could not audit one or more areas of the financial statements, and although they could not be verified, the rest of the financial statements were audited and they conform GAAP. Examples of this include an auditor not being able to observe and test a company's inventory of goods. If the auditor audited the rest of the financial statements and is reasonably sure that they conform with GAAP, then the auditor simply states that the financial statements are fairly presented, with the exception of the inventory which could not be audited.

The wording of the qualified report is very similar to the Unqualified opinion, but an explanatory paragraph is added to explain the reasons for the qualification after the scope paragraph but before the opinion paragraph. The introductory paragraph is left exactly the same as in the unqualified opinion, while the scope and the opinion paragraphs receive a slight modification in line with the qualification in the explanatory paragraph. The scope paragraph is edited to include the following phrase in the first sentence, so that the user may be immediately aware of the qualification. This placement also informs the user that, except for the qualification, the rest of the audit was performed without qualifications:

> *"Except as discussed in the following paragraph, we conducted our audit..."*

The opinion paragraph is also edited to include an additional phrase in the first sentence, so that the user is reminded that the auditor's opinion explicitly excludes the qualification expressed. Depending on the type of qualification, the phrase is edited to either state the qualification and the adjustments needed to correct it, or state the scope limitation and that adjustments could have but not necessarily been required in order to correct it.

For a qualification arising from a deviation from GAAP, the following phrase is added to the opinion paragraph, using the depreciation example mentioned above:

> *"In our opinion, except for the effects of the Company's incorrect determination of depreciation expense, the financial statement referred to in the first paragraph presents fairly, in all material respects, the financial position of..."*

For a qualification arising from a scope of limitation, the following phrase is added to the opinion paragraph, using the inventory example mentioned above:

> *"In our opinion, except for the effects of such adjustments, if any, as might have been determined to be necessary had we been able to perform proper tests and procedures on the Company's inventory, the financial statement referred to in the first paragraph presents fairly, in all material respects, the financial position of..."*

Due to the phrases added to the scope and opinion paragraphs, many refer to this report as the Except-For Opinion.

Adverse Opinion Report

An Adverse Opinion is issued when the auditor determines that the financial statements of an auditee are materially misstated and, when considered as a whole, do not conform with GAAP. It is considered the opposite of an unqualified or clean opinion, essentially stating that the information contained is materially incorrect, unreliable, and inaccurate in order to assess the auditee's financial position and results of operations. Investors, lending institutions, and governments very rarely accept an auditee's financial statements if the auditor issued an adverse opinion, and usually request the auditee to correct the financial statements and obtain another audit report. Generally, an adverse opinion is only given if the financial statements pervasively differ from GAAP. An example of such a situation would be failure of a company to consolidate a material subsidiary.

The wording of the adverse report is similar to the qualified report. The scope paragraph is modified accordingly and an explanatory paragraph is added to explain the reason for the adverse opinion after the scope paragraph but before the opinion paragraph.

However, the most significant change in the adverse report from the qualified report is in the opinion paragraph, where the auditor clearly states that the financial statements are not in accordance with GAAP, which means that they, as a whole, are unreliable, inaccurate, and do not present a fair view of the auditee's position and operations.

> *"In our opinion,* because of the situations mentioned above *(in the explanatory paragraph), the financial statements referred to in the first paragraph* do not *present fairly, in all material respects, the financial position of..."*

Disclaimer of Opinion Report

A Disclaimer of Opinion, commonly referred to simply as a Disclaimer, is issued when the auditor could not form, and consequently refuses to present, an opinion on the financial statements. This type of report is issued when the auditor tried to audit an entity but could not complete the work due to various reasons and does not issue an opinion. The disclaimer of opinion report can be traced back to 1949, when the Statement on Auditing Procedure No. 23: *Recommendation Made To Clarify Accountant's Representations When Opinion Is Not Expressed* was published in order to provide guidance to auditors in presenting a disclaimer.

Statements on Auditing Standards (SAS) provide certain situations where a disclaimer of opinion may be appropriate:

- A lack of independence, or material conflict(s) of interest, exist between the auditor and the auditee (SAS No. 26)

- There are significant scope limitations, whether intentional or not, which hinder the auditor's work in obtaining evidence and performing procedures (SAS No. 58);
- There is a substantial doubt about the auditee's ability to continue as a going concern or, in other words, continue operating (SAS No. 59)
- There are significant uncertainties within the auditee (SAS No. 79).

Although this type of opinion is rarely used, the most common examples where disclaimers are issued include audits where the auditee willfully hides or refuses to provide evidence and information to the auditor in significant areas of the financial statements, where the auditee is facing significant legal and litigation issues in which the outcome is uncertain (usually government investigations), and where the auditee has going concern issues (the auditee may not continue operating in the near future). Investors, lending institutions, and governments typically reject an auditee's financial statements if the auditor disclaimed an opinion, and will request the auditee to correct the situations the auditor mentioned and obtain another audit report.

A disclaimer of opinion differs substantially from the rest of the auditor's reports because it provides very little information regarding the audit itself, and includes an explanatory paragraph stating the reasons for the disclaimer. Although the report still contains the letterhead, the auditee's name and address, the auditor's signature and address, and the report's issuance date, every other paragraph is modified extensively, and the scope paragraph is entirely omitted since the auditor is basically stating that an audit could not be realised.

In the introductory paragraph, the first phrase changes from "We have audited" to "We were engaged to audit" in order to let the user know that the auditee commissioned an audit, but does not mention that the auditor necessarily completed the audit. Additionally, since the audit was not completely and/or adequately performed, the auditor refuses to accept any responsibility by omitting the last sentence of the paragraph.

The scope paragraph is omitted in its entirety since, effectively, no audit was performed. Similar to the qualified and the adverse opinions, the auditor must briefly discuss the situations for the disclaimer in an explanatory paragraph. Finally, the opinion paragraph changes completely, stating that an opinion could not be formed and is not expressed because of the situations mentioned in the previous paragraphs.

The following is a draft of the three main paragraphs of a disclaimer of opinion because of inadequate accounting records of an auditee, which is considered a significant scope of limitation: We *were engaged to audit* the accompanying balance sheet of ABC Company, Inc. (the "Company") as of December 31, 20XX and the related statements of income and cash flows for the year then ended. These financial statements are the responsibility of the Company's management. The Company does not maintain adequate accounting records to provide sufficient information for the preparation of the basic financial statements. The Company's accounting records do not constitute a double-entry system which can produce financial statements.

Because of the significance of the matters discussed in the preceding paragraphs, the scope of our work was not sufficient to enable us to express, and we do not express, an opinion of the financial statements referred to in the first paragraph.

Auditor's Report on Internal Controls of Public Companies

Following the enactment of the Sarbanes-Oxley Act of 2002, the Public Company Accounting Oversight Board (PCAOB) was established in order to monitor, regulate, inspect, and discipline audit and public accounting firms of public companies. The PCAOB Auditing Standards No. 2 now requires auditors of public companies to include an additional disclosures in the opinion report regarding the auditee's internal controls, and to opine about the company's and auditor's assessment on the company's internal controls over financial reporting. These new requirements are commonly referred to as the COSO Opinion. The auditor's report is modified to include all necessary disclosures by either presenting the report subsequent to the report on the financial statements, or combining both reports into one auditor's report. The following is an example of the former version of adding a separate report immediately after the auditor's report on financial statements.

Internal Control Over Financial Reporting

We have also audited management's assessment, included in the accompanying Management's Annual Report on Internal Control Over Financial Reporting, that the Company maintained effective internal control over financial reporting as of December 31, 20XX, based on criteria established in Internal Control—Integrated Framework issued by the Committee of Sponsoring Organisations of the Treadway Commission ("COSO"). The Company's management is responsible for maintaining effective internal control over financial reporting and for its assessment of the effectiveness of internal control over financial reporting. Our responsibility is to express an opinion on management's assessment and on the effectiveness of the Company's internal control over financial reporting based on our audit. We conducted our audits in accordance with the standards of the Public Company Accounting Oversight Board (United States). Those standards require that we plan and perform the audit to obtain reasonable assurance about whether effective internal control over financial reporting was maintained in all material respects. Our audit of internal control over financial reporting included obtaining an understanding of internal control over financial reporting, evaluating management's assessment, testing and evaluating the design and operating effectiveness of internal control, and performing such other procedures as we considered necessary in the circumstances. We believe that our audit provides a reasonable basis for our opinion.

A company's internal control over financial reporting is a process designed to provide reasonable assurance regarding the reliability of financial reporting and the preparation of financial statements for external purposes in accordance with generally accepted accounting principles. A company's internal control over financial reporting includes those policies and procedures that (1) pertain to the maintenance of records that, in reasonable detail, accurately and fairly reflect the transactions and dispositions of the assets of the company; (2) provide reasonable assurance that transactions are recorded as necessary to permit preparation of financial statements in accordance with generally accepted accounting principles, and that receipts and expenditures of the company are being made only in accordance with authorisations of management and directors of the company; and (3) provide reasonable assurance regarding prevention or timely detection of unauthorised acquisition, use, or disposition of the company's assets that could have a material effect on the financial statements.

Because of its inherent limitations, internal control over financial reporting may not prevent or detect misstatements. Also, projections of any evaluation of effectiveness to future periods are subject to the risk that controls may become inadequate because of changes in conditions, or that the degree of compliance with the policies or procedures may deteriorate. In our opinion, management's assessment that ABC Company maintained effective internal control over financial reporting as of December 31, 20XX, is fairly stated, in all material respects, based on criteria established in Internal Control—Integrated Framework issued by COSO. Furthermore, in our opinion, ABC Company maintained, in all material respects, effective internal control over financial reporting as of December 31, 20XX, based on criteria established in Internal Control—Integrated Framework issued by COSO.

Going Concern

Going concern is a term which means that an entity will continue to operate in the near future which is generally more than next 12 months, so long as it generates or obtains enough resources to operate. If the auditee is not a going concern, it means that it is either dissolved, bankrupt, shutdown, etc. Auditors are required to consider the going concern of an auditee before issuing a report. If the auditee is a going concern, the auditor does not modify his/her report in any way. However, if the auditor considers that the auditee is not a going concern, or will not be a going concern in the near future, then the auditor is required to include an explanatory paragraph before the opinion paragraph or following the opinion paragraph, in the audit report explaining the situation, which is commonly referred to as the going concern disclosure. Such as opinion is called an "unqualified modified opinion".

Unfortunately, many auditors are increasingly reluctant to include this disclosure in their opinions, since it is considered a "self-fulfilling prophesy" by some. This is because a disclosure for a lack of going concern is viewed negatively by investors, lending institutions, and credit agencies, and therefore reduces the chance that the auditee may obtain the capital or borrowing it needs to survive once the disclosure is made. If this situation occurs, the auditee is more likely to stop being a going concern while the auditor loses potential future audit engagements, and so the auditor may be pressured to avoid including a going concern disclosure. In a study performed on 2001 bankruptcies, nearly half (48%) of selected public companies who faced bankruptcy in 2001 did not have a "going concern disclosure" in the previous auditor's reports. Additionally, 12 of the 20 largest bankruptcies in U.S. history occurred between 2001 and 2002 and none of them had a "going concern disclosure" in their previous auditor's report. As for the actual wording of the auditor's report, when a lack of going concern is determined by the auditor, the disclosure paragraph should state the situation, state the auditor's determination, and state the auditee's plan to correct the situation. The disclosure paragraph should immediately follow the opinion paragraph. The following is the most widely used format of the paragraph which, in this case, deals with a company that has recurring losses: The accompanying financial statements have been prepared assuming that the Company will continue as a going concern. As discussed in Note (X) to the financial statements, the Company has suffered recurring losses and has a net capital deficiency. These conditions raise substantial doubt about its ability to continue as a going concern. Management's plans in regard to these matters are also described in Note (X). The financial statements do not include any adjustments relating to the recoverability and classification of asset carrying amounts or the amount and classification of liabilities that might result should the Company be unable to continue as a going concern.

5

Trends in State Corporate Tax Revenues

If we compare state corporate tax receipts to gross state product (GSP), we have a rough measure of whether the corporate income tax is keeping up with the general movement in a state's economy. Figure depicted earlier demonstrates this point more directly; it shows a divergence between state corporate income tax revenues and GSP (the alues were normalized to 1980). The trend line for SCIT is below that of GSP for the entire period. While the divergence is evident from 1980, there is a significant drop in 1989 and another downward adjustment in 1995. It appears that something other than changes in the economy impacted state corporate revenues throughout the period. A simple regression of normalized state corporate income taxes on time and normalized gross state product suggests that over the 1981–2000 period, the percentage change in state corporate income taxes for a one percent change in gross state product is 0.84.

Interestingly, if we break up the series and run separate regression for 1981–1989 and 1990–2000, the elasticity of the state corporate income tax falls from 1.08 for the 1981–1989 period to 0.78 for the latter period. There are some differences among the states regarding this trend. Out of the 44 states for which we have data on state corporate income taxes, 30 states (68 percent) have trends reflecting the divergence between GSP and state corporate income tax revenues illustrated. For 23 of these 30 states, there is a continuous divergence between GSP and corporate income tax revenue over the period. Some of these 30 states, including Maine, New Hampshire, North Carolina, Illinois, Nebraska, Arizona, and Arkansas, show relatively minor divergence between the growth of corporate income tax receipts and

GSP; in fact, in the early 2000s, state corporate income tax growth closely approaches that of GSP in Maine and New Hampshire. On the other hand, some states, for example, Hawaii, Ohio, Oregon, Rhode Island, and South Carolina, show very large divergences over the period. Finally, 14 states show mixed or opposite trends. In seven states (Michigan, Montana, North Dakota, Delaware, Missis- sippi, Oklahoma, and Utah), the growth in state corporate income tax tracks very closely the growth in GSP. West Virginia is an outlier in that it has relatively large reported growth in state corporate income taxes relative to GSP over the period, per- haps due to the state's frequent changes in corporate income tax rate. Fox and Luna (2002) present a rather comprehensive list of factors that may have inûuenced state corporate income taxes.

They discuss each of the factors and provide some data relevant to them, but for most of the factors they are unable to estimate the magnitude of the effect. In fact, there exists little research that provides estimates of the magnitude of the effect of the various factors that are thought to be responsible for the downward trend in state corporate income tax revenue relative to GSP. We now turn to a discussion of the few studies that do exist. The amount of state corporate income tax that is avoided through passive investment schemes, more commonly known as "Delaware holding companies," is generally unknown, but the Center on Budget and Policy Priorities (Mazerov, 2003) suggests that based on several important court cases where the value of the tax saving was disclosed, the revenue loss to states is quite substantial. Unfortunately, no data are available that allow a direct investigation of the growth in passive holding companies.

Fox and Luna (2003) explore the extent to which limited liability companies (LLCs) account for the recent decline in SCIT revenues. LLCs were first adopted in 1977 but gained popularity in the 1990s and are now an option in all states. LLCs combine the advantages of partnerships (no corporate tax) and corporations (limited liabilities) and they avoid the restrictions on ownership associated with S–corporations. To measure the effect of LLCs on SCIT revenue, Fox and Luna (2003) use panel data from states over the period of 1988 to 2000, although there are several missing observations. The dependent variable in the revenue equation is SCIT revenue measured as a percentage of personal income. The independent variable of interest is the percentage of businesses in a given year that choose the LLC structure. In order to account for the likelihood that the extent of adoption of LLCs by firms in a state is a function of the level of corporate income taxes, they estimate a simultaneous model. For the average state, Fox and Luna's (2003) regression analysis implies that a ten percent increase in the share of LLC firms reduces SCIT revenue as a percent of personal income by 3.6 percent. This implies that the rise of LLCs has reduced state tax revenue by about one–third.

The multistate tax commission (MTC) (2003) estimated that domestic and international corporate tax sheltering reduced state corporate income tax revenue by 35 percent (of actual collections) in 2001. A breakdown by state of the revenue loss was calculated, and mid–range estimated losses extend from a low of 10.3 percent for Michigan to a high of 57.8 percent for West Virginia. Fisher (2002) explores the effect of changes in apportionment formulas, tax rates, and tax incentives on effective corporate tax rates in 20 states during the period 1990 to 1998.

He relies on a hypothetical firm model developed by Fisher and Peters (1998). The major limitation of the model is that it applies only to manufacturing firms and only to 20 states, although these states account for 75 per- cent of U.S. manufacturing. Fisher finds that for manufacturing investment in the 20 states, the effective corporate income tax rate before incentives fell from 4.91 percent in 1990 to 4.42 percent in 1998, a decrease of 11.4 percent.

Considering the effective corporate income tax rate net of incentives, Fisher ûnds that it fell from 4.42 percent in 1990 to 3.12 percent in 1998, a decrease of 29.4 percent. It appears from Fisher's analysis that for manufacturing firms, the decrease in effective tax rates is largely due to the increase in the use of tax incentives. In fact, tax incentives increased from 9.9 percent of gross income from manufacturing investment in 1990 to 29.4 percent in 1998.

Fisher (2002) also investigates whether shifts in manufacturing to low–tax states has had an effect on the national trend of declining effective SCIT rates. For manufacturing investment in the 20 states, he ûnds that tax rates after incentives were higher among those states gaining manufacturing shares.

Thus, a shift to low–tax states does not appear to explain the declining effective SCIT rate for manufacturing firms. He also ûnds that increased local property tax (a deductible expense) is not a significant factor in explaining the decrease in the effective SCIT rate. There are a few studies that have estimated point–in–time revenue losses from specific legislative actions. Illinois, for example, estimated that the adoption of the single–sales factor apportionment formula in 1998 reduced 2001 revenues by approximately $63 million, which is 6 percent of gross corporate income tax revenues (Illinois Economic and Fiscal Commission, 2002). Massachusetts adopted several corporate tax changes in the 1990s, including an increased weight on the sales factor.

The estimated revenue loss from this shift from the three factor formula is $221.3 million for FY 2004 (Executive Office for Administration and Finance, 2003). Other changes in Massachusetts during the 1990s included a reduction in the tax rate for banks (a $32 million reduction in revenue), a tax rate reduction for insurance firms (a $39 million revenue reduction), a research and development (R&D) tax credit (a $94 million reduction), and an investment tax credit (a $13 million reduction). Actual corporate tax revenue for FY 2003 was $799 million.

Changes in Federal Taxable Income

Most states use federal corporate taxable income as the basis for their corporate income tax. Thus, policies at the federal level that affect corporate taxable income should affect state corporate income tax collections. Fox and Luna (2002), as part of their summary exploration of the factors driving the trends in SCIT revenue, focus on changes in federal corporate taxable income. They calculate the effective tax rate measured as the ratio of federal corporate income tax revenue to corporate proûts, as reported in the NIPA, for the period of 1960 to 2000.

We use their calculations and add two subsequent years. They report two ratios, one using actual tax receipts and one using tax receipts adjusted for changes in the federal tax rate; we consider only the latter. From 1960 to 1982, the adjusted effective tax rate declined from 40 to 20 percent (its low point for the post–1960 period). Changes in the early 1980s, culminating in the Tax Reform Act of 1986(TRA86), resulted in a substantial increase in the adjusted effective tax rate to about 42 percent in 1987.

TRA86 created a rate structure under which the statutory corporate tax rate exceeded the statutory individual income tax rate for the ûrst time in the modern history of both income taxes, while also changing the tax base. These federal changes increased the incentive for businesses to ûnd a way to distribute income so that it could be taxed at the lower individual income tax rate. This could be accomplished if business income were to flow through to individuals via partnerships, S–corps or LLCs. If this change occurred, the number of corporate income tax returns and corporate tax liabilities at the state level could fall as businesses "disincorporated."3 The effect of these changes, including changes in organisation arrangements, is to reduce the federal corporate tax base and, by extension, the state tax base. TRA86 also changed the definition of taxable income.

The investment tax credit was eliminated, the research and development tax credit was reduced, the preferential rate of capital gains taxation was eliminated, depreciation allowances were reduced, and business and entertainment expenses were reduced, among other changes. Because of the close coupling of most state corporate income tax bases to the federal corporate tax base, states were also subject to significant changes in their corporate income tax bases. Post–1987, additional changes occurred that reduced adjusted effective (statutory) rates through the early 1990s. Between 1993 and 2000, the adjusted effective rate increased from about 31 to about 36 percent.

Additional tax changes were made in 2002 (retroactive to 2001), when depreciation allowances and expensing for small businesses were made more lucrative, allowing an immediate deduction of 30 percent of new equipment purchases. For 2002, the adjusted effective tax rate had fallen to 25 percent. The effect of federal base changes on state corporate tax revenue depends on the period under consideration. If we compare the federal adjusted effective tax rate for 1960 to that for 2002, we ûnd that for that period, the adjusted effective tax rate did not change by very much and, thus, federal base changes accounted for a relatively small portion of the fall–off in state corporate income tax revenues.

However, for the period we consider, i.e., 1980 to 2002, the federal adjusted effective tax rate increased and, thus, changes in the federal tax base, ceteris paribus, should have substantially increased state corporate tax revenue. Most of the change in the effective tax rate during that later period occurred in the 1980s and, thus, changes at the federal level since the late 1980s have resulted in a modest decline in the federal tax base relative to proûts. Therefore, for the period we consider, changes at the federal level do not appear to be the cause of the decrease in state corporate income taxes.

Empirical Evidence: Survey of State Tax Administrators

For this part of the study, we used a mail survey to examine the opinions of state tax administrators on the importance of various economic, legislative, and administrative factors in explaining SCIT trends. The officials we surveyed were chosen based on recommendations from the Federation of Tax Administrators (FTA). The professional leadership of the FTA identified two administrative professionals in each state with a SCIT who have been recognised for their expertise and knowledge of state–specific SCIT issues.

Surveys were sent to 90 tax administrators, and we received 41 completed surveys from 24 states. The sample size is small by conventional standards. But given the nature of the questions and the extensive time frame covered by the survey, the population of experts with both an understanding of the issues and a historical perspective on the SCIT within the context of a state's legislative, administrative, and economic history is small. Thus, we have a small but well–informed sample. To motivate responses to the survey, we included with the survey a figure similar to Figure given for each recipient's individual state to illustrate the relative year–over–year trends in GSP and SCIT.

Based on the relationship between a state's GSP index and a state's SCIT index, we defined state–specific subperiods for analysis that were distinguished by the degree to which the trend in the SCIT index corresponded to the trend in the GSP index. We then solicited opinions of the experts regarding the importance of a set of policy and economic factors in explaining the various trends in SCIT relative to GSP for each subperiod that we identiûed. The issues on which we sought opinions can be classified into six general areas. The ûrst area included issues that are under the direct control of the firm's corporate tax departments and questions about the perceived importance of corporate tax planning and corporate tax compliance. The second area solicited views on the ef- fects of national and state business cycles on SCIT revenue.

The third general section had ten questions exploring the revenue importance of SCIT policies over which the state has policy and legislative control. These policies are all directly related to the definition of the SCIT tax base. Examples of such polices are the allowance of passive investments (Delaware holding companies), subchapter "S" corporations, economic development credits, LLC entities, carry forward and throwback rules, and state depreciation schedules.

The fourth general area of inquiry included two questions about changes in the federal corporate income tax code, both federal depreciation and general code changes. The final two general areas included questions about the importance of state corporate tax rates and of the state's administrative efforts, e.g., audits and enforcement.

When replying to the questions, respondents were asked to rate the effect of the various factors in terms of the perceived effect on SCIT revenue. The responses and the assigned score were "substantial increase in revenue" (1), "increase in revenue" (2), "no effect on revenue" (3), "decline in revenue" (4), and "substantial decline in revenue" (5).

We received returned questionnaires that allowed evaluations of 57 periods when revenue from the SCIT was decreasing relative to GSP and 49 periods when revenue was increasing at about the same rate or faster than the change in GSP. When the indices were moving in the same upward directions, we reported the interval as an "increasing" period, and if the SCIT index was decreasing as the GSP index was increasing, the phase was reported as a "decreasing" period.

Each state had at least two distinct revenue periods and in many states there were three or four periods. We made no mention in our instructions to the respondents about the relative direction of the GSP or SCIT indices, we only asked the respondents to comment on the importance of the above listed items for each distinct period in the state. The results are summarised in Table 1.9 For the factors on which the experts expressed an opinion, the most common response (47 percent) was that the factor had no observable effect on the change in SCIT revenue. Given the level of rhetoric that often surrounds the SCIT, we did not expect this outcome; we thought the views expressed would be more polarized.

The second somewhat surprising outcome was that the next most common response (35 percent) was that when an issue was perceived to trigger a change in revenue, it was reported as a decline, but was only viewed as a modest decline. This was true for factors like formula apportionment, combined reporting, and nexus confusion. Also, many state policies (for example, rate or base changes) had little reported effect because the policies were not commonly adopted. Less than eight percent of the responses reported any policy that created a substantial decline in SCIT revenue.

Respondents believed that most of the factors we inquired about decreased revenue regardless of whether SCIT was increasing or decreasing relative to GSP. This result suggests that tax administrators see most factors as having a negative effect on revenues and that the trend in SCIT is the result of many factors, each of which has had at best a small effect on the trend in SCIT. Consistent with the finding of the previous section, responses to the survey suggest that state administrators do not believe state SCIT revenue was overwhelmed by the changes at the federal level. We were also surprised by the numour instructions to the respondents about the relative direction of the GSP or SCIT indices, we only asked the respondents to comment on the importance of the above listed items for each distinct period in the state. The results are summarised in Table 1.9

For the factors on which the experts expressed an opinion, the most common response (47 percent) was that the factor had no observable effect on the change in SCIT revenue. Given the level of rhetoric that often surrounds the SCIT, we did not expect this outcome; we thought the views expressed would be more polarized. The second somewhat surprising outcome was that the next most common response (35 percent) was that when an issue was perceived to trigger a change in revenue, it was reported as a decline, but was only viewed as a modest decline. This was true for factors like formula apportionment, combined reporting, and nexus confusion.

Also, many state policies (for example, rate or base changes) had little reported effect because the policies were not commonly adopted. Less than eight percent of the responses reported any policy that created a substantial decline in SCIT revenue. Respondents believed that most of the factors we inquired about decreased revenue regardless of whether SCIT was increasing or decreasing relative to GSP. This result suggests that tax administrators see most factors as having a negative effect on revenues and that the trend in SCIT is the result of many factors, each of which has had at best a small effect on the trend in SCIT. Consistent with the finding of the previous section, responses to the survey suggest that state administrators do not believe state SCIT revenue was overwhelmed by the changes at the federal level. We were also surprised by the num-Cross–sectional data from Utah that al- lowed us to identify firms by their North American Industry Classification System

(NAICS) classification suggests that the magnitude of the state corporate tax differs, and quite dramatically, depending on the type of industry.10 Data does not exist to allow us to calculate tax revenue as a percent of GSP by industry. Instead we consider multi–state firms and compare by NAICS the ratio of corporate income taxes to the value of each of the three standard apportionment factors—property, sales, and payroll. These comparisons are made using data from the 2001 state corporate tax returns filed in Utah. (We are limited to such ratios because taxable income is not reported on Utah state tax returns.) Figure suggests that there are substantial differences across industries in the values of the ratios of Utah corporate income tax to each of the three factors. Consider, for example, the payroll factor, which is the largest income component of GSP. The ratio of corporate taxes to payroll varies significantly across industries. For example, the professional, scientific, technical sector has low corporate income tax relative to payroll as compared to the finance and insurance sector.

Thus, growth of the former sector would cause GSP to grow more rapidly than corporate tax revenue, all else equal. A second way of considering the effect of the industrial sector is to compare Utah corporate income taxes to federal corporate income taxes. The beginning point of the Utah law is federal taxable income.

Thus, if there were no differences across industrial sectors in the ability of firms to engage in tax planning or in the state's corporate tax provision, we would expect that the ratio of Utah to federal corporate income tax would be very similar across industries. The evidence in Figure given seems quite clear—there are substantial differences across industries in the state corporate tax burden relative to the federal corporate tax burden. We calculated the correlation between the growth in each industrial sector, as measured by employment growth between 1990 and 2003, and the values of the ratios reported. For the ratio of taxes to payroll and of Utah taxes to

Federal taxes, the correlation coefficients with employment growth are –0.35 and –0.49, respectively. This implies that the growth in the Utah economy was focused on those industries in which corporate taxes are a small percentage of payroll and in which Utah corporate taxes are a small percentage of Federal corporate taxes. This suggests that differential growth by industries may have reduced corporate income taxes as a percentage of GSP.

Empirical Evidence: A Georgia Case Study

In this section, we report on an analysis of the change in SCIT conducted with a panel of Georgia CIT returns. Table 2 shows the aggregate Georgia tax liability of multistate corporations from 1992 to 2002, along with the dollar and percentage change from the previous year. The early 1990s saw significant growth in aggregate tax liability, with annual increases of over 41 percent in 1993 and roughly 25 percent in 1994. Other than a 21.7 percent upturn in 1998, growth in aggregate tax liability slowed or turned slightly negative for the remainder of the decade. Growth turned significantly negative beginning in 2000. Aggregate tax liability fell 18.0 percent in 2001 and 47.8 percent in 2002. From 1999 to 2002, aggregate tax liability of multi- state corporations fell from $601 million to $238 million. These large changes in aggregate tax liability can be broken down into their component parts in order to isolate the predominant factor or factors that explain the change. To accomplish this, we considered only firms with a non–negative tax liability in each year, since firms with a negative tax liability are charged no tax, and movements in the various determinants of tax liability do not alter aggregate collections except to the extent that they come into or fall out of the tax umbrella.

Tax Credits

Aggregate Georgia tax liability for multistate corporations in any given year is given by: Taxt = Σi max{0, τt,π Tit – δit}, where τ is the statutory corporate income tax rate, π T is Georgia taxable income, and δ is tax credits taken. Table 3 decomposes aggregate Georgia tax liability for corporations reporting non–negative taxable income into the amount of pre–credit tax liability (τπ T) and tax credits taken. The aggregate Georgia tax liability of multistate corporations was boosted in the early 1990s largely by increases in taxable income,11 but also by reductions in tax credits taken (with the exception of 1994). Increased use of tax credits mitigated increases in taxable income in the late 1990s.

By 2000, large declines in taxable income drove aggregate tax liability down precipitously. The impact of tax credits on tax collections varied widely from year–to–year, being as low as 2.4 percent of pre–credit tax liability in 1993 and as high as 19.6 percent in 1992, averaging 10.8 percent over the period. Overall, the use of tax credits seems to have increased over time, averaging 8.8 percent from 1992 to 1997 and 13.0 percent since 1998.

Allocation and Apportionment

The aggregate Georgia taxable income of multi–state corporations can be writ- ten as: [2] π Tt = Σi = where π A is income subject to apportionment, φ is the share of income apportioned to Georgia, α is taxable (non–business) income specifically allocated to Georgia, and η is net operating loss (NOL) deductions (NOL reflects apportionment of prior year income).

Individual corporations are indexed by i, and years are indexed by t. φ * represents the weighted average apportionment ratio for all multistate corporations filing a Georgia income tax return. Table 4 presents values for the decomposition of changes in aggregate taxable income according to [2]. Changes in specific allocation (Δα) to Georgia account for little of the total changes in aggregate taxable income. The only exceptions are 1996 and 1997, where the large values reflect activity on a single corporate income tax return from a firm that allocated \$4.6 billion in nonbusiness income to Georgia in 1996 and took an NOL ($\Delta\eta$) for the same amount. These are then represented in opposite values of roughly the same magnitude in allocation and NOL in the following year.

Changes in apportionment percentages vary by a surprisingly large margin from year to year, resulting in large year–to–year differences in $\Delta\varphi$ *. This suggests that corporations are able to manage apportionment factors in an effort to manage taxable income. Other than the large increase in 1995 and a moderate increase in 1998, the change in taxable income apportioned to Georgia due to changes in φ * has been negative in the aggregate, with especially large declines in 2000 and 2002. One possible policy–oriented explanation for this pattern is the 1995 switch to a double-weighted sales apportionment formula. The most salient item in Table 4 is an increase in taxable income of \$3.5 billion, arising from changes in the apportionment percentage in 1995 ($\Delta\varphi$ *).

Because 1995 was the ûrst year in which multistate firms were subjected to a double–weighted sales apportionment formula, the most obvious explanation is that the large increase in taxable income is due to the change in factor weights. Much of the initial increase in revenues arising from a change in the apportionment formula depends on the relative sales or production intensity of corporations in the state. Previous research has shown Georgia to be a production–intensive state.

Thus, with all else equal, Georgia should have seen an initial decrease in the share of income apportioned to it rather than an increase as a result of the shift to a double–weighted sales factor. The anomaly arises because of dramatic differences in the growth of reported sales (S), payroll (P), and property (R) in Georgia relative to the nation as a whole from 1994 to 1995 (for firms with positive taxable income) (Table 5). For example, Georgia property was down 6.5 percent from 1994 to 1995, but national property reported on Georgia income tax returns (with positive taxable income) decreased by 46.5 percent. Payroll reported on tax returns was up 3.9 percent in Georgia in 1995, but down 42.2 percent nationally.

Similar magnitudes held for sales. Thus, changes in the factors themselves, not changes in the weights of these factors, explain the increase in π A between 1994 and 1995. If not for the offsetting effect of the change to double–weighted sales, the increase in taxable income due to the change in the aggregate apportionment ratio (Δφ *) would have been even larger in 1995. Placing a relatively larger weight on sales in the apportionment formula increases the implicit sales tax embodied in the formula and reduces the implicit payroll and property taxes, and discourages sales in the state and encourages the sitting of productive factors (Edmiston, 2002).

If relative changes in sales exceed changes in payroll and property, the apportionment percentage will decrease. Edmiston and Arze (2002) found that the elasticity of in–state sales with respect to the implicit sales tax in the apportionment formula in Georgia is –0.116, while the analogous elasticities for payroll and property are –0.069 and –0.035, respectively. Double–weighting increases the sales factor weight by 50 percent and reduces payroll and property factor weights by 25 percent.

Thus, the impact of double–weighting should lead to a 5.8 percent decrease in sales, but an increase in payroll and property of only 1.7 percent and 0.9 percent, respectively. The ûrst few years following Georgia's 1995 change to double–weighted sales supports this (Table 5). In 1996, Georgia sales as reported on tax returns declined 30.1 percent, while property and payroll declined only 13.9 percent and 3.8 percent. In 1998, Georgia sales declined 43.3 percent, while Georgia property increased by 24.2 percent and Georgia payroll increased by 15.3 percent.

In later years, property and payroll in the state declined relatively faster than in the nation as a whole. In 2000, Georgia property declined by 6.6 percent, while property nationally increased by a fairly substantial 10.5 percent. Moreover, payroll increased in Georgia in 2000 at about half the national rate of increase. In 2002, sales, payroll, and property saw substantial declines both in Georgia and nationally, which is not surprising given the nature of the economic climate in 2002. But declines were much more substantial in Georgia.

Property declined 46.4 percent in Georgia and 28.1 percent nationally in 2002. Payroll declined 33.8 percent in Georgia, compared to 23.4 percent nationally. Declines in sales were about the same in Georgia as in the nation as a whole. Growth in Georgia' GSP was in the second lowest quintile nationally over this period,13 and, thus, the decline in Georgia's share of apportionable income in 2002 may reûect the overall macroeconomic environment rather than state–specific policies.

Apportionable Income

Other than changes in apportionment percentages, changes in taxable income tend to mirror changes in apportionable income, which can be decomposed as: π At = FTIt + GAaddt – GAsubt – At, where FTI t is federal taxable income, GAaddt is Georgia additions to federal taxable income, GAsubt is amounts subtracted from federal taxable income, and At is income allocated everywhere (and therefore not subject to apportionment). Table 6 decomposes changes in apportionable income according to. Changes in apportionable income (ΔπA) largely reûect changes in federal taxable income (ΔFTI), and reductions in federal taxable income explain the bulk of the sizeable losses to πA in 2001 and 2002. A substantial increase in the share of national income apportioned to Georgia reversed what would have been a considerable decrease in revenue collections for 1995, due entirely to a reduction in federal taxable income.

No sizeable trends are apparent in goeorgia additions and subtractions from federal taxable income, but both factors do appear to be quite volatile relative to federal taxable income. Other than a single firm's activity in 1994 and 1995, allocations nationally appear to be relatively stable with no discernible trend in either direction. A decomposition of multistate corporate income tax returns in the State of Georgia reveals that recent declines in corporate income tax collections are largely cyclical in nature in that apportionable income is determined largely by federal taxable income, which is highly cyclical (compare ΔπA and ΔFTI in Table 6). Further, the close relationship between state and federal taxable income suggests that to the extent that federal policy changes reduced federal taxable income, Georgia taxable income suffered as well.

In terms of state–specific determinants, movements in Georgia taxable income were due largely to changes in apportionment percentages, and the data reveal that the bulk of these changes arose from changes in the apportionment factors (e.g., Georgia's share of total payroll) rather than from changes in the formula weights (Table 6). These changes in apportionment factors may be due in large part to the dynamic effects of Georgia's move to a double–weighted sales apportionment formula in 1995. Specific allocation of non–business income (Δα in Table 4) seems to have had little effect on corporate income tax collections. Although additions and subtractions to federal taxable income were very volatile relative to federal taxable income (ΔGAadd and ΔGAsub in Table 6), the magnitudes of the changes mattered little for tax collections overall.

Switch to S–Corps

Using the panel of Georgia C–corp returns along with a panel of S–corp tax returns over the same period, we identified the C–Corps that converted to S–Corps in each year. The SCIT paid by these firms in the year prior to their conversion ranged from $1.7 million to $6.6 million. To determine a cumulative revenue effect, we adjusted the taxes paid by the annual growth in taxes per firm for all corporations with a non–zero tax, essentially "inflating" these taxes to 2002. For corporations that switched from C–Corps to S–Corps over the period 1991 to 2002, the estimated SCIT revenue that was lost as a result of switching was 9.5 percent of actual 2002 SCIT revenue. Thus, even in the 1990s, long after S–Corps were allowed, Georgia experienced a small but significant decrease in SCIT revenue as a result of the conversions to S–Corps.

Empirical Evidence: An Analysis of Panel Data

In this section we employ panel data to explore the importance of tax policy, tax planning, and economic factors on the trend in state corporate tax receipts. We use a panel data set of states that covers the period 1980–1999 to estimate the impact of structural and economic factors on state corporate tax revenues to determine how much of the change in SCIT can be explained by these factors. It is very difficult to identify a variable to capture the effects of tax planning (setting up S–corporations, LLCs, tax shelters, off–shore banking, transfer pricing, and the like) on SCIT. Fox and Luna (2003) note the difficulties of gathering data on one of these strategies: LLCs.

They ultimately used data from Lexis/Nexis, augmented with their own survey, and they were able to account for about 83 percent of potential observations for the 50 states from 1988 to 2000. However, they note that there is a substantial degree of measurement error in their LLC variable.

To uncover the impact of tax planning on the trend in state corporate income tax collections, we take an empirical approach that controls for most of the structural and economic changes that are thought to influence corporate income taxes. We suggest that the residual includes the effects of "other" factors including tax planning, which we cannot easily incorporate directly into the regression. We estimate the following two equations incorporating time (γt), and state (αi) fixed effects:

$$SCITrevit = \alpha i + \gamma t + Xit2\ \beta + Yit2\ \zeta + Zit2\ \eta$$
$$+ \theta^{*}Demoit + \varepsilon it;$$

$$SCITrev/GSPit = \alpha i + \gamma t + Xit2\ \beta + Yit2\ \zeta$$
$$+ Zit2\ \eta + \theta^{*}Demoit + \varepsilon it.$$

The dependent variable in the ûrst equation is total SCIT revenue and uses GSP as a control variable, while the dependent variable in the second equation is the ratio of SCIT to GSP. The issue in selecting between the two equations is how we should measure the effect of a policy variable, i.e., by considering its effect on total SCIT revenue or on the share of the state's economy that goes to SCIT revenue. We expect these two measures of state corporate income taxes would be affected by similar sets of variables, but since both have been analyzed in the literature, we use both for ease of comparison with previous literature.

The X–vector includes variables that capture components of the state tax systems, including the maximum SCIT rate, various tax exemptions, and depreciation allowances. In general, the adoption of or increase in most of these specific factors is expected to reduce corporate tax liability. If these factors and incentives have that impact, they could reduce state corporate tax revenue in the short run, but increase it in the long run through increased investment and corporate activity. Because of this possible long–term effect, it is difficult, a priori, to hypothesize a speciûc relationship between these policy variables and state corporate tax revenues.

The Y–vector includes variables that attempt to capture the impact of federal policies on state corporate tax revenues. We explored the use of several variables, such as federal individual income tax revenues (as a proxy for changes in forms of incorporation), which proved insignificant and did not increase the ability of our regressions to explain state corporate income tax revenue growth or decline. In some cases, these variables were highly collinear with other variables, so we eventually dropped these control variables.

We were left with one variable—federal income tax revenue (adjusted for tax rate changes) as a share of total corporate proûts—and employ it as a proxy for major base changes. The Zvector includes economic–base variables that we expect should explain part of the growth or decline in the corporate income tax. The unemployment rate is used as a general measure of strength in the economy, and we expect it to be negatively related to the state corporate income tax. As suggested, the ability to tax some industries may be stronger than the ability to tax other sectors. To test this hypothesis, we include a variable equal to the ratio of manufacturing output to total GSP.

All else being equal, we expect that states with a relatively large manufacturing sector will experience smaller decline in SCIT revenue.

Finally, we include a dummy variable to control for the possible effects of politics on tax collections. The dummy variable, Demo, equals one if the state legislature is controlled by Democrats and equals to zero otherwise. Our expectation is that a Democratic legislature will be less likely to adopt tax measures that reduce SCIT revenue. Our results are found in Table 7 for both the level of state corporate tax revenue and for tax revenue as a share of GSP (the state and time fixed effect results are not reported).

The regression results suggest strong explanatory power. In both regressions, higher state tax rates are positively and significantly related to corporate tax revenues. The existence of some incentives (tax exemption on land and capital improvements, research and development credit, and inventory tax exemption on goods in transit) is associated with increased state corporate tax revenues, while that of others (accelerated depreciation, corporate income tax exemption, tax incentive for industrial development, tax exemption on manufacturers' inventory, and tax incentive for industrial development) is associated with reduced revenue.

Perhaps, as suggested above, some of these policies affect long–term economic development and, thus, increase the tax base. The economic variables performed in line with expectations in both of the regressions. Higher GSP yields higher revenue, higher unemployment is correlated with lower revenue, and a larger manufacturing base is correlated with higher revenue. This confirms the findings from the analysis of the Georgia data but runs somewhat counter to the survey results.

The coefficient on the ratio of federal corporate tax revenue to corporate profits is positive in both equations, as expected, but significant only in the ûrst equation. The coefficient on the legislative control dummy variable is insignificant in both equations. What do the results suggest? First, they suggest that the types of state corporate income tax incentives and speciûc structures seem to have had an impact on the growth of state corporate income taxes over the last 20 years. However, the impact of any speciûc incentive is very difficult to predict. The size (as measured byGSP) and condition (as measured by the unemployment rate) of the state's economy have the expected effect on the state corporate tax revenues. Overall, our regressions suggest that a significant portion of the change in state corporate income tax can be explained by the factors we list. In the ûrst equation, the R2 is very large, a fact that results from the high correlation between SCIT revenues and GSP. For the second, the R2 is 0.74. The unexplained variation may represent in part the effect of tax planning that we could not directly control for, including tax shelters, changes in forms of incorporation, and transfer pricing.

We also ran the regressions without the state and time effects and found that, in the case of total state corporate tax collections, these fixed effects add only marginal explanatory power to the analysis. In the case of the state tax collections as a share of GSP, the time and state effects are very important, as the R2 of the regression without these effects is only about 0.23.

To shed more light on the impact of changes in state tax policy variables (the X–vector of variables), we compared the difference in the predicted levels of state corporate tax revenue in 1985 and 1999 (based on the results of the regression analysis for SCIT revenue as presented in Table 7) to the difference in the predicted revenue in 1985 and a hypothetical prediction for 1999. For the hypothetical prediction, we used the regression coefficients applied to the 1985 values of the policy variables and the 1999 values for GSP, the effective federal corporate income tax rate, legislative control dummy, unemployment rate, and the ratio of manufacturing value added to total GSP. The general form of this analysis is:

(StTxCollhathypo – StTxCollhat85)

/ (StTtxCollhat99 – StTxCollhat85), where hat refers to the predicted value, and StTxCollhathypo is the predicted value of

SCIT revenue for 1999 assuming that the state corporate tax policy variables remain at 1985 levels. In the latter case, we are effectively holding state corporate tax policy constant at the level of the 1985 law, so by comparing the two sets of changes, we can estimate how much of the growth in state corporate tax revenue is due to changes in the policy variables.

When we compare the growth or decline in state–predicted state corporate tax revenues in these two cases, we ûnd that, on average, the changes in the policy variables account for about 24 percent of the growth in the predicted values of state corporate tax revenue. This is a substantial amount that helps to explain the trend in the state corporate income tax, but also suggests that another 75 percent of the change in level of state corporate tax revenue is the result of other factors. These other factors may include tax planning or other uncontrolled–for economic effects.

Summary and Conclusions

For most states over the period 1980 to 2002, SCIT revenue declined relative to GSP. This article attempts, using a variety of approaches, to identify the factors that have driven the changes in state corporate income tax revenue. The results of our analyses are suggestive, but not definitive, as to the factors that are associated with the relative decline in SCIT revenue. We are not able to identify one factor that explains the trend, but we are able to provide evidence about the relative importance of several factors.

Given that most states couple their corporate income tax base to the federal base, changes in tax structure at the federal level should translate into changes in corporate tax revenue at the local level. But based on the trend in the effective federal tax rate, it does not appear that changes in the federal tax code explain much of the change in state CIT revenue over the period of 1980 to 2002. This result is supported through our survey, in which state tax officials put only modest weight on changes in the federal tax code as a cause of the trend in state corporate income tax revenue.

We ûnd evidence that suggests corporate tax planning is an important factor in explaining the decline in SCIT relative to GSP. While our regression explains a substantial percentage of the changes in SCIT over the 20–year period, a significant amount of variation is not accounted for by our economic and policy variables. In this regard, we suggest that much of the unexplained variance may be a result of an increase in tax planning.

This is reinforced by the survey results; on balance, the most striking and consistent result of the survey was the opinion of state tax administrators that tax planning was the most important reason that revenue from the SCIT was declining. We find little evidence in the Georgia data that firms are shifting non–business income to low tax rate states, but we do ûnd a significant number of firms changing their forms of incorporation in Georgia, as evidenced by our link of C–corp and S–corp returns in the state.

Our analysis of Georgia corporate income tax returns also suggests that changes in apportionment factors, rather than changes in apportionment factor weights, inûuenced SCIT revenue in the state. While macroeconomic changes likely are responsible for much of the change in the relative magnitudes of factors in Georgia, which in turn reduced corporate tax revenue, part of the story is tax planning, as manifested in apportionment factor management. We ûnd for Georgia that the growth in economic development credits had a significant effect on corporate tax revenue, as the use of credits increased over the period and measured up to 19.6 percent of pre–credit tax liability. The regression analysis also revealed a dampening of revenues by some tax incentives, although others lead to an increase in revenue in the long term.

Most respondents to our survey revealed that economic development credits have lead to "decreases" (44 percent) or "substantial decreases" (23 percent) in revenue during periods of declining revenue relative to GSP. We also ûnd evidence that the changing composition of the industrial structure has resulted in decreased corporate tax revenue. Using tax return for Utah, we ûnd that industries that are growing have smaller proût per employee.

While state corporate income tax revenues move closely with the business cycle, as evidenced by the regression of revenues on GSP and unemployment rates and by the federal taxable income proportion of changes in Georgia apportionable income (Table 6), the consistency of the decline in state corporate income tax collections (relative to GSP) suggests that the business cycle does not explain much of the trend, which would require a downward trend in economy wide growth over the period. Our survey findings support this conclusion.

Sharply declining profits likely do explain a substantial amount of the decline in revenues in the ûrst part of this decade, however. Our analysis suggests that much of the decline in state corporate income tax revenues is explained by economic factors (such as changes in industrial structure) and tax planning (such as changes in corporate form and apportionment factor management). Federal policy that would alter taxable income does not seem to be much of a causal factor. Tax officials do not believe that state policy changes have had a significant effect on SCIT revenue either, and our other analyses support their views, except those relating to tax rates and tax incentives. While we believe that our analysis has contributed to the understanding of recent trends in SCIT revenue, there is still much work to be done to fully understand the factors that drive SCIT revenue.

A Review of Taxes and Corporate Finance

Modigliani and Miller (1985) and Miller and Modigliani (1961) demonstrate that corporate financial decisions are irrelevant in a perfect, frictionless world. During the past 45 years, research has focused on whether financial decisions become relevant if capital markets are not perfect. This paper reviews the literature that investigates the consequences of allowing taxation, with emphasis on how taxes can affect corporate policies and firm value. This role is potentially very important, given the sizable tax rates that many corporations and individuals face.

Modigliani and Miller (MM) argue that corporate financial policies do not add value in equilibrium, and therefore firm value equals the present value of operating cash flows. Once imperfections are introduced, however, corporate financial policies can affect firm value, and firms should pursue a given policy until the marginal benefit of doing so equals the marginal cost.

A common theme in tax research involves expressing how various tax rules and regulations affect the marginal benefit of corporate actions. For example, when tax rules allow interest deductibility, a \$1 interest deduction provides tax savings of \$1xτ_C(.). $_C$(.) measures corporate marginal tax benefits and is a function of statutory tax rates, nondebt tax shields, the probability of experiencing a loss, international tax rules about dividend imputation and interest allocation, organisational form, and various other tax rules.

A common theme that runs throughout this paper is the demonstration of how various tax rules affect the $_C$(.) benefit function, and therefore how they affect corporate incentives and decisions. A second but less common theme in tax research is related to how market imperfections affect costs. Given that this chapter reviews tax research, I emphasize research that describes how taxes affect costs and benefits - and only briefly discuss the influence of nontax factors.

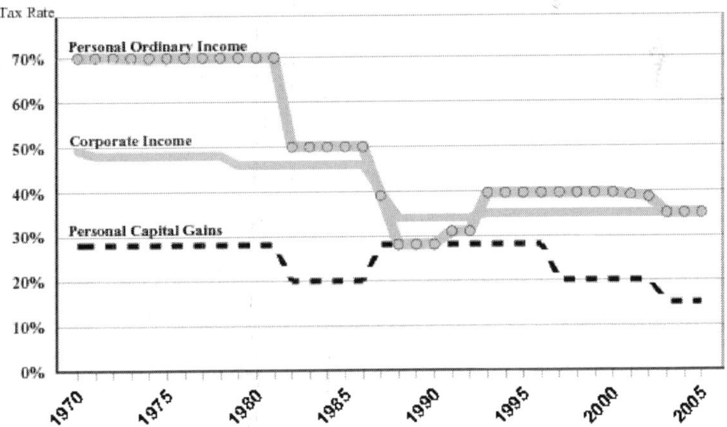

Figure: Corporate and Personal Income Tax Rates

The highest tax bracket statutory rates are shown for individuals and C corporations. The corporate capital gains tax rate (not shown) was equal to the corporate income taxrate every rate after 1987. In May 2003 President Bush signed into law a reduction in the top personal income tax rate to 35%. This same law reduced top personal tax rateson capital gains and dividends to 15%. Source for pre-2003 numbers: Commerce ClearingHouse, annual publications.

There are multiple avenues for taxes to affect corporate decisions. Taxes can affect capital structure decisions (both domestic (Section 1) and multinational (Section 2)), organisational form and restructurings (Section 3), payout policy (Section 4), compensation policy (Section 5), risk management (Section 6), and the use of tax shelters (Section 7). For each of these areas, the sections that follow provide a theoretical framework describing how taxes might affect corporate decisions, empirical predictions based on the theory, and summaries of the related empirical evidence.

This approach is intended to highlight important questions about how taxes affect corporate decisions, and to summarise and critique the answers that have been thus far provided. Each section concludes with a discussion of unanswered questions and possible avenues for future research. Overall, substantial progress has been made investigating if and how taxes affect corporate financial decisions - but much work remains to be done. Section 8 concludes and proposes directions for future research.

Making Financial Decisions

Does your relationship to your money define you? It's an important question, because your emotional attachment to money can significantly influence your investing results.

Money of course is neutral-it has no feelings and it doesn't care. When you identify *your* emotional connection to your money; and learn to deal with it objectively, you can move from a "present orientation" in your thinking towards a "future vision" for accumulating more capital (saving rather than spending), taking better care of it (stewardship) and sharing it with family members (reciprocity).

This is important because you may think you want to get rich more quickly these days, given all the market volatility. In reality, it's important to keep your eye on the ball.

Most people simply want to be affluent. I like to define affluence as having three main outcomes:

- Independence, resulting from the use of your financial skills
- Peace of mind, resulting from use of your financial knowledge

- Confident and purposeful decision-making, behaviour which enables you to live and retire in dignity, with enough resources to cover both needs and wants.

Most important, thinking about affluence over time, rather than just for today, requires an afer-tax focus. In the end, it's what you keep that matters.

So you can stop thinking emotionally about your investing activities, today. Instead, from a "Real Wealth Management" perspective we want to anticipate how much money is available now and in the future when we need or want it. This requires three skill sets:

1. Always Include a Tax Filter. To understand the amount of cash flow that is available, we must be able to measure income and capital on an after-tax basis at all times. Measuring wealth "before tax" can over-exaggerate the true amount of capacity one may have to use money when and how we need it.
2. Measure Active and Passive Income. If one of the primary purposes of wealth is to have enough financial resources to replace your actively earned income from employment or self-employment, then we must have a plan to build income sources that stem from invested capital. Your money is your business, and therefore needs to be managed with strategy and accountable purpose.
3. Liquidity and Purchasing Power. Will cash flow be available in the future when needed? What will it be worth? You may need to focus more on this in making investing decisions today, if you think the costs of fees, interest, taxes and inflation may rise.

It can certainly help you greatly to be assisted by a professional services community that follows an inter-advisory, client-centred process for managing your family's wealth. But in the end, it's your money. You're the boss of it. Thinking about the flow of your money over the long term, and on an inter-generational basis, can help you think about current market volatility over several economic cycles, rather than just the current one. Your decision-making will likely be different through such a lens.

Why is Income Tax Important When Making Investment Decisions

When we talk investing, not all types of investments are equal: At least as far as the Income Tax Act is concerned. If you have investments outside of a tax-deferred account like an RRSP, be aware of how income tax erodes your investment returns.

Every time you receive dividends, interest or have capital gains, the taxman wants a cut. This reduces the amount you have available to re-invest in the stock market. And while there are strategies to defer income tax over time, such as using an RRSP or timing capital gains, income tax can never be completely avoided.

Interest, Dividends and Capital Gains

Interest received from debt instruments such as bonds, GICs and T-bills, are taxed just like regular income. There is no special treatment and no special tax credits. You simply add interest to your taxable income. Dividends From Canadian Companies are payments made from a corporation to its shareholders. These payments are made from after-tax income. If you own shares in a Canadian public corporations there is a combination "gross-up" and "tax credit" designed to reduce the impact of tax already paid by the corporation.

Dividends From Foreign Corporations. Dividends received from foreign corporations are taxed just like interest. If a foreign withholding tax was withheld, you may claim the foreign tax credit. Capital Gains are a special type of income. One-half of the gain is included in your income and taxed, but only when you sell the share. Thus, you have the opportunity to time when you will receive a capital gain.

Comparing Interest, Dividends and Capital Gain

Interest, dividends and capital gains have different tax treatment. While we can generally say that dividends from Canadian corporations and capital gains are more tax efficient than interest income, the actual amount of tax varies depending on your province of residence and income level.

Final Thoughts

It is important to consider income taxes when making investment decisions. As a general rule, interest generating investments are less tax efficient than interest and dividends and are best held in tax-deferred accounts such as RRSPs. Similarly, dividend and capital gains generating securities should generally be held outside of registered accounts.

6

Income Taxes

Progressivity in the income tax is accomplished mainly by establishing tax "brackets" - branches of income that are taxed at progressively higher rates. For example, for tax year 2006 an unmarried person with no dependents will pay 10% tax on the first $7,550 of taxable income. The next $23,100 (i.e. taxable income over $7,550, up to $30,650) is taxed at 15%. The next $43,550 of income is taxed at 25%. Additional brackets of 28%, 33%, and 35% apply to higher levels of income. So, if a person has $50,000 of taxable income, his next dollar of income earned will be taxed at 25% - this is referred to as "being in the 25% tax bracket," or more formally as having a marginal rate of 25%. However, the tax on $50,000 of taxable income figures to $9,058. This being 18% of $50,000, the taxpayer is referred to as having an effective tax rate of 18%.

Effective Income Tax Rates

While the top marginal tax rate on ordinary income is 35 percent, average rates that a household in the upper income bracket pays is less. Much of the earnings of those in the top income bracket come from capital gains, interest and dividends, which are taxed at 15 percent. Also because only income up to $106,800 is subject to payroll taxes of 15.3%, which are paid by the employer and employee, individuals in the upper income bracket pay on average an effective rate not much different than that of other income brackets. The effective tax rate paid by an individual in the upper income bracket is highly dependent on the ratio of income they earn from capital gains, interest and dividends. As discussed in a Wall Street Journal article, the effective tax rate of income tax directly paid may differ from the effective economic incidence. When all taxes paid to local, state, and federal government are included, low, middle, and high income groups pay a similar share of their income to government. The article, using 2011 estimates of total income received versus total taxes paid, reported that the lowest 20% in income paid 2.1% of total taxes while receiving 3.4% of income. The middle 20% paid 10.3% of taxes while getting 11.4% of the income, and the top 1%, those with yearly incomes averaging $1,371,000, paid 21.6% of taxes while getting 21% of total income. Across eight income groups whose data were reported, the largest difference between total taxes paid and total income received was just 1.7%. When total taxes paid are compared to income received, payments to government are just mildly progressive across income groups.

Capital Gains Taxes

In recent years, a reduction in the tax rates applicable to capital gains and received dividends payments, has significantly reduced the tax burden on income generated from savings and investing. An argument is often made that these types of income are not generally received by low-income taxpayers, and so this sort of "tax break" is anti-progressive. Further clouding the issue of progressivity is that far more deductions and tax credits are available to higher-income taxpayers.

A taxpayer with $40,000 of wage income may only have the "standard" deductions available to him, whereas a taxpayer with $200,000 of wage income might easily have $50,000 or more of "itemized" deductions. Allowable itemized deductions include payments to doctors, premiums for medical insurance, prescription drugs and insulin expenses, state taxes paid, property taxes, and charitable contributions. In those two scenarios, assuming no other income, the tax calculations would be as follows for a single taxpayer with no dependents in 2006:

Wage income	$40,000	$200,000
Allowable deductions	8,450	51,430
Taxable income	31,550	148,570
Income tax	4,445	46,725
Statutory rate	14%	31%

This would appear to be highly progressive - the person with the higher taxable income pays tax at twice the rate. However, if you divide the tax by the amount of gross income (i.e., before deductions), the effective rates are 11% and 23%: the higher income person's rate is still twice as high, but his deductions drive down the effective rate more quickly ((14%-11%)/14% = a 21.4% effective tax rate savings or discount at the low income bracket; (31%-23%)/31% = a 29% effective tax rate savings or discount at the higher income tax bracket). To make the two tax rates realise an equal savings or discount from taking the maximum allowable deductions, the higher income tax bracket would have to have an effective tax rate of ~24.35% (31%-24.35%/31% = 21.4% or the same discount as the lower tax bracket) instead of 23%. This would necessitate an additional income tax of $1,975 from the higher tax bracket ($200,000*24.35% [new and equal effective tax rate] = $48,700), or an extra 0.99% in this model.

FICA Taxes

Discussions of income tax progressivity often do not factor the payroll taxes (FICA - social security and medicare taxes), which have a "ceiling". This is because these insurance benefits are directly determined by individual contributions over that individual's lifetime. Thus, since payroll taxes serve as direct individual premiums for direct individual benefits, most do not include these taxes in the calculation of the progressive nature of federal taxes, just as they do not include similar private automobile, homeowners, and life insurance policy premiums.

Another factor is that the social benefits themselves are paid in a progressive nature; individuals with lower lifetime average wages receive a larger benefit (as a percentage of their lifetime average wage income) than do individuals with higher lifetime average wages. However, if one were to expand the tax distribution example to include social security insurance taxes:

Social security tax	$3,060	$8,740
Total tax	7,505	55,465
Rate paid on gross income	19%	28%

Some lower income individuals pay a proportionately higher share of payroll taxes for Social Security and Medicare than do some higher income individuals in terms of the *effective tax rate*. All income earned up to a point, adjusted annually for inflation ($106,800 for the year 2010) is taxed at 7.65% (consisting of the 6.2% Social Security tax and the 1.45% Medicare tax) on the employee with an additional 7.65% in tax incurred by the employer.

The annual limitation amount is sometimes called the "Social Security tax wage base amount" or "Contribution and Benefit Base." Above the annual limit amount, only the 1.45% Medicare tax is imposed. In terms of the effective rate, this means that a worker earning $20,000 for 2010 pays at an effective rate of 7.65% (i.e., $20,000 x 7.65% = $1,530.00), while a worker earning $200,000 pays at an effective rate of only about 4.76% (i.e., the 7.65% rate is multiplied by $106,800, not by $200,000, resulting in a tax of $8,170.20, plus the $1,351.40 tax, at 1.45%, on the remaining $93,200, for a total tax of $9,521.60, which is about 4.7608% of $200,000).

When an individual's Social Security benefit is calculated, income in excess of each year's Social Security Tax wage base amount is disregarded for purposes of the calculation of future benefits. Although some lower income individuals pay a proportionately higher share of payroll taxes than do higher income individuals in terms of the "effective tax rate", the lower income individuals also receive a proportionately higher share of Social Security benefits than do some higher income individuals, since the lower income individuals will receive a much higher income replacement percentage in retirement than higher income individuals affected by the Social Security tax wage base cap.

If the higher income individuals want to receive an income replacement percentage in retirement that is similar to the income replacement percentage that lower income individuals receive from Social Security, higher income individuals must achieve this through other means such as 401(k)s, IRAs, defined benefit pension plans, personal savings, etc. As a percentage of income, some higher income individuals receive less from Social Security than do lower income individuals.

Breakdowns

These tables show the share of taxes, and effective tax rate, for each quintile of household income. In addition to the income tax and payroll tax, computations of the tax burden of each segment of the population usually contain estimates of taxes that people do not pay by themselves directly. An example is the corporate income tax, which may be thought of as indirectly taxing the corporation's customers (through higher prices) or its owners (through lower dividends or profits). Another example is excise taxes, e.g. on gasoline, which may be paid from throughout the economy without recording individual contributions.

The Congressional Budget Office computes household taxes as the sum of income tax, payroll tax, corporate income tax, and excise taxes. It attributes corporate taxes to households "according to their share of capital income" and apportions excise taxes "according to their consumption of the taxed good or service." The CBO report shows each part of the taxes (income, payroll, corporate and excise) separately in addition to showing the totals we report here.

Tax Burden by Income Bracket

The Congressional Budget Office breaks down the 2007 share of the tax burden according to each segment of the population as follows:

- The highest quintile in total earned 55.9% of all income. It paid 86.0% of federal income taxes and 68.9% of all federal taxes
  - o The top 1% earned 19.4% of all income. It paid 39.5% of income taxes and 28.1% of all federal taxes
  - o The next 4% earned 12.9% of income. It paid 21.5%. of income taxes and 16.2% of all federal taxes
  - o The next 5% earned 9.7% of income. It paid 11.7% of income taxes and 10.7% of all federal taxes
  - o The next 10% earned 13.9% of income. It paid 13.3% of income taxes and 13.9% of all federal taxes.
- The fourth quintile earned 19.3% of income. It paid 12.7% of income taxes and 16.5 of all federal taxes.
- The third quintile earned 13.1% of income. It paid 4.6% of income taxes and 9.2% of all federal taxes.
- The second quintile earned 8.4%. It paid a net -0.3% of income taxes, meaning in aggregate this quintile received slightly more back in income tax credits than it paid in income taxes. It paid 4.4% of all federal taxes.
- The lowest quintile earned 4.0% of all income and received a net -3.0% income tax credits. It paid 1.0% of all federal taxes.

Proportional Tax

A proportional tax is a tax imposed so that the tax rate is fixed. The amount of the tax is in proportion to the amount subject to taxation. "Proportional" describes a distribution effect on income or expenditure, referring to the way the rate remains consistent (does not progress from "low to high" or "high to low" as income or consumption changes), where the marginal tax rate is equal to the average tax rate.

It can be applied to individual taxes or to a tax system as a whole; a year, multi-year, or lifetime. Proportional taxes maintain equal tax incidence regardless of the ability-to-pay and do not shift the incidence disproportionately to those with a higher or lower economic well-being. It is not a progressive tax.

Flat taxes, implemented as well as proposed, usually exempt from taxation household income below a statutorily determined level that is a function of the type and size of the household. As a result, such a flat marginal rate is consistent with a progressive average tax rate. A progressive tax is a tax imposed so that the tax rate increases as the amount subject to taxation increases. The opposite of a progressive tax is a regressive tax, where the tax rate decreases as the amount subject to taxation increases.

The French *Declaration of the Rights of Man and of the Citizen* of 1789 proclaims: A common contribution is essential for the maintenance of the public forces and for the cost of administration. This should be equitably distributed among all the citizens in proportion to their means.

Proportional Rates

Proportional taxes on consumption are considered by some to be regressive; that is, low income people tend to spend a greater percentage of their income in taxable sales (using a cross section timeframe) than higher income people. A regressive tax is when the average tax rate is lower, with higher income. So income and average tax rate have an inverse relationship. However, this calculation is derived when the tax paid is divided not by the tax base (the amount spent) but by income, which is argued to create an arbitrary relationship. The tax rate itself is proportional, with people with higher incomes paying more tax but at the same rate as they consume more

If a consumption tax is to be related to income, the unspent income can be treated as tax-deferred (spending savings at a later point in time), at which time it is taxed creating a proportional rate using an income base. However, consumption taxes such as a sales tax can often exclude items or provide rebates in an effort to create progressive effects. In many locations, “necessary” items such as non-prepared food, clothing, or prescription drugs are exempt from sales tax to alleviate the burden on the poor.

Regrresive Tax

A regressive tax is a tax imposed in such a manner that the tax rate decreases as the amount subject to taxation increases. “Regressive” describes a distribution effect on income or expenditure, referring to the way the rate progresses from high to low, where the average tax rate exceeds the marginal tax rate. In terms of individual income and wealth, a regressive tax imposes a greater burden (relative to resources) on the poor than on the rich — there is an inverse relationship between the tax rate and the taxpayer's ability to pay as measured by assets, consumption, or income.

It can be applied to individual taxes or to a tax system as a whole; a year, multi-year, or lifetime. Regressive taxes tend to reduce the tax incidence of people with higher ability to pay, as they shift the incidence disproportionately to those with lower ability to pay. The opposite of a regressive tax is a progressive tax, in which the average tax rate increases as the amount subject to taxation increases. In between is a flat or proportional tax, where the tax rate is fixed as the amount subject to taxation increases.

The term is frequently applied in reference to fixed taxes, in which every person has to pay the same amount of money. The regressivity of a particular tax often depends on the propensity of the taxpayers to engage in the taxed activity relative to their income. In other words, if the activity being taxed is more likely to be carried out by the poor and less likely to be carried out by the rich, the tax may be considered regressive. To determine whether a tax is regressive, the income elasticity of the good being taxed as well as the income substitution effect must be considered.

Common Examples

- A tax with a cap, above which no taxes are paid. The United States payroll tax is an example of this.
- A value added tax or other sales tax on food and other essentials such as clothing, transport, and residential rents can be regressive. Since the income elasticity of demand of food is usually less than 1 (inelastic), it tends to take up a higher percentage of the budget of a person or family with a lower income.
- A poll tax (a discriminatory tax that was a pre-condition of the exercise of the ability to vote) is a *fixed* tax for each person. Since each person pays the same amount of money, it is a lower proportion for people with higher incomes.
- Television licences that are implemented in many countries, especially in Europe, are considered regressive taxes and in most cases consist of a *flat* annual payment for the use of a television.
- The so called sin taxes are also criticized for being regressive, as it is assumed that they are often consumed more (or at least

at a greater proportion) by the lower classes. For example, "people in the bottom income quintile spend a 78% larger share of their income on alcohol taxes than people in the top quintile." Tobacco in particular is highly regressive, with the bottom quintile of income paying an effective rate 583% higher than that of the top quintile.

- An allowance reduction in an income tax systems allows for an individuals personal allowance to be withdrawn making a higher marginal tax for a limited band before returning to the underlying rate. In the UK there is an effective 60% band at £100,000 that returns to 40% at £113,000.

United States

According to Congressional Budget Office estimates, the federal tax system is a progressive tax system for earners all but the richest 1% of Americans. According to the study, the lowest earning 20% of Americans (24.1 million households earning an average of $15,900 in 2005) paid an effective federal tax rate of 3.9%, when taking into account income tax, social insurance tax, and excise tax. The highest earning 5% (5.8 million households earning an average of $520,200 in 2005) paid an effective federal tax rate of 21.5%. However, the highest earning 1% of Americans (1.1 million households earning an average of $1,558,500 in 2005) paid an "effective" federal tax rate of 21.3%.

Investor and multi-billionaire Warren Buffett has criticized the US tax code as highly regressive, citing himself as anecdotal evidence: Buffett stated that with an income of over $46 million, he pays a tax rate of 17.7%, whereas his receptionist pays a tax rate of 30%. Buffett's critique focuses on significantly lower tax rates applied to certain forms of investment income including capital gains.

However, progressive or regressive taxation often must be considered as part of an overall system since tax codes have many interdependent variables. The marriage penalty, particularly on those engaged in Shared Earning/Shared Parenting Marriage, creates a regressive tax system in the United States, so much so that economist Justin Wolfers has said that there is strong disincentive to have children within marriage or to marry at all. The National Bureau of Economic Research has also reported a study showing "that two earner couples—the horses that pull our economic plow—pay for the second job with taxes that are far beyond the well known marriage penalty."

The issue includes not only regressive tax, but also progressive benefits, where two-earner couples and single people are subsidizing one-earner/one-nonearner parent couples in a number of ways.

For example, in Social security and Medicare, two-earner couples pay for their own benefits through employment taxes, while one-earner couples receive an extra, unfunded benefit of 50% or more in Social Security (a total of 150% or more) and 100% or more in Medicare (a total of 200% or more).

Tax Advantages

Tax advantage refers to the economic bonus which applies to certain accounts or investments that are, by statute, tax-reduced, tax-deferred, or tax-free. Governments establish the tax advantages to encourage private individuals to contribute money when it is considered to be in the public interest.

An example is retirement plans, which often offer tax advantages to incentivize savings for retirement. In the United States, many government bonds (such as state bonds or municipal bonds) may also be exempt from certain taxes. In countries in which average age of the population is increasing, tax advantages may put pressure on pension schemes.

For example, where benefits are funded on a pay-as-you-go basis, the benefits paid to those receiving a pension come directly from the contributions of those of working age. If the proportion of pensioners to working-age people rises, the contributions needed from working people will also rise proportionately. In the United States, the rapid onset of Baby Boomer retirement is currently causing such a problem.

In order to reduce the burden on such schemes, many governments give privately funded retirement plans a tax advantaged status in order to encourage more people to contribute to such arrangements.

Governments often exclude such contributions from an employee's taxable income, while allowing employers to receive tax deductions for contributions to plan funds. Investment earnings in pension funds are almost universally excluded from income tax while accumulating, prior to payment.

Payments to retirees and their beneficiaries also sometimes receive favourable tax treatment. In return for a pension scheme's tax advantaged status, governments typically enact restrictions to discourage access to a pension fund's assets before retirement.

Tax Bracket

Tax brackets are the divisions at which tax rates change in a progressive tax system (or an explicitly regressive tax system, although this is much rarer). Essentially, they are the cutoff values for taxable income — income past a certain point will be taxed at a higher rate.

Example

Imagine that there are three tax brackets: 10%, 20%, and 30%. The 10% rate applies to income from $1 to $10,000; the 20% rate applies to income from $10,001 to $20,000; and the 30% rate applies to all income above $20,000. Under this system, someone earning $10,000 would be taxed at a rate of 10%, paying a total of $1,000. Someone earning $5,000 would pay $500, and so on.

Meanwhile, someone earning $35,000 would face a more complicated calculation. The rate on the first $10,000 would be 10%; the rate from $10,001 to $20,000 would be 20%; and the rate above that would be 30%. Thus, he would pay $1,000 for the first $10,000 of income; $2,000 for the second $10,000 of income; and $4,500 for the last $15,000 of income; in total, he would pay $7,500, or about 21.4%.

Internal Revenue Code Terminology

Gross Salary is the amount your employer pays you, e.g., John gets paid $50/hour as an electrical engineer. His annual gross salary is $50/hour x 2,000 hours/year = $100,000/year. W-2 wages are the wages that appear on the employee's W-2 issued by his employer each year in January. A copy of the W-2 is sent to the Internal Revenue Service (IRS). It is the Gross Salary less any contributions to pre-tax plans. The W-2 form also shows the amount withheld by the employer for federal income tax.

W-2 Wages = Gross Salary less (contributions to employer retirement plan) less (contributions to employer health plan) less (contributions to some other employer plans) Total Income is the sum of all taxable income, including the W-2 wages. Almost all income is taxable. There are a few exemptions for individuals such as non-taxable interest on government bonds, a portion of the Social Security (SS) income (not the payments to SS, but the payments from SS to the individual), etc.

Adjusted Gross Income (AGI) is Total Income less some specific allowed deductions. Such as; alimony paid (income to the recipient), permitted moving expenses, self-employed retirement program, student loan interest, etc.

Itemized Deductions are other specific deductions such as; mortgage interest on a home, state income taxes or sales taxes, local property taxes, charitable contributions, state income tax withheld, etc. Standard Deduction is a sort of minimum Itemized Deduction. If you add up all your itemized Deductions and it is less than the Standard Deduction you take the Standard Deduction. In 2007 this was $5,350 for those filing individually and $10,700 for married filing jointly. Personal Exemption is a tax exemption in which the taxpayer can deduct an amount from their gross income for each dependent they can claim. It was $3,400 in 2007.

Sample Tax Calculation

Given the complexity of the United States' income tax code, individuals often find it necessary to consult a tax accountant or professional tax preparer. For example, John, a married 44-year old who has two children, earned a gross salary of $100,000 in 2007. He contributes the maximum $15,500 per year to his employer's 401(k) retirement plan, pays $1,800 per year for his employer's family health plan, and $500 per year to his employer's Flexfund medical expense plan. All of the plans are allowed pre-tax contributions.

Gross pay = $100,000

W-2 wages = $100,000–$15,500–$1,800–$500 = $82,200

John's and his wife's other income is $12,000 from John's wife's wages (she also got a W-2 but had no pre-tax contributions), $200 interest from a bank account, and a $150 state tax refund.

Total Income = $82,200 + $12,000 + $200 + $150 = $94,550.

John's employer reassigned John to a new office and his moving expenses were $8,000, of which $2,000 was not reimbursed by his employer.

Adjusted Gross Income = $94,550–$2,000 = $92,550.

John's itemized deductions were $22,300 (he had some big mortgage interest, property taxes, and state income tax withheld).

John had four personal exemptions—himself, his wife and two children. His total personal exemptions were 4 x $3,400 = $13,600.

Taxable Income = $92,550–$22,300–$13,600 = $56,650.

The tax on the Taxable Income is found in a Tax Table if the Taxable Income is less than $100,000 and is computed if over $100,000. Both will be used. The Tax Tables can be found in the 2007 1040 Instructions. The Tax Tables list income in $50 increments for all categories of taxpayers, single, married filing jointly, married filing separately, and head of household. For the Taxable Income range of "at least $56,650 but less than $56,700" the tax is $7,718 for a taxpayer who is married filing jointly.

The 2007 Tax Rates Schedule for married filing jointly is:

Over	*But not over*		*of the Amount Over*
$0	$15,650	10%	$0
$15,650	$63,700	$1,565+15%	$15,650
$63,700	$128,500	$8,772.50+25%	$63,700
$128,500	$195,850	$24,972.50+28%	$128,500
$195,850	$349,700	$43,830.50+33%	$195,850
$349,700	————	$94,601+35%	$349,700

The tax is 10% on the first $15,650 = $1,565.00

plus 15% of the amount over $15,650 up to $56,650 = $41,000 x 15% = $6,150.00

Total = $7,715.00

The difference is because of the use of the tax tables in the first determination, and these tables are in $50 increments. John's taxable income was at the bottom of the increment. If his taxable income had been $56,675, in the middle of the increment, then the calculated amount would be $7,718.75.

In addition to the Federal income tax, John will probably be paying state income tax, Social Security tax, and Medicare tax. The Social Security tax in 2007 for John is 6.2% on the first $97,500 of earned income (wages), or a maximum of $6,045. There are no exclusions from earned income for Social Security so John will pay the maximum of $6,045. His wife will pay $12,000 x 6.2% = $744. Medicare is 1.45% on all earned income with no maximum. John and his wife will pay $112,000 x 1.45% = $1,624 for Medicare in 2007. Most states also levy income tax, exceptions being Alaska, Florida, Nevada, South Dakota, Texas, Washington, New Hampshire, Tennessee and Wyoming.

Octroi

Octroi (French pronunciation: [Tkt□wa]; Old French: *octroyer*, to grant, authorize; Lat. *auctor*) is a local tax collected on various articles brought into a district for consumption.

Antiquity

Octroi taxes have a respectable antiquity, being known in Roman times as *vectigalia*. These vectigalia were either the *portorium*, a tax on the entry from or departure to the provinces (those cities which were allowed to levy the *portorium* shared the profits with the public treasury); the *ansarium* or *foricarium*, a duty levied at the entrance to towns; or the *edulia*, sales imposts levied in markets. *Vectigalia* were levied on wine and certain articles of food, but it was seldom that the cities were allowed to use the whole of the profits of the taxes. *Vectigalia* were introduced into Gaul by the Romans, and remained after the invasion by the Franks, under the name of *tonlieux* and *coutumes*.

Middle Ages

They were usually levied by the owners of seigniories. This is a tax which is levied by government for transfer of goods from one state to another state. The taxes did not remain strictly municipal, for an ordinance of Cardinal Mazarin (in 1647) ordered the proceeds of the octroi to be paid into the public treasury, and at other times the government claimed a certain percentage of the product, but this practice was finally abandoned in 1852.

Tax Farming

From an early time the octroi was farmed out to associations or private individuals, and so great were the abuses which arose from the system that the octroi was abolished during the French Revolution. But such a drastic measure meant the stoppage of all municipal activities, and in 1798 Paris was allowed to re-establish its octroi. Other cities were allowed gradually to follow suit, and in 1809 a law was passed laying down the basis on which octrois might be established.

Other laws were passed from time to time in France dealing with the octroi, especially those of 1816, 1842, 1867, 1871, 1884 and 1897. By the law of 1809 octroi duties were allowed on beverages and liquids, eatables, fuel, forage and building materials. A scale of rates was fixed, graduated according to the population, and farming out was strictly regulated. A law of 1816 enacted that an octroi could only be established at the wish of a municipal council, and that only articles destined for local consumption could be taxed. The law of 1852 abolished the 10% of the gross receipts paid to the treasury. Certain indispensable commodities were allowed to enter free, such as grain, flour, fruit, vegetables and fish.

French octroi duties were collected either by the (1) *regie simple*, i.e. by special officers under the direction of the mayor; (2) by the *bail à ferme*, i.e. farming, the contractor paying yearly a certain agreed upon sum calculated on the estimated amount; (3) the *regie interesse*, a variation of the preceding method, the contractor sharing the profits with the municipality when they reached a given sum; and (4) the *abonnement avec la regie des contributions indirectes*, under which a department of the treasury undertook to collect the duties. More than half the octrois were collected under (1), and the numbers tend to increase; (2) is steadily decreasing, while (3) has been practically abandoned; (4) tends to increase. The gross receipts in 1901 amounted to 11,132,870 francs. A law of 1897 created new sources of taxation, giving *communes* the option of (1) new duties on alcohol; (2) a municipal license duty on retailers of beverages; (3) a special tax on wine in bottle; (4) direct taxes on horses and carriages, clubs, billiard tables and dogs; (5) additional centimes to direct taxes.

From time to time there was agitation in France for the abolition of octroi duties, but it was never pushed very earnestly. In 1869 a commission was appointed to consider the matter, and reported in favour of their retention. Octrois were finally abolished in 1948. In Belgium, on the other hand, they were abolished in 1860, being replaced by an increase in customs and excise duties; and in 1903 those in Egypt were also abolished.

Rates (Tax)

Rates are a type of property tax system in the United Kingdom, and in places with systems deriving from the British one, the proceeds of which are used to fund local government. Some other countries have taxes with a more or less comparable role, for example France's *taxe d'habitation*.

Rates by Country

Australia

Local government levy rates usually called council or shire rates on property based on the nominal rental value of the property. The value is called gross rental value and is calculated by the land authority or agency.

Hong Kong

In Hong Kong, rates on property is based on the nominal rental value of the property. Unlike in England and Wales, it is still levied on domestic property as well as non-domestic premises. Prior to 2000, it was used to fund municipal services, responsible by the now-abolished Urban Council and Regional Council, through the Urban Services Department and Regional Services Department. The revenue now goes to the treasury. The bill is issued quarterly.

Israel

Israel has a similar tax known as *arnona* that goes back to the days of the British Mandate of Palestine. It is levied by the municipality (or, in smaller localities, by the *moatza eizorit*, i.e., Regional Council) based (currently) on the square meterage of dwelling or business. Specific rates vary widely among municipalities, with Jerusalem and Rehovot having the highest rates in the country. In rental dwellings, tenants (rather than owners) generally pay the arnona. Single parents and some forms of economic hardship qualify for discounts or even exemptions.

New Zealand

Numerous Rating Acts and their amendments have sustained Territorial Authorities of New Zealand for over a century. Rental value is not the commonest criterion: land value and improved value have been more commonly used. Many exceptions are provided in legislation to reduce perceived unfairness of whichever system the council is using.

United Kingdom

Further information: Business rates in England and Wales and Business rates in Scotland. The modern system of rates had their origin in the Poor Law Act 1601, for parishes to levy rates to fund the Poor Law, although parishes often adopted property rates to fund earlier poor law measures. Indeed, the Court of Appeal in 2001 called the rating an “ancient system”, suggesting that it had medieval origins. In the United Kingdom, rates on residential property were based on the nominal rental value of the property, the value being reassessed periodically in revaluations.

By the Rating and Valuation Act 1925, revaluations were supposed to take place every five years but in practice they were frequently delayed or suspended. Revaluations took place in 1928/1929, 1934, 1956 (but based on 1939 values), 1963, and 1973. A revaluation due in the early 1980s was scrapped by the Secretary of State for the Environment Michael Heseltine in June 1979, with Heseltine urging householders to tear up the forms already sent out by the Valuation

Office. Whilst still levied in Northern Ireland, they were generally abolished in Scotland in 1989 and England and Wales in 1990 and replaced with the Community Charge (so called "poll tax"), a fixed tax per head that was the same for everyone. This was soon replaced with the Council Tax, a system based on the estimated market value of property assessed in bands of value, with a discount for people living alone.

As of 2007, domestic properties in Northern Ireland have moved to a rateable value based on the capital value of properties (similar to the Council Tax) as they stood on 1 January 2005; non-domestic properties are still rated based on their rental value. Non-domestic properties are currently being revalued, so a new list with 2008 values will come into effect in 2010. The Crown Estate Paving Commission still levies rates on residential property within its jurisdiction, in the area of Regent's Park, London, under the provisions of the Crown Estate Paving Act 1851.

Rates on non-residential property (business rates) are still charged, at a uniform rate set by central government. Rates are collected by local councils, but the moneys collected are distributed nationally according to population. Rating assessments (rateable values) are made on all non-domestic properties. As well as business, this includes village halls and other non-business occupations. The exception to this is where a hereditament is exempt by virtue of Schedule 6 of the Local Government Finance Act 1988 which specifies exempt classes.

The rateable value should represent the reasonable rental value of the occupation according to the circumstances at the "Material Day" and according to rental values at the "Antecedent Valuation Date". (For the compiled 2005 Rating List the "Material Day" is 1 April 2005 and the "Antecedent Valuation Date" is 1 April 2003). Later physical changes will have a later Material Day but the Antecedent Valuation Date will still be 1 April 2003 for the currency of the 2005 Rating List. The Rating List is a public document.

United States

Real estate taxes which are based on a percentage of the property's actual or nominal value are the prime funding method for local government.

Staple Right

The staple right (also translated stacking right or storage right, both from the German *Stapelrecht*) was a medieval right accorded to certain ports, the staple ports, that required merchant barges or ships to unload their goods at the port, and display them for sale for a certain period, often three days. Only after this option had been given to the local customers was the trader allowed to reload his cargo and travel onwards with the remaining unsold freight. Limited staple rights were sometimes given to towns along major trade-routes, e.g. Görlitz obtained staple rights for Salt and Woad.

Germany

The staple right can be compared to the market right (the right to hold a regular market) as being extremely important for the economic prosperity of the river cities that possessed the right, such as Leipzig, Mainz, or Cologne (where a *Stapelhaus* still stands as a reminder of the former right). At the same time it erected a strong barrier against long-distance trade due to the increased costs and the time required to unload and load ships - especially as a river might have multiple staple-right cities in a row.

This especially affected the transport of perishable goods like foodstuffs, though traders could often pay a fee to avoid having to display their wares, thus turning the staple right into a form of trade taxation, with similar, but less severe results.

The staple right was probably introduced by Charles the Great (ruled 768-814); while the Congress of Vienna decided to abolish the staple right in 1815. This took effect on the river Rhine by means of the Mainzer Akte in 1831 and for the whole of Germany by means of the German Customs Union in 1834.

Use Tax

A use tax is a type of excise tax levied in the United States. It is assessed upon otherwise "tax free" tangible personal property purchased by a resident of the assessing state for use, storage or consumption of goods in that state (not for resale), regardless of where the purchase took place. The use tax is typically assessed at the same rate as the sales tax that would have been owed (if any) had the same goods been purchased in the state of residence. Use tax applies when sales tax has not been charged. Purchases made either over the Internet or out-of-state are the most common transactions subject to a use tax.

For example, a resident of Massachusetts, with a 6.25% "sales and use tax" on certain goods and services, purchases non-exempt goods or services in New Hampshire for use, storage or other consumption in Massachusetts. Under New Hampshire law, the New

Hampshire vendor collects no sales taxes on the goods but the purchaser/user must still pay 6.25% of the sales price directly to the Department of Revenue in Massachusetts as a use tax. If the same goods are purchased in a US state that does collect sales tax for such goods at time of purchase, whatever taxes were paid by the purchaser to that state can be deducted (as a tax credit) from the 6.25% owed for subsequent use, storage or consumption in Massachusetts.

With few exceptions, no state's vendors will charge the native sales tax on goods shipped out of state. New Hampshire vendors, however, do not omit tax because something was shipped to Massachusetts or some other state; rather, they omit sales tax because New Hampshire does not impose a sales tax in the first place.

The assessing jurisdiction may make the use tax payable annually, but some states require a monthly payment. For example, where a Vermont resident has not paid at least 6% sales tax on property brought in for use in the state, Vermont law requires filing a tax return (Form SU-452 and payment) by the 20th day of the month following non-exempt purchases to avoid a $50 late fee, a 5% penalty per month, to a maximum of 25%, plus statutory interest on the unpaid tax and penalties.

Typical exemptions include purchases by charitable non-profit organisations or governmental agencies, purchases for resale in commerce, and purchases via "casual sales" by individuals not in the ordinary course of business. Also note that there are thousands of tax jurisdictions in the U.S. and many have ever-changing lists of specific types of goods and services that are not taxable.

As an illustration of the complexities: a 2006 Massachusetts law requires payment of tax on "pre-written" (not custom) software purchased and downloaded over the Internet for installation and use in Massachusetts, regardless of where it originates. However, the actual use of the same software downloaded by a Massachusetts resident to a server in another state remains a non-taxed "service".

In contrast, Arkansas generally does not tax anything delivered over the Internet (such as downloaded software or music), except VoIP which is specifically defined as taxable "telecommunications services". Software (pre-written or custom) "delivered thru a tangible medium" (i.e., on disk) in Arkansas is taxable even if ordered online, except "custom software for a particular customer" which is non-taxable "programming services" even if delivered on a disk. In most cases, this complexity is part of the underlying sales tax laws; but while a brick-

and-mortar store has to deal with only the sales tax laws of its own location, remote sellers have to deal with the use tax laws of many jurisdictions—up to every US state and locality that assesses them, if the company has a presence or "nexus" in every state (as large "brick-and-mortar" sellers like Wal-Mart and Best Buy do).

Self-Assessment

Not all use tax derives from sales transactions. There are also internal transactions a company might initiate that will trigger use tax consequences. For example, ABC Furniture Company buys its inventory tax-free with a resale certificate, then charges sales tax to its customers. But if this company removes furniture from inventory for use in the retail store by its sales staff, it has triggered a tax incident: use tax is due on the converted inventory that is being used, not sold. The states differ in the tax basis of such a transaction: some tax [cost], others [cost + overhead], and still others [cost + overhead + markup].

For another example, suppose a carpet manufacturer sends swatches of carpet to its sales people to use as samples. That is a taxable use of carpeting to the manufacturer (or distributor as the case may be). Large manufacturers purchase many items that are used in both exempt and nonexempt manners. To facilitate determination of the correct tax due, they use a Direct Pay Permit that authorizes them to omit sales tax to their vendors, while requiring them to self-assess their purchases and remit the correct amount of use tax to the proper taxing authority.

It is also possible that equipment purchased under a manufacturing or mining exemption in one state is later relocated across a state line—into a jurisdiction where the exemption no longer applies. In this case, the company must recognise the book value of the capital item when it was relocated as the basis of the use tax due to the nonexempt state. Another form of use tax related to this example is referred to as *reciprocity.*

Reciprocity is triggered when items taxed at a lower rate are transferred or put to use (subsequent to first use) in a taxing jurisdiction with a higher rate. The use tax due, where StateA is the sending state and StateB is the receiving state, is typically StateB rate - StateA rate] + local rateB] x tax basis]. Most states do not offer reciprocity for their local rates, and they may have specific states they will reciprocate with or they may reciprocate on a *quid pro quo* basis with the other state.

Tax practitioners in large corporations must always be vigilant of transactions such as the above examples that trigger tax consequences for two reasons: to make sure they are in compliance with state laws, and to take advantage of all possible planning opportunities to minimise or avoid tax. Where the tax consequence is substantive and/or the law is vague, assistance will often be sought from outside professionals such as consultants, CPAs, or attorneys who specialise in sales and use tax and who keep up to date with the changing laws and case law history of the various states.

Enforcement

In 2007, 22 states including New York, California, Ohio and Virginia have included an entry on their state individual income tax return for taxpayers to voluntarily calculate an amount for use tax liability. Taxpayers however have not been so quick to reach into their wallets and forward these taxes to the state. A few of these states have tried another approach by pre-determining the tax liability owed by every taxpayer via a tax table based on the individual's adjusted gross income.

For example, a Michigan taxpayer with $45,000 of income can use the state's use tax table to estimate his use tax liability as $36. Use of this table is limited, however, to purchases of less than $1,000 and may be challenged during an audit. For purchases over $1,000, the taxpayer must calculate the tax for each item and add this amount to the use tax from the table. States using this method have seen an increase in voluntary compliance over those states that have the taxpayers calculate the use tax themselves.

As the amount of e-commerce sales continues to rise ($34 billion for just the second quarter of 2008) states recognise that the key to collecting these taxes rests not only in educating the individual taxpayer but with coordinating their efforts with other states. Currently, there are 19 full member states and 3 associate member states that belong to the Streamlined Sales Tax Project (SSTP). The SSTP assists states in collection of sales and use tax by registering merchants who charge out-of-state consumers the appropriate state sales tax and remit the tax to the appropriate state through a certified service provider.

SSTP has also been in the forefront of an effort to push Congress to amend the laws to make collection of sales tax less burdensome. In fact, in August 2007 a bill was introduced in the House that would have given the states authority to require sellers to collect sales tax on out-of-state sales; however, the bill appears to have never made it out of committee. States may also work with adjacent states via interstate use tax agreements. These agreements allow states to exchange tax audit records from businesses that have shipped goods to out of state consumers. Reciprocal states will then use those records and send a tax bill including penalties and interest to the individual taxpayer.

States have also pursued their collection efforts through the court system. In 2007, a California appeals court ruled that Borders Online owed California sales tax for online purchases that the store failed to collect from 1998 to 1999 since customers were able to return merchandise bought on-line to Border's retail stores in California.

Methods

Country of Residence

One way a company may chose to avoid taxes is by establishing their company or subsidiaries in an offshore jurisdiction. Individuals may also avoid tax by moving their tax residence to a tax haven, such as Monaco, or by becoming a perpetual traveler. However some countries, such as the U.S., tax their citizens, permanent residents, and companies on all their worldwide income. In these cases, taxation cannot be avoided by simply transferring assets or moving abroad.

The United States is unlike many other countries in that its citizens and permanent residents are subject to U.S. federal income tax on their worldwide income even if they reside temporarily or permanently outside the United States. U.S. citizens therefore cannot avoid U.S. taxes simply by emigrating from the U.S. According to *Forbes* magazine some nationals choose to give up their United States citizenship rather than be subject to the U.S. tax system; however, U.S. citizens who reside (or spend long periods of time) outside the U.S. may be able to exclude some salaried income earned overseas (but not other types of income unless specified in a bilateral tax treaty) from income in computing the U.S. federal income tax. The 2010 limit on the amount that can be excluded was US$91,500.

Double Taxation

Most countries impose taxes on income earned or gains realised within that country regardless of the country of residence of the person or firm. Most countries have entered into bilateral double taxation treaties with many other countries to avoid taxing nonresidents twice—once where the income is earned and again in the country of residence (and perhaps, for US citizens, taxed yet again in the country of citizenship)—however, there are relatively few double-taxation treaties with countries regarded as tax havens. To avoid tax, it is usually not enough to simply move one's assets to a tax haven. One must also personally move to a tax haven (and, for U.S. nationals, renounce one's citizenship) to avoid tax.

Legal Entities

Without changing country of residence (or, if a U.S. citizen, giving up one's citizenship), personal taxation may be legally avoided by the creation of a separate legal entity to which one's property is donated. The separate legal entity is often a company, trust, or foundation. These may also be located offshore, such as in the case of many private foundations. Assets are transferred to the new company or trust so that gains may be realised, or income earned, within this legal entity rather than earned by the original owner. If assets are later transferred back to an individual, then capital gains taxes would apply on all profits. Also income tax would still be due on any salary or dividend drawn from the legal entity. For a settlor (creator of a trust) to avoid tax there may be restrictions on the type, purpose and beneficiaries of the trust. For example, the settlor of the trust may not be allowed to be a trustee or even a beneficiary and may thus lose control of the assets transferred and/or may be unable to benefit from them.

Legal Vagueness

Tax results depend on definitions of legal terms which are usually vague. For example, vagueness of the distinction between "business expenses" and "personal expenses" is of much concern for taxpayers and tax authorities. More generally, any term of tax law, has a vague penumbra, and is a potential source of tax avoidance.

Tax Shelters

Tax shelters are investments that allow, and purport to allow, a reduction in one's income tax liability. Although things such as home ownership, pension plans, and Individual Retirement Accounts (IRAs) can be broadly considered "tax shelters", insofar as funds in them are not taxed, provided that they are held within the Individual Retirement Account for the required amount of time, the term "tax shelter" was originally used to describe primarily certain investments made in the form of limited partnerships, some of which were deemed by the U.S. Internal Revenue Service to be abusive.

The Internal Revenue Service and the United States Department of Justice have recently teamed up to crack down on abusive tax shelters. In 2003 the Senate's Permanent Subcommittee on Investigations held hearings about tax shelters which are entitled *U.S. TAX SHELTER INDUSTRY: THE ROLE OF ACCOUNTANTS, LAWYERS, AND FINANCIAL PROFESSIONALS*. Many of these tax shelters were designed and provided by accountants at the large American accounting firms.

Examples of U.S. tax shelters include: Foreign Leveraged Investment Program (FLIP) and Offshore Portfolio Investment Strategy (OPIS). Both were devised by partners at the accounting firm, KPMG. These tax shelters were also known as "basis shifts" or "defective redemptions."

Prior to 1987, passive investors in certain limited partnerships (such as oil exploration or real estate investment ventures) were allowed to use the passive losses (if any) of the partnership (i.e., losses generated by partnership operations in which the investor took no material active part) to offset the investors' income, lowering the amount of income tax that otherwise would be owed by the investor. These partnerships could be structured so that an investor in a high tax bracket could obtain a net economic benefit from partnership-generated passive losses.

In the Tax Reform Act of 1986 the U.S. Congress introduced the limitation (under 26 U.S.C. § 469) on the deduction of passive losses and the use of passive activity tax credits. The 1986 Act also changed the "at risk" loss rules of 26 U.S.C. § 465. Coupled with the hobby loss rules (26 U.S.C. § 183), the changes greatly reduced tax avoidance by taxpayers engaged in activities only to generate deductible losses.

7

Debt Financing - Pros and Cons

What is Debt Financing?

Debt is borrowing money from an outside source with the promise to return the principal, in addition to an agreed-upon level of interest. Although the term tends to have a negative connotation, startup companies often turn to debt to finance their operations. In fact, even the healthiest of corporate balance sheets will include some level of debt. In finance, debt is also referred to as "leverage." The most popular source for debt financing is the bank, but debt can also be issued by a private company or even a friend or family member.

Advantages to Debt Financing

- Maintain ownership: When you borrow from the bank or another lender, you are obligated to make the agreed-upon payments on time. But that is the end of your obligation to the lender. You can choose to run your business however you choose without outside interference.
- Tax deductions: This is a huge attraction for debt financing. In most cases, the principal and interest payments on a business loan are classified as business expenses, and thus can be deducted from your business income taxes. It helps to think of the government as a "partner" in your business, with a 30 percent ownership stake (or whatever your business tax rate is). If you can cut the government out of the equation, then it's beneficial to your business.
- Lower interest rate: Furthermore, you should analyze the impact of tax deductions on the bank interest rate. If the bank is charging you 10 percent for your loan, and the government

taxes you at 30 percent, then there is an advantage to taking a loan you can deduct. Take 10 percent and multiply it by (1-tax rate), in this case it's: 10 percent times (1-30 percent), which equals 7 percent. After your tax deductions, you'll be paying the equivalent of a 7 percent interest rate.

Drawbacks to Debt Financing

- Repayment: As mentioned above, your sole obligation to the lender is to make your payments. Unfortunately even if your business fails, you will still have to make these payments. And if you are forced into bankruptcy, your lenders will have claim to repayment before any equity investors.
- High rates: Even after calculating the discounted interest rate from your tax deductions, as explained above, you may still be faced with a high interest rate. Interest rates will vary with macroeconomic conditions, your history with the banks, your business credit rating and your personal credit history
- Impacts your credit rating: It might seem attractive to keep bringing on debt when your firm needs money, a practice knowing as "levering up," but each loan will be noted on your credit rating. And the more you borrow, the higher the risk to the lender, and the higher interest rate you'll pay.
- Cash and collateral: Even if you plan to use the loan to invest in an important asset, you'll need to make sure your business will be generating sufficient cash flows by the time loan repayment starts. Also you'll likely be asked to put up collateral on the loan in case you default on your payments.

Alternatives to Debt Financing

- Equity financing: This involves selling shares of your company to interested investors, or putting your own money into the company.
- Mezzanine financing: Lenders who set up this debt tool offer the business unsecured debt (no collateral is required). The tradeoff is a high interest rate, in the 20- 30 percent range. Plus there's a catch. The lender has the right to convert the debt into equity in the company if the company defaults on payments. Despite the high interest rate, mezzanine financing appeals to entrepreneurs because it offers quick liquidity, and even though it can be converted to equity, the issuing bank usually does not want to be an equity holder, meaning they're not looking to control the company.

- Hybrid financing: Most likely you'll turn to a combination of debt and equity financing to fund your venture. The question then becomes: What is the proper combination? When deciding optimal capital structure, a common finance theory is the Modigliani-Miller theorem, which states that in a perfect market, without taxes, the value of a firm is the same whether it is financed completely by debt or equity or a hybrid. This, however, is considered too theoretical since real companies do have to pay taxes, and there are costs associated with bankruptcy. There are several other theories and formulas on determining optimal capital structures.

Debt/Equity Ratio

This is simply dividing your total debt amount by your total equity amount. Both lenders and investors will want to see this number to get an idea of how financially viable your firm is and where their investment stands in case your firm goes bankrupt, since debt holders get priority over equity-holders in recovering funds during bankruptcy. You will most likely take on some debt in the early stages but make sure to monitor how "levered up" your firm is, compared to the rest of your industry. Bizstats.com offers an easy way to gut-check your debt-to-equity ratio against a list of industry benchmarks. Reading this list shows investment banking is among the more risk-seeking industries, with a ratio of 29, while the electrical equipment industry comes in at a conservative 0.7.

When to Use Debt Financing

As mentioned above, the lender will be seeking installment payments on his loan shortly after the money is lent. That means in order to begin making payments you will need cash. Even a thriving business can be short on cash if its money is tied up in equipment, or customers aren't paying. When considering debt, ask yourself:

- Am I using this money to invest in fixed or variable costs? If you're investing in fixed costs, such as a new piece of equipment, then you likely won't see any cash returns from it in the near-term. If you need the money to invest in variable costs such as materials for the product you make or costs associated with each new client, than the debt investment should have associated cash inflow
- What are my customers like? Customers who consistently pay on time are critical to cash flow and the ability to repay debt. Learn the payment habits of your customers and consider

incentives to get them to pay early. Also, check with associations and competitors to make sure your payment terms are in line with industry standards.

- Where am I in my business lifecycle? In the early stages of a firm, debt financing can be dangerous. You will likely be losing money at first, thus hurting your ability to make payments. Also, since your net income will be low, the tax advantages of debt will be minimal. As your business grows and matures, debt becomes a stronger option. The tax advantage will be greater, your cash flow will be more predictable, and the risk you face in bankruptcy decreases since you have been operating longer.

Set Up a Debt Collection System to Get Paid by Customers

Every small business runs on cash, and cash only comes in when you collect money that is due you. Set up a debt collection system, with billing, accounts receivable management, and collection practices that include small claims court and which abide by the Fair Debt Collection Practices Act. Start now to get the money your customers owe you.

How to Get Paid

Rule #1 in collecting debts: The longer a debt is owed, the less likely you are to collect it. Rule #2 in collecting debts: Some people won't pay, no matter what. A system for collecting the money your customers owe can help you keep going, with Rule #1 in mind and minimising the number of people who become Rule #2. Set up your debt collection system when you first start your business, keep tweaking it to improve your collections, and you will maximise your cash flow from receivables.

Set up Your Billing System

Before you start your business, take some time to determine how you will bill customers. Putting together a billing system and plan will help you collect more money faster. How often will you bill? How will you communicate with customers who owe you money? Will you make phone calls? Send letters? Both? Don't wait until you have a ton of receivables to collect. Start now to develop that system, always remembering Rule #1.

Abide by the Fair Debt Collections Practices Act (FDCPA)

The Fair Debt Collections Practices Act (FDCPA) does not apply to business debtors, but you must abide by it when attempting to collect money from consumers. The Act protects consumers against harassment and privacy violation by creditors and it regulates who you can contact, how often, and how you can represent yourself. Consumers can bring lawsuits against bill collectors, so please read this article before you contact customers about debts owed to your business.

Use an Accounts Receivable Aging Report to Monitor Collections

An accounts receivable aging report is an important tool to help you monitor outstanding bills and see what needs to be collected. This report can show you who owes how much and how long it has been unpaid. With this information, you can set your collections strategy for individual customers.

Take Your Collections Case to Small Claims Court

Small claims court is a good possibility for collecting money owed you, if the amount owed is small (under the small claims limit for your state) and you don't expect to do business with this customer again.

If Your Collections Efforts Don't Work

Remember Rule #2 above? Some people just won't pay, no matter what you do. So, what now? Find out how to write off a bad debt at the end of a year and take a tax deduction for the loss of sales.

Sell Your Accounts Receivable

Selling accounts receivable is a common business practice called "factoring." You can sell your receivables to someone who will pay you for them - at a discounted value, of course. Then the factor collects the money. If you are short of cash, factoring can be a good way to raise some quickly.

Debt vs. Equity Financing

Debt vs. equity financing is one of the most important decisions facing managers who need capital to fund their business operations. Debt and equity are the two main sources of capital available to businesses, and each offers both advantages and disadvantages. "Absolutely nothing is more important to a new business than raising capital," Steve Jefferson wrote in *Pacific Business News* (Jefferson, 2001). "But the way that money is raised can have an enormous impact on the success of a business."

Debt Financing

Debt financing takes the form of loans that must be repaid over time, usually with interest. Businesses can borrow money over the short term (less than one year) or long term (more than one year). The main sources of debt financing are banks and government agencies, such as the Small Business Administration (SBA).

Debt financing offers businesses a tax advantage, because the interest paid on loans is generally deductible. Borrowing also limits the business's future obligation of repayment of the loan, because the lender does not receive an ownership share in the business.

However, debt financing also has its disadvantages. New businesses sometimes find it difficult to make regular loan payments when they have irregular cash flow. In this way, debt financing can leave businesses vulnerable to economic downturns or interest rate hikes. Carrying too much debt is a problem because it increases the perceived risk associated with businesses, making them unattractive to investors and thus reducing their ability to raise additional capital in the future.

Debt to Equity

The debt to equity ratio is a measure of the company's total long-term debt divided by shareholder's equity. The debt to equity ratio gives the proportion of a company (or person's) assets that are financed by debt versus equity. It is a common measure of the long-term viability of a company's business and, along with current ratio, a measure of its liquidity, or its ability to cover its expenses. As a result, debt to equity calculations often only include long-term debt rather than a company's total liabilities.

A high debt to equity ratio implies that the company has been aggressively financing its activities through debt and therefore must pay interest on this financing. If the company's assets generate a greater return than the interest payments, then the company can generate greater earnings than it would without the debt. If not, however, and the company's debt outweighs the return from its assets, then the debt cost may outweigh the return on assets. Over the long-term, this would lead to bankruptcy . Investors should take this into consideration when investing in a company with a high debt to equity ratio, especially in times of rising interest rates.

Debt to equity ratios vary across industries. Capital intensive industries such as airplane manufacturers tend to have higher debt to equity ratios — typically greater than 2. Less capital intensive industries, such as a software company, can have lower debt to equity ratios of under .5.

Examples

- To start, Widgets Inc. has long term debt of $1 million and shareholder's equity of $1 million for a debt to equity ratio of 1, which is fairly standard in the widget industry.
- To increase production, Widgets Inc. enters into a loan of $2 million in order to finance a new widget manufacturing facility, which increases its debt to equity ratio to 3 (=[$1 million previous debt + $2 million in new debt]/[$1 million in equity]) . The company pays 5% interest on the loan while its new facilities generate a 7% return. In this case, a higher debt to equity ratio allows the company to increase earnings beyond what would have been possible otherwise. The high debt to equity ratio is worthwhile for the company.
- One year later, however, interest rates on the loan rise to 9%. Now, the company is paying more for its debt than the 7% it is generating out of its new facilities. The company's high debt to equity ratio and increasing debt payments now put the company at risk of going bankrupt.

Debt and Equity Tests: Overview

When did the Measures Start?

Division 974 of the *Income Tax Assessment Act 1997* contains rules to determine what is equity in a company and what is debt in an entity for tax purposes with effect from 1 July 2001.

Transitional rules existed for amounts paid on all interests issued before 1 July 2001. The law as it existed prior to 1 July 2001 continued to operate in relation to those interests until 1 July 2004 unless:

- the terms of the interest were materially altered
- the interest was rolled over
- the original term of the interest was extended, or
- the issuer elected that the new debt and equity rules applied. This transitional election must have been lodged with the Tax Office, generally by 31 December 2001.

What are the Measures?

The tests for debt and equity interests determine whether a particular interest is a debt interest or an equity interest. The law:

- identifies when a scheme gives rise to a debt interest as distinct from an equity interest

- is used to identify debt for *thin capitalisation* purposes, and
- is also used to identify debt for the *consolidation* measure.

The debt and equity tests determine whether a return on an interest in an entity may be frankable and non-deductible (like a dividend), or may be deductible to the entity and not frankable (like interest payments).

If an interest passes one or more items of the *equity* test table, then, subject to the overriding operation of the debt test, it will be an equity interest. If the equity interest is classified as a non-share equity interest, a non-share capital account is maintained. For more details about the non-share capital account, refer to the guide to the debt and equity tests.

In determining what is a *debt* interest, the rules use a single organising principle - the effective obligation of an issuer to return to the investor an amount at least equal to the amount invested. This test has regard to the substance of the arrangement, and is not based purely on legal form.

If an interest can meet both the debt and equity tests, a tiebreaker test applies so that the interest will be a debt interest.

Special Applications of the Debt and Equity Measures

At Call Loans

Where the debt and equity rules apply to an interest, a transitional exception from the equity test contained within those rules applied until 30 June 2005 to 'connected entity at call loans' (certain loans between connected entities that are repayable on demand by the lender).

The debt and equity rules were amended by the *Tax Laws Amendment (2005 Measures No. 5) Act 2005* to ensure that certain connected entity at call loans to smaller entities would continue to receive exceptional debt treatment after 1 July 2005. For a more detailed explanation of connected entity at call loans (also referred to as 'credit shareholder loans' or 'related party loans'), refer to the guide to at call loans between connected entities.

Upper Tier 2 Instruments of Certain Authorised Deposit-Taking Institutions

On 4 March 2003 the former Minister for Revenue and Assistant Treasurer, Senator Helen Coonan, announced that a regulation would be developed to ensure that certain Upper Tier 2 capital instruments issued by Authorised Deposit-Taking Institutions (ADIs) that are banks would be treated as debt for taxation purposes. On 5 August 2004, the former Minister for Revenue and Assistant Treasurer, the Hon. Mal Brough, announced an extension until 1 July 2005 of the existing transitional provisions for certain Upper Tier 2 instruments issued by authorised ADIs that are banks or non-mutual building societies. On 25 October 2005 Mr Brough announced a further extension until 1 July 2007. The existing transitional provisions will apply to instruments which have been issued prior to 1 July 2001, and amended after 4 March 2003, but before the announced Upper Tier 2 regulation is gazetted, provided the instruments maintain their Upper Tier 2 status.

Non-Equity Shares not to Give Rise to a Capital Gains Tax Event

Various technical amendments of the debt/equity provisions of income tax law were enacted by the *Tax Laws Amendment (2005 Measures No. 5) Act 2005.* One of these amendments ensured that the issue of non-equity shares after 1 July 2001 would not give rise to a capital gains tax (CGT) event by virtue of sections 104-35 or 104-155 of the *Income Tax Assessment Act 1997.*

Why are the Debt and Equity Measures Needed?

The debt and equity rules aim to improve certainty in the tax law by establishing tests that provide a clearer and more coherent distinction between equity and debt interests.

Impacts on Taxpayers

The major impact will be on financial institutions, life insurers, superannuation funds and large corporates. Small business and individuals are affected to a lesser extent.

Should I Raise Debt or Equity?

If you raise convertible debt for a seed round, you should negotiate simple and short documents, close quickly and cheaply, and maintain your options for the Series A. But first, determine if you should raise debt or equity—debt is better for small financings with small discounts. Startups often raise their seed round by selling convertible debt instead of equity because debt is simpler and cheaper. Read Yokum Taku's excellent series on convertible debt for a primer.

Seed stage convertible debt agreements are fairly simple, especially if your investors are angels. There isn't a lot to hack in these agreements. You should be more careful if your debt investors are VCs, but these debt financings are still much easier to negotiate than an equity financing. Later stage convertible debt can get complicated and adversarial. We know companies that took convertible debt from a corporate investor and couldn't pay the debt back on time—which triggered the corporate investor's right to take over the company. Fun stuff. If you are raising convertible debt, you should focus on negotiating simple and short documents, closing quickly and cheaply, and maintaining your options for the Series A. But first...

What are the Differences between Debt and Equity Markets?

First, Some Definitions

The debt market is the market where debt instruments are traded. Debt instruments are assets that require a fixed payment to the holder, usually with interest. Examples of debt instruments include bonds (government or corporate) and mortgages. The equity market (often referred to as the stock market) is the market for trading equity instruments. Stocks are securities that are a claim on the earnings and assets of a corporation (Mishkin 1998). An example of an equity instrument would be common stock shares, such as those traded on the New York Stock Exchange.

How are Debt Instruments Different from Equity Instruments?

There are important differences between stocks and bonds. Let me highlight several of them:

1. Equity financing allows a company to acquire funds (often for investment) without incurring debt. On the other hand, issuing a bond does increase the debt burden of the bond issuer because contractual interest payments must be paid— unlike dividends, they cannot be reduced or suspended.
2. Those who purchase equity instruments (stocks) gain ownership of the business whose shares they hold (in other words, they gain the right to vote on the issues important to the firm). In addition, equity holders have claims on the future earnings of the firm. In contrast, bondholders do not gain ownership in the business or have any claims to the future profits of the borrower. The borrower's only obligation is to repay the loan with interest.
3. Bonds are considered to be less risky investments for at least two reasons. First, bond market returns are less volatile than stock market returns. Second, should the company run into trouble, bondholders are paid first, before other expenses are paid. Shareholders are less likely to receive any compensation in this scenario.

Debt vs. Equity Financing: Which is the Best Way for Your Business to Access Capital?

Deciding between equity financing and taking on a loan for your business is a challange for all small business owners when they need capital to expand a business. Should you go to a bank and apply for a business loan? Or should you look for an investor? Consider the advantages and disadvantages of each to determine which type of financing is best for your business:

Equity Financing

Having an investor write you a check may seem like the perfect answer if you want to expand your business but don't want to take on debt. After all, it's money without the hassle of repayment or interest. But the dollars come with huge strings attached: You must share the profits with the venture capitalist or angel investor.

Advantages to equity financing:

- It's less risky than a loan because you don't have to pay it back, and it's a good option if you can't afford to take on debt.
- You tap into the investor's network, which may add more credibility to your business.
- Investors take a long-term view, and most don't expect a return on their investment immediately.
- You won't have to channel profits into loan repayment.
- You'll have more cash on hand for expanding the business.
- There's no requirement to pay back the investment if the business fails.

Disadvantages to equity financing:

- It may require returns that could be more than the rate you would pay for a bank loan.
- The investor will require some ownership of your company and a percentage of the profits. You may not want to give up this kind of control.
- You will have to consult with investors before making big (or even routine) decisions — and you may disagree with your investors.
- In the case of irreconcilable disagreements with investors, you may need to cash in your portion of the business and allow the investors to run the company without you.
- It takes time and effort to find the right investor for your company.

New Products Development

In business and engineering, new product development (NPD) is the term used to describe the complete process of bringing a new product to market. A product is a set of benefits offered for exchange and can be tangible (that is, something physical you can touch) or intangible (like a service, experience, or belief). There are two parallel paths involved in the NPD process: one involves the idea generation, product design and detail engineering; the other involves market research and marketing analysis. Companies typically see new product development as the first stage in generating and commercializing new product within the overall strategic process of product life cycle management used to maintain or grow their market share.

The Process

1. Idea Generation is often called the "fuzzy front end" of the NPD process
   - o Ideas for new products can be obtained from basic research using a SWOT analysis (Strengths, Weaknesses, Opportunities & Threats). Market and consumer trends, company's R&D department, competitors, focus groups, employees, salespeople, corporate spies, trade shows, or ethnographic discovery methods (searching for user patterns and habits) may also be used to get an insight into new product lines or product features.
   - o Lots of ideas are being generated about the new product. Out of these ideas many ideas are being implemented. The ideas use to generate in many forms and their generating places are also various. Many reasons are responsible for generation of an idea.
   - o Idea Generation or Brainstorming of new product, service, or store concepts - idea generation techniques can begin when you have done your OPPORTUNITY ANALYSIS to support your ideas in the Idea Screening Phase (shown in the next development step).
2. Idea Screening
   - o The object is to eliminate unsound concepts prior to devoting resources to them.
   - o The screeners should ask several questions:
     - – Will the customer in the target market benefit from the product?

- What is the size and growth forecasts of the market segment / target market?
- What is the current or expected competitive pressure for the product idea?
- What are the industry sales and market trends the product idea is based on?
- Is it technically feasible to manufacture the product?
- Will the product be profitable when manufactured and delivered to the customer at the target price?

3. Concept Development and Testing
   - o Develop the marketing and engineering details
     - Investigate intellectual property issues and search patent databases
     - Who is the target market and who is the decision maker in the purchasing process?
     - What product features must the product incorporate?
     - What benefits will the product provide?
     - How will consumers react to the product?
     - How will the product be produced most cost effectively?
     - Prove feasibility through virtual computer aided rendering and rapid prototyping
     - What will it cost to produce it?
   - o Testing the Concept by asking a number of prospective customers what they think of the idea - usually via Choice Modelling.
4. Business Analysis
   - o Estimate likely selling price based upon competition and customer feedback
   - o Estimate sales volume based upon size of market and such tools as the Fourt-Woodlock equation
   - o Estimate profitability and break-even point
5. Beta Testing and Market Testing
   - o Produce a physical prototype or mock-up
   - o Test the product (and its packaging) in typical usage situations
   - o Conduct focus group customer interviews or introduce at trade show

- o Make adjustments where necessary
- o Produce an initial run of the product and sell it in a test market area to determine customer acceptance

6. Technical Implementation
   - o New program initiation
   - o Finalize Quality management system
   - o Resource estimation
   - o Requirement publication
   - o Publish technical communications such as data sheets
   - o Engineering operations planning
   - o Department scheduling
   - o Supplier collaboration
   - o Logistics plan
   - o Resource plan publication
   - o Program review and monitoring
   - o Contingencies - what-if planning
7. Commercialization (often considered post-NPD)
   - o Launch the product
   - o Produce and place advertisements and other promotions
   - o Fill the distribution pipeline with product
   - o Critical path analysis is most useful at this stage
8. New Product Pricing
   - o Impact of new product on the entire product portfolio
   - o Value Analysis (internal & external)
   - o Competition and alternative competitive technologies
   - o Differing value segments (price, value and need)
   - o Product Costs (fixed & variable)
   - o Forecast of unit volumes, revenue, and profit

These steps may be iterated as needed. Some steps may be eliminated. To reduce the time that the NPD process takes, many companies are completing several steps at the same time (referred to as concurrent engineering or time to market). Most industry leaders see new product development as a *proactive* process where resources are allocated to identify market changes and seize upon new product opportunities before they occur (in contrast to a *reactive strategy* in which nothing is done until problems occur or the competitor introduces an innovation). Many industry leaders see new product development as an ongoing process (referred to as *continuous development*) in which the entire organisation is always looking for opportunities. For the more innovative products indicated on the diagram above, great amounts of uncertainty and change may exist which makes it difficult or impossible to plan the complete project before starting it. In this case, a more flexible approach may be advisable.

Because the NPD process typically requires both engineering and marketing expertise, cross-functional teams are a common way of organising projects. The team is responsible for all aspects of the project, from initial idea generation to final commercialization, and they usually report to senior management (often to a vice president or Program Manager). In those industries where products are technically complex, development research is typically expensive and product life cycles are relatively short, strategic alliances among several organisations helps to spread the costs, provide access to a wider skill set and speeds up the overall process.

Also, notice that because both engineering and marketing expertise are usually critical to the process, choosing an appropriate blend of the two is important. Observe that this article is slanted more toward the marketing side. People respond to new products in different ways. The adoption of a new technology can be analyzed using a variety of diffusion theories such as the Diffusion of Innovations theory. A new product pricing process is important to reduce risk and increase confidence in the pricing and marketing decisions to be made. Bernstein and Macias describe an integrated process that breaks down the complex task of new product pricing into manageable elements. The Path to Developing Successful New Products points out three key processes that can play critical role in product development: Talk to the customer; Nurture a project culture; Keep it focused.

Fuzzy Front End

The Fuzzy Front End is the messy "getting ended" period of new product engineering development processes. It is in the front end where the organisation formulates a concept of the product to be developed and decides whether or not to invest resources in the further development of an idea. It is the phase between first consideration of an opportunity and when it is judged ready to enter the structured development process (Kim and Wilemon, 2002; Koen et al., 2001). It includes all activities from the search for new opportunities through the formation of a germ of an idea to the development of a precise concept. The Fuzzy Front End ends when an organisation approves and begins formal development of the concept.

Although the Fuzzy Front End may not be an expensive part of product development, it can consume 50% of development time, and it is where major commitments are typically made involving time, money, and the product's nature, thus setting the course for the entire project and final end product. Consequently, this phase should be considered as an essential part of development rather than something that happens "before development," and its cycle time should be included in the total development cycle time.

Koen et al. (2001, pp. 47–51) distinguish five different front-end elements (not necessarily in a particular order):

1. Opportunity Identification
2. Opportunity Analysis
3. Idea Genesis
4. Idea Selection
5. Concept and Technology Development

The first element is the opportunity identification. In this element, large or incremental business and technological chances are identified in a more or less structured way. Using the guidelines established here, resources will eventually be allocated to new projects.... which then lead to a structured NPPD (New Product & Process Development) strategy. The second element is the opportunity analysis. It is done to translate the identified opportunities into implications for the business and technology specific context of the company. Here extensive efforts may be made to align ideas to target customer groups and do market studies and/or technical trials and research.

The third element is the idea genesis, which is described as evolutionary and iterative process progressing from birth to maturation of the opportunity into a tangible idea. The process of the idea genesis can be made internally or come from outside inputs, e.g. a supplier offering a new material/technology or from a customer with an unusual request. The fourth element is the idea selection.

Its purpose is to choose whether to pursue an idea by analyzing its potential business value. The fifth element is the concept and technology development. During this part of the front-end, the business case is developed based on estimates of the total available market, customer needs, investment requirements, competition analysis and project uncertainty. Some organisations consider this to be the first stage of the NPPD process (i.e., Stage 0). The Fuzzy Front End is also described in literature as "Front End of Innovation", "Phase 0", "Stage 0" or "Pre-Project-Activities". A universally acceptable definition for Fuzzy Front End or a dominant framework has not been developed so far.

In a glossary of PDMA, it is mentioned that the Fuzzy Front End generally consists of three tasks: strategic planning, concept generation, and, especially, pre-technical evaluation. These activities are often chaotic, unpredictable, and unstructured. In comparison, the subsequent new product development process is typically structured, predictable, and formal.

The term *Fuzzy Front End* was first popularized by Smith and Reinertsen (1991). R.G.Cooper (1988) describes the early stages of NPPD as a four step process in which ideas are generated (I), subjected to a preliminary technical and market assessment (II) and merged to coherent product concepts (III) which are finally judged for their fit with existing product strategies and portfolios (IV). In a more recent paper, Cooper and Edgett (2008) affirm that vital predevelopment activities include:

1. Preliminary market assessment
2. Technical assessment
3. Source-of-supply-assessment: suppliers and partners or alliances
4. Market research: market size and segmentation analysis, VoC (voice of the customer) research
5. Product concept testing
6. Value-to-the customer assessment
7. Product definition
8. Business and financial analysis

These activities yield vital information to make a Go/No-Go to Development decision.

In the in-depth study by Khurana and Rosenthal front-end activities include:

- product strategy formulation and communication
- opportunity identification and assessment
- idea generation
- product definition
- executive reviews

Economical analysis, benchmarking of competitive products and modelling and prototyping are also important activities during the front-end activities.

The outcomes of FFE are the

- mission statement
- customer needs
- details of the selected concept
- product definition and specifications
- economic analysis of the product
- the development schedule
- project staffing and the budget
- a business plan aligned with corporate strategy

In a paper by Husig, Kohn and Huskela (2005) a conceptual model of Front-End Process was proposed which includes early Phases of Innovation Process. This model is structured in three phases and three gates:

- Phase 1: Environmental screening or opportunity identification stage in which external changes will be analysed and translated into potential business opportunities.
- Phase 2: Preliminary definition of an idea or concept.
- Phase 3: Detailed product, project or concept definition, and Business planning.

The gates are:

- Opportunity screening
- Idea evaluation
- Go/No-Go for development

The final gate leads to a dedicated new product development project. Many professionals and academics consider that the general features of Fuzzy Front End (fuzziness, ambiguity, and uncertainty) make it difficult to see the FFE as a structured process, but rather as a set of interdependent activities (e.g. Kim and Wilemon, 2002).

However, Husig et al., 2005 [10] argue that front-end not need to be fuzzy, but can be handled in a structured manner. Peter Koen argues that in the FFE for incremental, platform and radical projects, three separate strategies and processes are typically involved. The traditional Stage Gate (TM) process was designed for incremental product development, namely for a single product. The FFE for developing a new platform must start out with a strategic vision of where the company wants to develop products and this will lead to a family of products. Projects for breakthrough products start out with a similar strategic vision, but are associated with technologies which require new discoveries.

It is worth mentioning what incremental, platform and breakthrough products are.

- *Incremental products* are considered to be cost reductions, improvements to existing product lines, additions to existing platforms and repositioning of existing products introduced in markets.
- *Breakthrough products* are new to the company or new to the world and offer a 5-10 times or greater improvement in performance combined with a 30-50% or greater reduction in costs.
- *Platform products* establish a basic architecture for a next generation product or process and are substantially larger in scope and resources than incremental projects.

New Product Development Process

Because introducing new products on a consistent basis is important to the future success of many organisations, marketers in charge of product decisions often follow set procedures for bringing products to market. In the scientific area that may mean the establishment of ongoing laboratory research programs for discovering new products (e.g., medicines) while less scientific companies may pull together resources for product development on a less structured timetable.

In this section we present a 7-step process comprising the key elements of new product development. While some companies may not follow a deliberate step-by-step approach, the steps are useful in showing the information input and decision making that must be done in order to successfully develop new products. The process also shows the importance market research plays in developing products.

We should note that while the 7-step process works for most industries, it is less effective in developing radically new products. The main reason lies in the inability of the target market to provide sufficient feedback on advanced product concepts since they often find it difficult to understand radically different ideas. So while many of these steps are used to research breakthrough ideas, the marketer should exercise caution when interpreting the results.

Idea Generation

The first step of new product development requires gathering ideas to be evaluated as potential product options. For many companies idea generation is an ongoing process with contributions from inside and outside the organisation.

Many market research techniques are used to encourage ideas including: running focus groups with consumers, channel members, and the company's sales force; encouraging customer comments and suggestions via toll-free telephone numbers and website forms; and gaining insight on competitive product developments through secondary data sources.

One important research technique used to generate ideas is brainstorming where open-minded, creative thinkers from inside and outside the company gather and share ideas. The dynamic nature of group members floating ideas, where one idea often sparks another idea, can yield a wide range of possible products that can be further pursued.

Screening

In Step 2 the ideas generated in Step 1 are critically evaluated by company personnel to isolate the most attractive options. Depending on the number of ideas, screening may be done in rounds with the first round involving company executives judging the feasibility of ideas while successive rounds may utilise more advanced research techniques.

As the ideas are whittled down to a few attractive options, rough estimates are made of an idea's potential in terms of sales, production costs, profit potential, and competitors' response if the product is introduced. Acceptable ideas move on to the next step.

Concept Development and Testing

With a few ideas in hand the marketer now attempts to obtain initial feedback from customers, distributors and its own employees. Generally, focus groups are convened where the ideas are presented to a group, often in the form of concept board presentations (i.e., storyboards) and not in actual working form.

For instance, customers may be shown a concept board displaying drawings of a product idea or even an advertisement featuring the product. In some cases focus groups are exposed to a mock-up of the ideas, which is a physical but generally non-functional version of product idea. During focus groups with customers the marketer seeks information that may include: likes and dislike of the concept; level of interest in purchasing the product; frequency of purchase (used to help forecast demand); and price points to determine how much customers are willing to spend to acquire the product.

Managing Existing Products

Marketing strategies developed for initial product introduction almost certainly need to be revised as the product settles into the market. While commercialization may be the last step in the new product development process it is just the beginning of managing the product. Adjusting the product's marketing strategy is required for many reasons including:

- Changing customer tastes
- Domestic and foreign competitors
- Economic conditions
- Technological advances

To stay on top of all possible threats the marketer must monitor all aspects of the marketing mix and make changes as needed. Such efforts require the marketer to develop and refine the product's marketing plan on a regular basis. In fact, as we will discuss in The PLC and Marketing Planning tutorial, marketing strategies change as a product moves through time leading to the concept called the Product Life Cycle (PLC). We will see that marketers make numerous revisions to their strategy as product move through different stage of the PLC.

Have a New Product Idea?

Every Day, Bright Ideas are Turned into New Products.

Some of the best new product inventions come from average people from every walk of life who are trying to solve a problem or make life more enjoyable. These new products can be found on store shelves, in catalogs, for sale on television or via the Internet. While we can't guarantee that the product you've created will be a success, it is safe to suggest that if you never pursue it, you may never find out. If you'd like to learn more about turning your invention into a new product, we recommend that you complete the free information form and Davison will send you information on our exclusive development process. The products depicted on this page include both client-submitted products and products designed by Davison for its own benefit.

Product Design & Development

The Generic Process for Developing New Products

Poductdevelopment is the process of creating a new product to be sold by a business or enterprise to its customers. In the document title, *Design* refers to those activities involved in creating the styling, look and feel of the product, deciding on the product's mechanical architecture, selecting materials and processes, and engineering the various components necessary to make the product work. *Development* refers collectively to the entire process of identifying a market opportunity, creating a product to appeal to the identified market, and finally, testing, modifying and refining the product until it is ready for production. A product can be any item from a book, musical composition, or information service, to an engineered product such as a computer, hair dryer, or washing machine. This document is focused on the process of developing discrete engineered products, rather than works of art or informational products.

The task of developing outstanding new products is difficult, time-consuming, and costly. People who have never been involved in a development effort are astounded by the amount of time and money that goes into a new product. Great products are not simply designed, but instead they evolve over time through countless hours of research, analysis, design studies, engineering and prototyping efforts, and finally, testing, modifying, and re-testing until the design has been perfected.

Few products are developed by a single individual working alone. It is unlikely that one individual will have the necessary skills in marketing, industrial design, mechanical and electronic engineering, manufacturing processes and materials, tool-making, packaging design, graphic art, and project management, just to name the primary areas of expertise. Development is normally done by a project team, and the team leader draws on talent in a variety of disciplines, often from both outside and inside the company. As a general rule, the cost of a development effort is a factor of the number of people involved and the time required to nurture the initial concept into a fully-refined product. Rarely can a production-ready product be developed in less than one year, and some projects can take three to five years to complete.

The impetus for a new product normally comes from a perceived market opportunity or from the development of a new technology. Consequently, new products are broadly categorized as either *market-*

pull products or *technology-push* products. With a market-pull product, the marketing center of the company first determines that sales could be increased if a new product were designed to appeal to a particular segment of its customers. Engineering is then be asked to determine the technical feasibility of the new product idea.

This interaction is reversed with a technology-push product. When a technical breakthrough opens the way for a new product, marketing then attempts to determine the idea's prospects in the marketplace. In many cases, the technology itself may not actually point to a particular product, but instead, to new capabilities and benefits that could be packaged in a variety of ways to create a number of different products.

Marketing would have the responsibility of determining how the technology should be packaged to have the greatest appeal to its customers. With either scenario, manufacturing is responsible for estimating the cost of building the prospective new product, and their estimations are used to project a selling price and estimate the potential profit for the company.

The process of developing new products varies between companies, and even between products within the same company. Regardless of organisational differences, a good new product is the result a methodical development effort with well defined product specifications and project goals. A development project for a market-pull product is generally organised along the lines shown.

Concept Development

Good concept development is crucial. During this stage, the needs of the target market are identified, competitive products are reviewed, product specifications are defined, a product concept is selected, an economic analysis is done, and the development project is outlined. This stage provides the foundation for the development effort, and if poorly done can undermine the entire effort. Concept development activities are normally organised according to Figure.

Identify Customer Needs: Through interviews with potential purchasers, focus groups, and by observing similar products in use, researchers identify customer needs. The list of needs will include hidden needs, needs that customers may not be aware of or problems they simply accept without question, as well as explicit needs, or needs that will most likely be reported by potential purchasers. Researchers develop the necessary information on which to base the performance, size, weight, service life, and other specifications of the product. Customer needs and product specifications are organised into a hierarchical list with a comparative rating value given to each need and specification.

Establish Target Specifications: Based on customers' needs and reviews of competitive products, the team establishes the target specifications of the prospective new product. While the process of identifying customer needs is entirely a function of marketing, designers and engineers become involved in establishing target specifications. Target specifications are essentially a wish-list tempered by known technical constraints. Later, after designers have generated preliminary products concepts, the target specifications are refined to account for technical, manufacturing and economic realities.

Analyze Competitive Products: An analysis of competitive products is part of the process of establishing target specifications. Other products may exhibit successful design attributes that should be emulated or improved upon in the new product. And by understanding the shortfalls of competitive products, a list of improvements can be developed that will make the new product clearly superior to those of others. In a broader sense, analyzing competitive products can help orient designers and provide a starting point for design efforts. Rather than beginning from scratch and re-inventing the wheel with each new project, traditionally, the evolution of design builds on the successes and failures of prior work.

Generate Product Concepts: Designers and engineers develop a number of product concepts to illustrate what types of products are both technically feasible and would best meets the requirements of the target specifications. Engineers develop preliminary concepts for the architecture of the product, and industrial designers develop renderings to show styling and layout alternatives. After narrowing the selection, non-functional appearance models are built of candidate designs.

Select a Product Concept: Through the process of evaluation and tradeoffs between attributes, a final concept is selected. The selection process may be confined to the team and key executives within the company, or customers may be polled for their input. Candidate appearance models are often used for additional market research; to obtain feedback from certain key customers, or as a centerpiece of focus groups.

Refine Product Specifications: In this stage, product specifications are refined on the basis of input from the foregoing activities. Final specifications are the result of tradeoffs made between technical feasibility, expected service life, projected selling price, and the financial limitations of the development project. With a new luggage product, for example, consumers may want a product that is lightweight, inexpensive, attractive, and with the ability to expand to carry varying amounts of luggage.

Unfortunately, the mechanism needed for the expandable feature will increase the selling price, add weight to the product, and introduce a mechanism that has the potential for failure. Consequently, the team must choose between a heavier, more costly product, or one that does not have the expandable feature. When product attributes are in conflict, or when the technical challenge or higher selling price of a particular feature outweighs its benefits, the specification may be dropped or modified in favour of other benefits.

Perform Economic Analysis: Throughout the foregoing activities, important economic implications regarding development expenses, manufacturing costs, and selling price have been estimated. A thorough economic analysis of the product and the required development effort is necessary in order to define the remainder of the development project. An economic model of the product and a review of anticipated development expenses in relation to expected benefits is now developed.

Plan the Remaining Development Project: In this final stage of concept development, the team prepares a detailed development plan which includes a list of activities, the necessary resources and expenses, and a development schedule with milestones for tracking progress.

System-Level Design

System-level design, or the task of designing the architecture of the product, is the subject of this stage. In prior stages, the team was focused on the core product idea, and the prospective design was largely based on overviews rather than in-depth design and engineering. Once the development plan is approved, marketing may begin to develop ideas for additional product options and add-ons, or perhaps an extended product family. Designers and engineers develop the product architecture in detail, and manufacturing determines which components should be made and which should be purchased, and identifies the necessary suppliers.

The product architecture defines the product in *chunks,* or the primary functional systems and subsystems, and how these systems are arranged to work as a unit. For example, an automobile is comprised of a body and a chassis with an engine, a transmission, final drive, frame, suspension and braking system. The architecture of an automobile design determines the platform layout, whether the vehicle is front-wheel-drive or rear-wheel-drive, the size and location of the engine, transmission and final drive, the overall design of suspension system, and the layout and type of other necessary subsystems such as brakes, wheels, and steering. The architecture may determine the layout of the exhaust system, but it would not provide the detailed engineering needed to determine the diameter and thickness of the exhaust pipe, the detailed design of mufflers, nor the engineering of motor mounts and exhaust hangers needed to isolate vibrations from the passenger compartment.

The architecture of the product, how it is divided into chunks and how the chunks are integrated into the total product, impacts a number of important attributes such as standardization of components, modularity, options for change later on, ease of manufacture, and how the development project is divided into manageable tasks and expenses. If a family of products or upgrades and add-ons are planned, the architecture of the product would determine the commonality of components and the ease with which upgrades and add-ons can be installed. A system or subsystem borrowed from another product within the company's line will economize on development, tooling and manufacturing costs. With outsourced components, the supplier may contribute much of the associated design and engineering.

Detail Design

Detail design, or design-for-manufacture, is the stage wherein the necessary engineering is done for every component of the product. During this phase, each part is identified and engineered. Tolerances, materials, and finishes are defined, and the design is documented with drawings or computer files. Increasingly, manufacturers and developers are turning to three-dimensional solid modelling using programs such as Pro-Engineer. Three-dimensional computer models form the core of today's rapid prototyping and rapid manufacturing technologies. Once the database has been developed, prototype components can be rapidly built on computerized machines such as CNC mills, fused deposition modelling devices, or stereo lithography systems.

Testing and Refinement

During the testing and refinement stage, a number of prototypes are built and tested. Even though they are not made from production components, prototypes emulate production products as closely as possible. These *alpha* prototypes are necessary to determine whether the performance of the product matches the specifications, and to uncover design shortfalls and gain in-the-field experience with the product in use. Later, *beta* prototypes are built from the first production components received from suppliers.

Production Ramp-up

During production ramp-up, the work force is trained as the first products are being assembled. The comparatively slow product build provides time to work out any remaining problems with supplier components, fabrication, and assembly procedures. The staff and supervisory team is organised, beginning with a core team, and line workers are trained by assembling production units.

Technology-Push Products

The generic development process is used with technology-push products, but with slight modification. With technology-push products, the company acquires or develops a new technology and then looks for appropriate markets in which to apply the technology. Consequently, an extra phase is added at the beginning during which the new technology is matched to an appropriate market opportunity. When the match has been made, the generic development process is carried out as described.

Models and Prototypes

The terms *prototype* and *model* are often used interchangeably to mean any full-scale pre-production representation of a design, whether functional or not. I prefer to use the term *model* to describe a non-functional representation and the term *prototype* to describe a functional item. An *appearance model* is a full-scale, non-functional representation that looks, as closely as possible, identical to the prospective new product. Modelling and prototyping serve a variety of purposes throughout the development effort.

Early on, engineering prototypes may be built of systems and subsystems to bench-test performance and debug the system before proceeding with the design. Appearance models prove out styling and ergonomics. A full-scale mockup of an automobile interior, for example, provides a real-world test of ease of ingress, seating position, access to controls, visibility and appearance. Models and prototypes are necessary because of the limitations of theoretical work and artificial mediums. A product can be designed and put into simulated use on computer, but one doesn't really know how it will work until the item is built and tested in its intended environment. Prototyping and modelling efforts begin virtually at the inception of the project and continue into production ramp-up.

The Role of Industrial Design

According to the definition given by the Industrial Designers Society of America (IDSA), industrial design (ID) is the "professional service of creating and developing concepts and specifications that optimize the function, value and appearance of products and systems for the mutual benefit of both user and manufacturer." An industrial designer combines artistic form with engineering necessities.

The ID practitioner blends the human meanings expressed through form, colour, and texture with the mechanical realities of function in a way that broadcasts a coherent and purposeful message to those who experience the product. Good industrial design can create additional product benefits through the selection of materials and the architecture of the design. Industrial designers have extensive training in art, as well as training in basic engineering, manufacturing and fabrication processes, and marketing practices. Dreyfuss (1967) lists five critical goals that industrial designers bring to a team when developing new products:

- *Utility:* The product's human interfaces should be safe, easy to use, and intuitive. Each feature should be shaped so that it communicates its function to the user.
- *Appearance:* Form, line, proportion, and colour are used to integrate the product into a pleasing whole.
- *Ease of Maintenance:* Products must also be designed to communicate how they are to be maintained and repaired.
- *Low Costs:* Form and features have a large impact on tooling and production costs, so they must be considered jointly by the team.
- *Communication:* Product designs should communicate the corporate design philosophy and mission through the visual qualities of the products.

Industrial design is costly and the value per dollar spent is often difficult to quantity. The value becomes obvious, however, when one experiences the results. When the purchaser intuitively understands a product's function, and senses the quality of its construction and the integrity of the company that produced it, these subliminal messages are normally the result of good industrial design. Industrial designers usually become involved in a development project almost at the outset. Enthusiasm within the development team increases when industrial designers develop an attractive concept early in the project. When members have a real concept to work towards, the effort ceases to be a purely cerebral exercise, and instead, comes alive with personal meaning.

New Product Ideas

The thirst for adventure and creative expression is intrinsic to the human spirit. Nothing is quite as gratifying as venturing into uncharted territory to give birth to a new idea. Add to this the prospect of generating wealth from the adventure, and the irresistible goddess of invention is born. This paper is dedicated to those brave individuals who would rather fly than sit on a fence and watch the birds. The following material explains the practical aspects of developing, protecting, and most importantly, marketing a new product idea. It is directed primarily to the inventor and entrepreneur.

Intellectual property information is based on U.S. Patent Law. Although information is readily available on patents and intellectual property rights, usually, an inventor or entrepreneur is on his own when it comes to marketing his intellectual property. Based on more than 20 years experience with new product development and startup operations, these pages provide an outline of how best to succeed at this most challenging and potentially fruitful endeavour.

At the outset I would like to challenge two opposing, but interrelated, myths. The first myth is the belief that if you invent a better mousetrap, the world will beat a path to your door. In truth, the world will hardly notice. What really counts is the time, effort, and resources that go into developing and marketing a product. The second myth is that one has to be tremendously lucky to beat the odds against success with a new invention. In reality, much depends on how well you know the field of your invention (the political, economic, and marketing factors), and then on the action you take to develop and promote it. A good product idea is important, but an average idea powered by well-targeted action is better than a great idea that stands alone.

Create Intellectual Property

If you are a private inventor with aspirations to license a manufacturer you must own your idea in order to license it. In other words, you must create some form of intellectual property (patent, copyright, trademark, etc.). With a startup operation, a patent will be considered an asset by investors and lenders. When intellectual property is included in the business plan, it will be easier to attract financing. For a company already in the widget manufacturing business, the decision on whether to proceed with a patent application will primarily be a business decision.

The protection afforded by a patent may not be as important as the potential benefits of allocating the same resources to building and/ or marketing the product itself. On the other hand, a small entity with limited marketing resources will benefit from the extra time in the marketplace, unchallenged, due to the exclusivity provided by patent protection.

What is Intellectual Property

Intellectual property is established by obtaining a copyright, trademark, or patent. A copyright protects literary, dramatic, musical, and artistic works. A trademark protects a word, name, symbol, or device used in trade to indicate the source or origin of the goods, and to distinguish them from the goods of others.

In our business, we are concerned primarily with patents and the patentability of product features that result from our development services. Such patents then become the property of the client through assignment. (The person who actually makes the invention or creates the patentable design must be listed on the patent application as the inventor. If the inventor and the rightful owner are not the same, such as in the case of work done for hire, ownership would then be assigned to the correct party.)

There are two types of patents: a design patent and a utility patent. A design patent protects the ornamental design of a product, such as a unique design for the face of a clock or the particular styling of a product. Normally, minor changes can circumvent a design patent. The most valued and effective patent is the utility patent.

Throughout the remainder of this document, the term "patent" will imply a utility patent. A utility patent protects any new and useful process, machine, manufacture, or composition of matter, or any new and useful improvements thereof.

The term "useful" means that the invention must have a purpose and it must work. A patent cannot be obtained on an idea or a concept. The invention must be a real and workable item, composition, or process. The term "new" implies novelty. A patent cannot be obtained if:

1. The invention was known or used by others in this country, or patented or described in a printed publication in this or a foreign country, before the invention by the applicant for patent, or

The invention was patented or described in a printed publication in this or a foreign country or in public use or on sale in this country more than one year prior to the application for the patent in the U.S. A patent attorney is the best source of patent information and the best judge of patentability. Typically, a patent attorney will provide a complementary consultation on the first visit.

The General Agreement on Tariffs and Trade

The recent General Agreement on Tariffs and Trade (GATT) has caused changes in U.S. Patent Law. Again, your patent attorney is the best source of detailed information, but significant changes already in effect are as follows:

- *Term:* The term of a patent is now 20 years from the application date. Prior to GATT, it was 17 years from issuance.
- *Provisional Patent Application:* You can now file a Provisional Patent Application, which is essentially a patent application without claims. The advantages include lower initial cost and one extra year of protection (1 year on the provisional application, plus 20 years on the patent itself). The disadvantages are that it delays the issuance of the patent, total cost is greater, and it carries the risk of inadequate disclosure.

Cost of a Patent

Although it is possible to save money by preparing and filing your own patent application, it is best to use a patent attorney. A correctly prepared patent application with correctly defined claims will provide the strongest foundation for subsequent commercialization efforts. In addition, a new product may have patentable features that may not be obvious to the untrained eye. A patent attorney can identify patentable design attributes, and then correctly structure the claims to obtain the broadest possible protection. The costs of obtaining a patent (for a small entity) are as follows:

Cost When Using a Patent Attorney

Utility Patent

- Professional Fees..........$3500
- Issue Fee......................$ 650

- Maintenance Fees.........$ 445 in 3.5 years, $1025 in 7.5 years, and $1575 in 11.5 years (from issuance date)

Design Patent

- Professional Fees..........$1300
- Issue Fee......................$ 215

Cost When Applying Yourself

Utility Patent

- Filing Fee......................$375
- Issue Fee.......................$650
- Maintenance Fees..........Same as above, due at 3.5, 7.5, and 11.5 years

Design Patent

- Filing Fee.......................$155
- Issue Fee........................$215

Prior to maintenance fees (introduced about 20 years ago), an inventor who filed his own patent applications could afford to have a number of active patents and take his time pursuing commercialization. Today, however, maintaining several active patents on uncommercialized inventions can be quite costly. In addition, the decreasing value of an uncommercialized patent (due to less time remaining on the patent), in combination with escalating maintenance fees, tends to discourage inventors from hanging on to older patents that may have little commercial value.

Patent Pitfalls

A number of potential pitfalls exist with patent law. A few of the primary areas of caution are as follows:

- Co-Inventors and Co-Owners: When co-inventors are listed on a patent, each inventor has full rights to manufacture, sell, and license others, without regard to the other inventors. The same rights extend to co-owners of a patent, no matter how small the percentage of ownership. Consequently, it is best to make a separate agreement with co-owners/co-inventors outlining mutual obligations and restrictions.
- Assignment or Sale: When possible, avoid an assignment or outright sale of a patent, unless you are happy with the initial payment. When a patent is sold or assigned, it becomes the property and asset of the assignee. In the event of financial difficulties, the patent could be lost to a lender.

- Infringement: When the owner of a patent becomes aware of an infringement, the owner must notify the infringing party, or risk jeopardizing his patent rights. However, when a party is accused of infringement, the accused party has the right to bring legal action against the accuser and claim an invalid patent. The patent owner will then have to defend the action in federal court. Expect to spend at least $100,000 in legal expenses on such a defence. If an infringement does occur, a patent attorney can notify the infringing party in a way that will not provide grounds for this type of counter litigation (normally by subtle suggestion, rather than overt accusation).

Turning a Patent into Income

After obtaining a patent, an inventor faces the prospect of marketing the invention to a manufacturer. In order to develop an effective marketing strategy, one must first see the world from the customer's perspective. From the licensee's perspective, the key factors that determine an idea's success potential are its technical and economic feasibility, and its market potential.

And regardless of a product's technical and economic feasibility, success will ultimately depend on market factors. Unfortunately, when a new product does reach the marketplace, nine out of ten fail. In the event of a failure, development and marketing expenses become a total loss. To put the impact of such a failure in business terms, consider that a manufacturer must sell at least $10.00 worth of profitable goods for every $1.00 lost to an unsuccessful venture..... just to break even on the loss.

As a result, a great deal of the effort that goes into evaluating a new product idea is oriented toward heading off a possible failure. Moreover, a substantial investment of time and resources is required to properly evaluate a new product idea and estimate its potential for success. So when a company executive declines a seemingly good product idea, what is probably being declined is the expense of properly evaluating the idea, and after having paid these expenses, the prospect of embarking on an expensive commercialization effort that has a 90 percent chance of failing.

Despite the foregoing, new products are essential if a manufacturer is to remain competitive, and successful new products translate into new markets, increased market share, and greater profits. The key is to avoid failure while pursuing success. In order to comfortably move ahead, a manufacturer must have accurate knowledge about the associated expenses, risks, and market factors. When soliciting a licensee, let the following guide your presentation:

- The most effective incentive is PROFIT.
- The biggest obstacle is FEAR.
- The most powerful antidote is KNOWLEDGE.

A well developed package of knowledge about the product and its market will provide the prospective licensee with essential information that he would otherwise have to develop.

Package the Product for the Buyer

The most common shortfall of efforts to solicit a licensee is the failure to develop a refined prototype and a well targeted presentation (package of knowledge). In a sense, one must package the new product idea for the prospective buyer. And from the inventor's perspective, two buyers exist: The end user and the prospective licensee. Consequently, the most effective packaging will contain elements that are directed to each of them.

Your presentation package should include a manufacturing cost study, a market study, and a working prototype. Ideally, the prototype will be fully refined and production-ready. If the product is not ready for production, an outline of additional development tasks and expenses, as well as an estimation of the time required, should be included.

The manufacturing study would include a review of production materials and processes, and an estimation of direct materials, components, and labour costs, along with economies of scale. The market study should include an overview of market trends, and a review of the various factors that will impact marketing strategy and expenses, as well as an estimation of potential sales. Sketches of display package design and advertising layouts might also be included. This will project the product visually and emotionally into the marketplace.

Depending on the magnitude of the information, each of the three categories (development, manufacturing, and marketing) may be formatted as individual reports, or they may be presented as chapters in a single report. The goal of the presentation package is to project the product into the marketplace according to your vision, and remove the unknowns for the prospective licensee. In addition to providing essential information and correctly framing your idea, a comprehensive presentation will also imply that the product has been professionally conceived and developed.

A Refined Prototype is an Essential Sales Tool

Unfortunately, most new product ideas are unnecessarily penalized because they have not been rendered in the correct technology. They have not been designed for production processes, and they have not been correctly packaged nor professionally styled. Manufacturers are rarely presented with anything resembling a production-ready new product. Consequently, an inventor with a well designed and well built prototype will be miles ahead when it comes to soliciting a licensee. Conversely, a poorly built prototype will psychologically project similar deficiencies into the product idea itself. The prospective licensee will then have to use his imagination to see the product in its finished (marketable) form. In the final analysis, a professionally developed prototype represents a bundle of knowledge about the product, and it represents development expenses that the potential licensee does not have to pay.

Tips on Market Research

A market study can indicate attributes about the product that should be modified or emphasized. It can point out distribution avenues, strengths, and weaknesses, suggest advertising appeals, and indicate potential sales. This information is an essential part of the presentation. However, market research studies can be expensive. Even the most basic study will cost $2,500 to 3,500. If marketing information is expensive to obtain, the cost can rapidly escalate. Actual expenses depend the particular product and the scope of the information necessary to analyze market factors.

It may be possible to save money by doing some of the work yourself. But unless you have a marketing background, it is probably unwise to attempt to design the study, interpret data or survey results, or prepare the final document yourself. Another way to save on costs is to solicit the participation of a local university. Perhaps a market study can be done as a class project.

The Wal-Mart Innovation Network (WIN) provides new-product evaluations that may be useful in a market study. The WIN process begins with an evaluation conducted by the College of Business Administration at Southwest Missouri State University (SMU). The cost is $175.00. If the product receives a high enough rating, it is then sent to a Wal-Mart buyer for a more extensive evaluation of its market potential. Although a successful outcome would be significant, neither the initial evaluation by SMU, nor the Wal-Mart buyer evaluation would suffice as a market study by itself.

One of the most powerful indicators of potential success is actual demonstrated success in a micro-marketing environment. If it is feasible to build a small run, offer the product for sale through an appropriate end user purchasing outlet. Price the product as though it were in production, even though each sale may result in a loss. The information obtained by test-marketing could dramatically document your product's potential. However, if the product is unrefined, poorly packaged, or inappropriately priced, the exercise could backfire and indicate poor sales of an otherwise potentially successful product.

Moreover, many products do not simply disappear off the shelves when they are offered for sale. Instead, sales are generated by the marketing effort, which undoubtedly will be lacking in a limited trial run. But if your product can stand the test of unsupported exposure, there is no better way to demonstrate its potential.

Distribution Related Marketing Considerations

The sales potential of a new product is not necessarily a function of end-user appeal. Distribution factors could be much more significant. In fact, an ordinary product with good distribution may experience excellent sales, whereas a superior product that is not well distributed would likely fade into oblivion. A popular adage in manufacturing circles is that one can sell almost anything, provided the price is right and the distribution is good.

To complicate matters, a manufacturer often has to pay a large initial fee ($5,000 to $30,000) to a retail chain in order to get a new product into their stores. Shelf space is a premium commodity, and retailers are increasingly unwilling to absorb the expense of stocking a new product that may turn out to be a poor seller. Consequently, the market study must address distribution realities that are likely to impact marketing efforts. These factors could be even more important than the benefits and appeal of the product itself.

Assuming that the limited test-marketing exercise mentioned in the previous section were feasible, it may be possible to achieve more than valid sales data. A test-marketing effort could be parlayed into a purchasing commitment from a large chain. Depending on the product and the particular chain, many large retailers will test-market a new product (after it is in production) by placing it into a limited number of stores. If the product sells well, the retailer will then order an appropriate quantity for the remaining outlets. Consider the effect on a prospective licensee if you were to negotiate a test-market through a large retailer, and on the basis of the results, obtained a commitment to purchase the product for the entire chain. As a rule, retailers tend to avoid such early-stage involvements. But regardless of conventional wisdom about today's impersonal business protocols, the vast majority of transactions are still based on personal relationships between individuals. Much depends on your ability to connect with a buyer on a human level and gain his support.

Avoid Building Weaknesses into the Presentation

A seemingly good presentation can backfire if any of its elements are poorly executed. For example, if you have invented a better widget and the potential licensee is in the widget manufacturing business, he will probably be an expert at manufacturing and marketing widgets. In other words, he will be an expert at evaluating the design of your widget and judging the validity of supportive information in your presentation. Poor design, inaccurate manufacturing cost estimations, or unsound market research methodology in support of unlikely sales projections will all be apparent to an experienced professional.

Should the presentation contain any of these shortfalls, the prospective licensee will then have more on which to base a rejection - possible uncertainties about the product itself, as well as unsound technique and improbable conclusions. Unless you have the elements professionally developed, you may have to rely on a more abbreviated, and possibly less powerful presentation. If you are refining the product and preparing the presentation yourself, the key is to provide the most complete and fully developed package, within the limits of your expertise. Above all, it is essential to maintain credibility with the prospective licensee.

The Option of a Joint Effort

Today, companies are turning more and more to "partnering" to cooperatively pioneer new products and markets. While a large commitment may be outside the capabilities of most inventors, some form of partnering may be feasible. In fact, the foregoing suggestions for promoting an invention actually amount to a form of limited partnering, wherein the inventor assumes responsibility for part of the development effort.

Recently, a client/inventor was able to get his product into production through a similar, but more expansive arrangement. The inventor approached the manufacturer with an offer to underwrite the direct costs of developing the product to production-ready status, and pay for direct tooling costs. Because of the inventor's commitment, the manufacturer agreed to put the product into production and market it internationally. The inventor retained U.S. distribution rights and received royalties on international sales. In this case, the license agreement was based as much on mutual business commitments as it was on the product itself.

Whether the foregoing are good terms depends on the value that each party places on their respective contributions and benefits. The point, however, is that business relationships can take many forms, and there are many roads to the same goal.

A New Product is Born

Tide Pods are palm-size, liquid detergent-filled tablets that are designed to be tossed in the washer to take the measuring cups — and messiness — out of laundry. P&G says the product, which hit store shelves last month, is its biggest innovation in laundry in about a quarter of a century. Tide Pods aren't the sexiest of inventions, but they illustrate how mature companies that are looking for growth often have to tweak things as mundane as soap and detergent. The story behind Tide Pods provides a window into the time, money and brainpower that goes into doing that.

P&G, the maker of everything from Pampers diapers to Pantene shampoo, has built its 175-year history on creating things people need and then improving them. (Think: Ivory soap in 1879; Swiffer Sweeper in 1999.) Each year, the company spends $2 billion on research and development and rolls out about 27 products worldwide — more than two a month. That focus on innovation has paid off. P&G says 98 percent of American households have at least one of its products in their cupboards, broom closets or bathrooms. And while about 15 to 20 percent of all new products succeed, P&G has claimed a 50 percent success rate. Four of the top 10 new consumer products in 2010 were made by P&G, according to research firm SymphonyIRI.

"What they've gotten very good at is being able to understand consumer expectations," says Robert Passikoff, president of Brand Keys Inc., a New York customer research firm.

But improving things like window cleaner and toilet paper can take years. It also can cost hundreds of millions of dollars — or up to 100 percent of first-year sales — to develop, make and market them. And even then, new products are a tough sell to consumers.

> *"You have to develop a product that is meaningfully better than the ones out there, which is tough because generally speaking consumer products work pretty well,"*

says Ali Dibadj, an analyst at Bernstein Research who follows P&G. "You then have to convince the consumer to try the product ... and then get that consumer to break their old habit to make a new one."

First Load: A Product is Born

The laundry detergent industry, with $6.5 billion in annual sales, is always looking for the next big thing. Over the years, fruity scents were introduced, along with suds that work in cold water. There also were concentrated and super-concentrated detergents that need less packaging. Liquid Tide, which costs about $15 for 32 loads, is the best-selling detergent, according to SymphonyIRI, the research firm. But cheaper rivals have been gaining: For instance, the number of units sold of Church & Dwight's Arm & Hammer Oxi-Clean Laundry, the No. 2 detergent brand that costs $8 for 35 loads, rose 13 percent in the past year. Unit sales of Liquid Tide were flat.

In 2004, P&G decided to try to freshen up the category. Surveys and observations of 6,000 consumers found that more than a third dreaded doing laundry. A big reason: Many apartment dwellers hated lugging a seven-pound detergent bottle downstairs to the laundry room or a Laundromat and back. Researchers also found that people rewashed loads about 20 percent of the time because they thought detergent didn't get their laundry clean enough. And many were confused about which detergent to use when they wash in different ways: in regular washers versus high-efficiency machines; in big loads or small; and in hot or cold water.

"We knew people felt laundry was complicated," says Alex Keith, vice president of P&G's unit that makes laundry detergents and fabric softeners. So P&G set about creating a product that weighed less, cleaned better and could be used with any washing machine, any size load and in water at any temperature. Pod-like products had been on the market before. P&G introduced tablets filled with powder detergent in 2000, but yanked them from stores shelves two years later. The problem was that powder tablets didn't always dissolve completely, leading to messiness. They also worked only in hot water.

To make sure Tide Pods would dissolve in cold water too, P&G turned to MonoSol, a company that makes water soluble films. MonoSol developed a polyvinyl alcohol film that not only dissolves in any temperature water, but even in sweaty palms. The film also is strong — it won't break even when stretched over the top of a can of marbles and shaken — but soft to the touch.

The film created another problem, though. Detergents, which mostly consist of water, would cause the pod to melt before it even got into the wash. So P&G made a detergent that is 10 percent water — compared with Liquid Tide, which is 50 percent water. Next, scientists had to figure out how to combine cleansers, brighteners and fabric softeners into one product, while keeping them separate until the pod dissolves in the wash. Doing so would ensure each liquid would work better. After 450 sketches and iterations, P&G developed a proprietary technology that sections the pod into three chambers for all three liquids. The result? A soft ball with three separate bubbles filled with liquids in Tide's trademark white, blue and orange colours.

Innovate, Rinse, Repeat

Making the product was half the battle. Consumer testing is at the heart of product development for P&G, which has more than 25 facilities across the globe where people can use the things it makes. The Beckett Ridge Innovation Center, about 30 minutes from P&G's Cincinnati headquarters, is one. Inside, there's a 3,000-square-foot grocery store packed with everything from Charmin diapers to Cascade dishwashing liquid. There's also a 2,000-square-foot mock clapboard house where researchers analyze how people do laundry, wash dishes, take showers and change babies' diapers.

About 50 P&G researchers work at the center, watching and videotaping about 20,000 people each year in their "natural" environment. The testers are picked by third-party companies and paid based on the task they complete. "When we watch consumers in action, we can see things they can't otherwise explain or articulate," says Jessica Hall White, director of P&G's unit that makes fabric care brands like Tide, Gain and Downy. When P&G researchers had consumers test Tide Pods at the center, they found that 97 percent were satisfied with their experience, compared with about 68 percent who were satisfied beforehand using regular detergent. People also liked how Tide Pods felt in their hands.

When it came to packaging, P&G took a more futuristic approach to testing. The company used three screens at the Innovation Center to project 3D images of a virtual grocery store. There, testers could see early designs of Tide Pod packaging on the virtual store shelves alongside regular detergents. Researchers learned that people sometimes overlooked the product. So P&G determined that in order to stand out, Tide Pods needed to have see-through packaging. The company developed a clear fishbowl-like container that shows the pods clearly.

The product was developed. The consumer tests were done. The packaging was complete. Next, it was time to get Tide Pods to market. P&G was poised to be the first detergent maker to get its new dissolvable pods into stores. They were to cost $20.89 for 57 pods and land on shelves by September 2011. But the company ran into problems making the pods, which require different equipment from what's used to manufacture regular detergent. At the same time, P&G was flooded with orders from supermarkets and retailers.

P&G declined to detail the manufacturing problems, but it says the issues forced it to push back the launch date of Tide Pods by five months to February. In the hyper-competitive world of consumer products, that might as well be an eternity. Tide Pods entered a market that was already getting crowded. Henkel's Purex UltraPacks and Sun Products' All Mighty Pacs came out in February, too. And Church and Dwight plans to launch its Toss 'N Done Power Packs— made of crystals — this month. All of the products are priced similarly — more expensive than liquid or powder detergents. But P&G has a big advantage. The Tide brand is one of the most recognised in the world, so P&G hopes to win over shoppers with performance and brand recognition. The company says it expects Tide Pods to ring up $300 million in sales during its first year.

John San Marco, an analyst with Janney Capital Markets, says P&G is at a slight disadvantage because it wasn't first to market its product. But he believes its Tide Pods product is likely to hit its first-year sales goal. "It seems when Procter does anything in the laundry category it makes a huge wave," he says. Still, P&G isn't taking chances. The company spent an estimated $150 million on a marketing campaign to roll out Tide Pods. The first commercial debuted during the Academy Awards, one of TV's biggest events.

Promotion

Promotion is one of the market mix elements. The specification of five promotional mix or promotional plan. These elements are personal selling, advertising, sales promotion, direct marketing, and publicity. A promotional mix specifies how much attention to pay to each of the five subcategories, and how much money to budget for each. A promotional plan can have a wide range of objectives, including: sales increases, new product acceptance, creation of brand equity, positioning, competitive retaliations, or creation of a corporate image. Fundamentally, however there are three basic objectives of promotion. These are:

1. To present information to consumers as well as others.
2. To increase demand.
3. To differentiate a product.

There are different ways to promote a product in different areas of media. Promoters use internet advertisement, special events, endorsements, and newspapers to advertise their product.

Many times with the purchase of a product there is an incentive like discounts, free items, or a contest. This is to increase the sales of a given product.

The term "promotion" is usually an "in" expression used internally by the marketing company, but not normally to the public or the market - phrases like "special offer" are more common. An example of a fully integrated, long-term, large-scale promotion are My Coke Rewards and Pepsi Stuff. The UK version of My Coke Rewards is Coke Zone.

How to Promote a New Product & Marketing Activities

Launching a new product can be both timely and costly, but what about promoting it? Have you thought how you will go about spreading the word about your product.

If you have or haven't, then here are a few ways you can promote a new product:

1. Through sending press releases to your local press and media and by getting editorials and features out of your press releases.
2. Through piggyback marketing. By working alongside another company that is normally well established or known.
3. By using cross promotion. For example if you have another produce for sale/in the marketplace then why not cross promote it with your new product. Let the products work together and compliment each other.
4. Through giving away freebies. Now this could be a free sample of a product, a free trial, free test or similar. It could even be a free gift such as a pen or umbrella - dependant of course on your marketing and promotions budget.
5. Use business cards, leaflets and flyers and get your product out there now. Give and hand out these pieces of marketing literature to both existing customers and potential customers. Give to people at networking events and anywhere else you can think of.

6. Send samples off to industry experts and other recognised bodies/individuals. Try to get as many reviews as possible of your product, reviews help sell products.
7. Through using and getting both testimonials and referrals. Nothing works better than word of mouth so once a product is available for sale then why not give a few away for a review/ testimonial in return. Testimonials really do sell products!

TOP TIP: It takes at least 7 times before someone buys your product or service, this means that on average a potential customer must see your product and marketing at least 7 times before they will part with their cash. So then, now that you have a few ways to promote a new product how do you go about putting all of this into action?

Well.... To start off with you will need to conduct market research to establish who your market is and where they are. You then need to collate and analyse the results which will allow you to do two main things, one of these being to see whether or not there is a market for your product. The second being how you can/will be able to reach your target audience/market, for example from market research you will be able to establish what they read, view, watch, listen to and so on.

After you have find out who your target market/audience is then you will have to start drawing up a budget. This budget will cover how much you have for promotions, sales events, marketing literature, websites, press releases and so on for at lest the next 12 months. TOP TIP: Ideally you will put together both a pre launch marketing plan and budget and a post launch marketing budget to see where you are spending your money and why. Now you have a budget, and your research you now need to produce a plan and put it into action. You should ideally produce a marketing plan for your product as soon as possible based on your budget and market research results.

Getting a new product out for customers to see and try out is the first step in selling that product successfully. Even the best product will do little good for the public if they do not know it exists. Therefore, business owners or marketing professionals must utilise various marketing techniques to guarantee that the right audience knows about the product and that they receive the knowledge as effectively as possible. Fortunately, there are a number of fairly simple marketing opportunities for spreading the word and ensuring sales.

Step 1

Offer promotional products. The majority of people love freebies, and creating an event at which you give away products is more likely to draw customers that might not otherwise have been interested. In addition, a promotional event creates an opportunity for you to send out a press release about the event—as well as the product—and thus utilise the local media outlets, such as newspapers and news programs, for getting the word to the public.

Step 2

Order printed promotional material that shares information about the products. Printed promotional material can range from simple flyers to more elaborate pamphlets that detail product specifications. In addition, business cards can be an excellent marketing tool. If the company features one product in particular, the business card can note that the company is “home of the ______ product,” or something along those lines, to keep the connection in mind for customers. And be sure to hand out as many of these printed promotional items as possible, to reach the widest desired audience.

Step 3

Create sample sizes of products and offer them to those who can review the products and offer feedback or a positive response. Focus on sending the samples to those with credibility in the industry, such as professionals or experts whose feedback will have more effect on convincing customers to try the product.

Step 4

Collect testimonials from customers who have used and enjoyed the product. Testimonials can be a powerful tool for convincing potential customers to take the plunge, because they create the link between customers who trust the opinions of others like themselves. Suppose, for instance, that you have designed and are marketing a new range of hand lotion. Testimonials from customers can be powerful for persuading others to pass by more familiar names to use your product. What is more, testimonials that speak to specific –such as reduced psoriasis or elimination of chapping on hands–can help to convince others with similar concerns.

8

Balance of Payments

A Balance of payments (BOP) sheet is an accounting record of all monetary transactions between a country and the rest of the world. These transactions include payments for the country's exports and imports of goods, services, and financial capital, as well as financial transfers. The BOP summarises international transactions for a specific period, usually a year, and is prepared in a single currency, typically the domestic currency for the country concerned. Sources of funds for a nation, such as exports or the receipts of loans and investments, are recorded as positive or surplus items. Uses of funds, such as for imports or to invest in foreign countries, are recorded as a negative or deficit item. When all components of the BOP sheet are included it must balance-that is, it must sum to zero-there can be no overall surplus or deficit. For example, if a country is importing more than it exports, its trade balance will be in deficit, but the shortfall will have to be counter balanced in other ways-such as by funds earned from its foreign investments, by running down reserves or by receiving loans from other countries.

While the overall BOP sheet will always balance when all types of payments are included, imbalances are possible on individual elements of the BOP, such as the current account. This can result in surplus countries accumulating hoards of wealth, while deficit nations become increasingly indebted. Historically there have been different approaches to the question of how to correct imbalances and debate on whether they are something governments should be concerned about. With record imbalances held up as one of the contributing factors to the financial crisis of 2007-2010, plans to address global imbalances are now high on the agenda of policy makers for 2010.

Standard Definition

Since 1973, the two principal divisions on the BOP have been the current account and the capital account. The *current account* shows the net amount a country is earning if it is in surplus, or spending if it is in deficit. It is the sum of the balance of trade (net earnings on exports-payments for imports), factor income (earnings on foreign investments-payments made to foreign investors) and cash transfers.

The *capital account* records the net change in ownership of foreign assets. It includes the reserve account (the international operations of a nations central bank), along with loans and investments between the country and the rest of world (but not the future regular repayments/dividends that the loans and investments yield, those are earnings and will be recorded in the current account). Expressed with the standard meaning for the *capital account*, the BOP identity is: (+ or-Balancing item).

The *balancing item* is simply an amount that accounts for any statistical errors and make sure the current and capital accounts sum to zero. At high level, by the principles of double entry accounting, an entry in the current account gives rise to an entry in the capital account, and in aggregate the two accounts should balance.

A balance isn't always reflected in reported figures, which might, for example, report a surplus for both accounts, but when this happens it always means something has been missed—most commonly, the operations of the country's central bank.

An actual balance sheet will typically have numerous sub headings under the principal divisions. For example, entries under Current account might include:

- *Trade*-buying and selling of goods and services.
  - o *Exports*-a credit entry
  - o *Imports*-a debit entry.
    - – *Trade balance*-the sum of Exports and Imports
- *Factor income*-repayments and dividends from loans and investments
  - o *Factor earnings*-a credit entry
  - o *Factor payments*-a debit entry
    - – *Factor income balance*-the sum of earnings and payments.

Especially in older balance sheets, a common division was between visible and invisible entries. Visible trade recorded imports and exports of physical goods (entries for trade in physical goods excluding services is now often called the *merchandise balance*). Invisible trade would record international buying and selling of services, and sometimes would be grouped with transfer and factor income as invisible earnings.

Discrepancies in the use of term "Balance of Payments"

According to economics writer J. Orlin Grabbe the term *Balance of Payments* is sometimes misused by people who aren't aware of the accepted meaning, not only in general conversation but in financial publications and the economic literature.

A common source of confusion is to exclude the *reserve account* entry which records the activity of the nation's central bank. Once this is done, the BOP can be in surplus (which implies the central bank is building up foreign exchange reserves) or in deficit (which implies the central bank is running down its reserves or borrowing from abroad) The term can also be misused to mean just relatively narrow parts of the BOP such as the trade deficit, which means excluding parts of the current account and the entire capital account. Another cause of confusion is the different naming conventions in use.

Before 1973 there was no standard way to break down the BOP sheet, with the separation into invisible and visible payments sometimes being the principal divisions. The IMF have their own standards for the BOP sheet, at high level it's the same as the standard definition, but it has different nomenclature, in particular with respect to the meaning given to the term *capital account*.

The IMF Definition

The IMF use a particular set of definitions for the BOP, which is also used by the OECD, and the United Nations' SNA.

The main difference with the IMF definition is that they use the term financial account to capture transaction that in the standard definition are recorded in the *capital account*. The IMF do use the term *capital account*, to designate a sub set of transactions that according to usage common in the rest of the world form a small part of the overall capital account. The IMF separate these transaction out to form an additional top level division of the BOP sheet. Expressed with the IMF definition, the BOP identity can be written: (+ or- Balancing item)

The IMF use the term *current account* with the same meaning as the standard definition, although they have their own names for their three leading sub divisions, which are:

- The *goods and services account* (the overall trade balance)
- The *primary income account* (factor income such as from loans and investments)
- The *secondary income account* (transfer payments).

Imbalances

While the BOP has to balance overall, surpluses or deficits on its individual elements can lead to imbalances between countries. In general there is concern over deficits in the current account. Countries with deficits in their current accounts will build up increasing debt and/or see increased foreign ownership of their assets. The types of deficits that typically raise concern are:

- A *visible trade deficit* where a nation is importing more physical goods than it exports (even if this is balanced by the other components of the current account.)
- An overall *current account deficit.*
- A *basic deficit* which is the current account plus foreign direct investment (but excluding other elements of the capital account like short terms loans and the reserve account.)

As discussed in the history section below, the *Washington Consensus* period saw a swing of opinion towards the view that there is no need to worry about imbalances. Opinion swung back in the opposite direction in the wake of *financial crisis of 2007-2009.* Mainstream opinion expressed by the leading financial press and economists, international bodies like the IMF—as well as leaders of surplus and deficit countries—has returned to the view that large current account imbalances do matter. Some economists do, however, remain relatively unconcerned about imbalances and there have been assertions, such as by Michael P. Dooley, David Folkerts-Landau and Peter Garber, that nations need to avoid temptation to switch to protectionism as a means to correct imbalances.

Causes of BOP Imbalances

There are conflicting views as to the primary cause of BOP imbalances, with much attention on the US who currently have by far the largest deficit. The conventional view is that current account factors are the primary cause-these include the exchange rate, the government's fiscal deficit, business competitiveness, and private behaviour such as the willingness of consumers to go into debt to finance extra consumption. An alternative view, argued at length in a 2005 paper by Ben Bernanke, is that the primary driver is the capital account, where a global savings glut caused by savers in surplus countries, runs ahead of the available investment opportunities, and is pushed into the US resulting in excess consumption and asset price inflation.

Reserve Asset

In the context of BOP and international monetary systems, the reserve asset is the currency or other store of value that is primarily used by nations for their foreign reserves. BOP imbalances tend to manifest as hoards of the reserve asset being amassed by surplus countries, with deficit countries building debts denominated in the reserve asset or at least depleting their supply. Under a gold standard, the reserve asset for all members of the standard is gold. In the Bretton Woods system, either gold or the US Dollar could serve as the reserve asset, though its smooth operation depended on countries apart from the US choosing to keep most of their holdings in dollars. Following the ending of Bretton Woods, there has been no *de jure* reserve asset, but the US dollar has remained by far the principal *de facto* reserve.

Global reserves rose sharply in the first decade of the 21st century, partly as a result of the 1997 Asian Financial Crisis, where several nations ran out of foreign currency needed for essential imports and thus had to accept deals on unfavourable terms. The IMF estimate that between 2000 to mid-2009, official reserves rose from $1,900bn to $6,800bn. As of 2009 approx 65% of the world's $6,800bn total is held in US dollars, with approx 25% in Euro. The UK Pound, Japanese yen, IMF SDRs, and precious metals also play a role. In 2009 Zhou Xiaochuan, governor of the People's Bank of China, proposed a gradual move towards increased use of SDRs, and also for the national currencies backing SDRs to be expanded to include the currencies of all major economies. Dr. Zhou's proposal has been described as one of the most significant ideas expressed in 2009. While the current central role of the dollar does give the US some advantages such as lower cost of borrowings, it also contributes to the pressure causing the US to run a BOP deficit, due to the Triffin dilemma. In a November 2009 article published in Foreign Affairs magazine, economist C. Fred Bergsten argued that Dr. Zhou's suggestion or a similar change to the international monetary system would be in the United States' best interests as well as the rest of the world's.

Balancing Mechanisms

One of the three fundamental functions of an international monetary system is to provide mechanisms to correct imbalances.

Broadly speaking, there are three possible methods to correct BOP imbalances, though in practice a mixture including some degree of at least the first two methods tends to be used. These methods are adjustments of exchange rates; adjustment of a nations internal prices along with its levels of demand; and rules based adjustment. Increasing the desirability of exports through other means can also help, though it is generally assumed a nation is always trying to develop and sell its products to the best of its abilities.

Rebalancing by Changing the Exchange Rate

An upwards shift in the value of a nation's currency relative to others will make a nation's exports less competitive and make imports cheaper and so will tend to correct a current account surplus. It also tends to make investment flows into the capital account less attractive so will help with a surplus there too. Conversely a downward shift in the value of a nation's currency makes it more expensive for its citizens to buy imports and increases the competitiveness of their exports, thus helping to correct a deficit (though the solution often doesn't have a positive impact immediately due to the Marshall-Lerner Condition.

Exchange rates can be adjusted by government in a rules based or managed currency regime, and when left to float freely in the market they also tend to change in the direction that will restore balance. When a country is selling more than it imports, the demand for its currency will tend to increase as other countries ultimately need the selling country's currency to make payments for the exports. The extra demand tends to cause a rise of the currencies price relative to others. When a country is importing more than it exports, the supply of its own currency on the international market tends to increase as it tries to exchange it for foreign currency to pay for its imports, and this extra supply tends to cause the price to fall. BOP effects are not the only market influence on exchange rates however, they are also influenced by differences in national interest rates and by speculative flows.

Rebalancing by Adjusting Internal Prices and Demand

When exchange rates are fixed by a rigid gold standard, or when imbalances exist between members of a currency union such as the Eurozone, the standard approach to correct imbalances is by making changes to the domestic economy. To a large degree, the change is optional for the surplus country, but compulsory for the deficit country. In the case of a gold standard, the mechanism is largely automatic. When a country has a favourable trade balance, as a consequence of selling more than it buys it will experience a net inflow of gold. The natural effect of this will be to increase the money supply, which leads to inflation and an increase in prices, which then tends to make its goods less competitive and so will decrease its trade surplus.

However the nation has the option of taking the gold out of economy (sterilising the inflationary effect) thus building up a hoard of gold and retaining its favourable balance of payments. On the other hand, if a country has an adverse BOP its will experience a net loss of gold, which will automatically have a deflationary effect, unless it chooses to leave the gold standard.

Prices will be reduced, making its exports more competitive, and thus correcting the imbalance. While the gold standard is generally considered to have been successful up until 1914, correction by deflation to the degree required by the large imbalances that arose after WWI proved painful, with deflationary policies contributing to prolonged unemployment but not re-establishing balance. Apart from the US most former members had left the gold standard by the mid 1930s.

A possible method for surplus countries such as Germany to contribute to re-balancing efforts when exchange rate adjustment is not suitable, is to increase its level of internal demand (i.e. its spending on goods). While a current account surplus is commonly understood as the excess of earnings over spending, and alternative expression is that it is the excess of savings over investment. That is:

{where CA = current account, NS = national savings (private plus government sector), NI = national investment.}

If a nation is earning more than it spends the net effect will be to build up savings, except to the extent that those savings are being used for investment. If consumers can be encouraged to spend more instead of saving, or if the government runs a fiscal deficit to offset private savings, or if investment is increased, then any current account surplus will tend to be reduced. However in 2009 Germany amended her constitution to prohibit running a deficit greater than 0.35% of her GDP and calls to reduce her surplus by increasing demand have not been welcome by officials, adding to fears that the 2010s will not be an easy decade for the eurozone.

Rules Based Rebalancing Mechanisms

Nations can agree to fix their exchange rates against each other, and then correct any imbalances that arise by rules based and negotiated exchange rate changes and other methods. The Bretton Woods system of fixed but adjustable exchange rates was an example of a rules based system, though it still relied primarily on the two traditional mechanisms.

Keynes, one of the architects of the Bretton Woods system had wanted additional rules to encourage surplus countries to share the burden of rebalancing, as he argued that they were in a stronger position to do so. Keynes suggested that traditional balancing mechanisms should be supplemented by the threat of confiscation of a portion of excess revenue if the surplus country did not choose to spend it on additional imports.

However his ideas were not accepted by the Americans at the time. In 2008 and 2009, American economist Paul Davidson had been promoting his revamped form of Keynes's plan as a possible solution to global imbalances which in his opinion would expand growth all round with out the downside risk of other rebalancing methods.

History of Balance of Payments Issues

Historically, accurate balance of payments figures were not generally available. However, this did not prevent a number of switches in opinion on questions relating to whether or not a nations government should use policy to encourage a favourable balance.

Pre 1820: Mercantilism

Up until the early 19th century, measures to promote a trade surplus such as tariffs were generally favoured. Power was associated with wealth, and with low levels of growth, nations were best able to accumulate funds either by running trade surpluses or by forcefully confiscating the wealth of others.

From about the 16th century, Mercantilism was a prevalent theory influencing European rulers, who sometimes strove to have their countries out sell competitors and so build up a "war chest" of gold.

This era saw low levels of economic growth; average global per capita income is not considered to have significantly risen in the whole 800 years leading up to 1820, and is estimated to have increased on average by less than 0.1% per year between 1700-1820.

1820-1914: Free Trade

From the late 18th century, mercantilism was challenged by the ideas of Adam Smith and other economic thinkers favouring free trade. After victory in the Napoleonic wars Great Britain began promoting free trade, unilaterally reducing her trade tariffs. Hoarding of gold was no longer encouraged, and in fact Britain exported more capital as a percentage of her national income than any other creditor nation has since.

Great Britain's capital exports further helped to correct global imbalances as they tended to be counter cyclical, rising when Britain's economy went into recession, thus compensating other states for income lost from export of goods. According to historian Carroll Quigley, Great Britain could afford to act benevolently in the 19th century due to the advantages of her geographical location, her naval power and her economic ascendancy as the first nation to enjoy an industrial revolution.

Though Current Account controls were still widely used (in fact all industrial nations apart from Great Britain and the Netherlands actually increased their tariffs and quotas in the decades leading up to 1914, though this was motivated more by a desire to protect "infant industries" than to encourage a trade surplus), capital controls were largely absent, and people were generally free to cross international borders without requiring passports. A gold standard enjoyed wide international participation especially from 1870, further contributing to close economic integration between nations. The period saw substantial global growth, in particular for the volume of international trade which grew tenfold between 1820-1870 and then by about 4% annually from 1870 to 1914.

1914-1945: Deglobalisation

The favourable economic conditions that had prevailed up until 1914 were shattered by the first world war, and efforts to re-establish them in the 1920s were not successful. Several countries rejoined the gold standard around 1925. But surplus countries didn't "play by the rules", sterilising gold inflows to a much greater degree than had been the case in the prewar period.

Deficit nations such as Great Britain found it harder to adjust by deflation as workers were more enfranchised and unions in particular were able to resist downwards pressure on wages. During the great depression most countries abandoned the gold standard, but imbalances remained an issue and international trade declined sharply. There was a return to mercantilist type "beggar thy neighbour" policies, with countries competitively devaluing their exchange rates, thus effectively competing to export unemployment.

1945-1971: Bretton Woods

Following World War II, the Bretton Woods institutions (the International Monetary Fund and World Bank) were set up to support an international monetary system designed to encourage free trade while also offer states options to correct imbalances without having to defalte their economies. Fixed but flexible exchange rates were established, with the system anchored by the dollar which alone remained convertible into gold, The Bretton Woods system ushered in a period of high global growth, known as the Golden Age of Capitalism, however it came under pressure due to imbalances related to the central role of the dollar, with imbalances causing gold to flow out of the US and a loss of confidence in the United States ability to supply gold for all future claims by dollar holders.

1971-2009: Transition, Washington Consensus, Bretton Woods II

The Bretton Woods system came to an end between 1971 and 1973. There were attempts to repair the system of fixed exchanged rates over the next few years, but these were soon abandoned, as were determined efforts for the US to avoid BOP imbalances. Part of the reason was displacement of the previous dominant economic paradigm-Keynesianism-by the Washington Consensus, with economists and economics writers such as Murray Rothbard and Milton Friedman arguing that there was no great need to be concerned about BOP issues. According to Rothbard:

Fortunately, the absurdity of worrying about the balance of payments is made evident by focusing on interstate trade. For nobody worries about the balance of payments between New York and New Jersey, or, for that matter, between Manhattan and Brooklyn, because there are no customs officials recording such trade and such balances.

In the immediate aftermath of the Bretton Woods collapse, countries generally tried to retain some control over their exchange rate by independently managing it, or by intervening in the Forex as part of a regional bloc, such as the Snake which formed in 1971. *The Snake* was a group of European countries who tried to retain stable rates at least with each other; the group eventually evolved into the ERM by 1979. From the mid 1970s however, and especially in the 1980s and early 90s, many other countries followed the US in liberalising controls on both their capital and current accounts, in adopting a somewhat relaxed attitude to their balance of payments and in allowing the value of their currency to float relatively freely with exchange rates determined mostly by the market. Developing countries who chose to allow the market to determine their exchange rates would often develop sizeable current account deficits, financed by capital account inflows such as loans and investments, though this often ended in crises when investors lost confidence.

A turning point was the 1997 Asian Financial Crisis, where unsympathetic responses by western powers caused policy makers in emerging economies to re-assess the wisdom of relying on the free market; by 1999 the developing world as a whole stopped running current account deficits while the US current account deficit began to rise sharply. This new form of imbalance began to develop in part due to the practice of emerging economies (principally China) in pegging their currency against the dollar, rather than allowing the value to freely float. The resulting state of affairs has been referred to as Bretton Woods II. According to economics writer Martin Wolf, in the eight years leading up to 2007, "three quarters of the foreign currency reserves accumulated since the beginning of time have been piled up".

2009 and Later: Post Washington Consensus

Speaking after the 2009 G-20 London summit, Gordon Brown announced "the Washington Consensus is over". There is now broad agreement that large imbalances between different countries do matter; for example mainstream US economist C. Fred Bergsten has argued the US deficit and the associated large inbound capital flows into the US was one of the causes of the financial crisis of 2007-2010. In 2007 when the crises began, the total BOP imbalance was $1680bn. On the credit side, the biggest current account surplus was China with approx. $362Bn, followed by Japan at $213Bn and Germany at £185BN, with oil producing countries such as Saudi Arabia also having large surpluses. On the debit side, the US had the biggest current account deficit at over £700Bn, with the UK, Spain and Australia together accounting for close to a further $300Bn. While there have been warnings of future cuts in public spending, deficit countries on the whole did not make these in 2009, in fact the opposite happened with increased public spending contributing to recovery as part of global efforts to increase demand. The emphases has instead been on the surplus countries, with the IMF, EU and nations such as the US, Brazil and Russia asking them to assist with the adjustments to correct the imbalances.

Economists such as Gregor Irwin and Philip R. Lane have suggested that increased use of pooled reserves could help emerging economies not to require such large reserves and thus have less need for current account surpluses. Writing for the FT in Jan 2009, Gillian Tett says she exspects to see policy makers becoming increasingly concerned about exchange rates over the comming year. Japan has allowed her currency to appreciate, but has only limited scope to contribute to the rebalancing efforts thanks in part to her ageing population. The Euro used by Germany is allowed to float fairly freely in value, however further appreciation would be problematic for other members of the currency union such as Spain, Greece and Ireland who run large deficits.

Therefore Germany has instead been asked to contribute by further promoting internal demand, but this hasn't been welcomed by German officials. China has been requested to allow the Renminbi to appreciate but has so far refused, the position expressed by her premier Wen Jiabao being that by keeping the value of the Renimbi stable against the dollar China has been helping the global recovery, and that calls to let her currency rise in value have been motivated by a desire to hold back China's development. After China reported favourable results for her December 2009 exports however, the Financial Times reported that analysts are optimistic that China will allow some appreciation of her currency around mid 2010. 2008 and 2009 did see some reduction in imbalances, but early indications towards the end of 2009 were that major imbalances such as the US current account deficit are set to begin increasing again, leaving the prospects for their resolution uncertain.

Capital Asset Pricing Model

In finance, the capital asset pricing model (CAPM) is used to determine a theoretically appropriate required rate of return of an asset, if that asset is to be added to an already well-diversified portfolio, given that asset's non-diversifiable risk. The model takes into account the asset's sensitivity to non-diversifiable risk (also known as systematic risk or market risk), often represented by the quantity beta (a) in the financial industry, as well as the expected return of the market and the expected return of a theoretical risk-free asset.

The model was introduced by Jack Treynor (1961, 1962), William Sharpe (1964), John Lintner (1965a,b) and Jan Mossin (1966) independently, building on the earlier work of Harry Markowitz on diversification and modern portfolio theory. Sharpe, Markowitz and

Merton Miller jointly received the Nobel Memorial Prize in Economics for this contribution to the field of financial economics.

Asset-specific Required Return

The CAPM returns the asset-appropriate required return or discount rate-i.e. the rate at which future cash flows produced by the asset should be discounted given that asset's relative riskiness. Betas exceeding one signify more than average "riskiness"; betas below one indicate lower than average.

Thus a more risky stock will have a higher beta and will be discounted at a higher rate; less sensitive stocks will have lower betas and be discounted at a lower rate. Given the accepted concave utility function, the CAPM is consistent with intuition-investors (should) require a higher return for holding a more risky asset.

Since beta reflects asset-specific sensitivity to non-diversifiable, i.e. market risk, the market as a whole, by definition, has a beta of one. Stock market indices are frequently used as local proxies for the market-and in that case (by definition) have a beta of one. An investor in a large, diversified portfolio (such as a mutual fund) therefore expects performance in line with the market.

Risk and Diversification

The risk of a portfolio comprises systematic risk, also known as undiversifiable risk, and unsystematic risk which is also known as idiosyncratic risk or diversifiable risk. Systematic risk refers to the risk common to all securities-i.e. market risk. Unsystematic risk is the risk associated with individual assets.

Unsystematic risk can be diversified away to smaller levels by including a greater number of assets in the portfolio (specific risks "average out"). The same is not possible for systematic risk within one market.

Depending on the market, a portfolio of approximately 30-40 securities in developed markets such as UK or US will render the portfolio sufficiently diversified such that risk exposure is limited to systematic risk only. In developing markets a larger number is required, due to the higher asset volatilities.

A rational investor should not take on any diversifiable risk, as only non-diversifiable risks are rewarded within the scope of this model. Therefore, the required return on an asset, that is, the return that compensates for risk taken, must be linked to its riskiness in a portfolio context-i.e. its contribution to overall portfolio riskiness-as opposed to its "stand alone riskiness." In the CAPM context, portfolio risk is represented by higher variance i.e. less predictability. In other words the beta of the portfolio is the defining factor in rewarding the systematic exposure taken by an investor.

The Efficient Frontier

The CAPM assumes that the risk-return profile of a portfolio can be optimized-an optimal portfolio displays the lowest possible level of risk for its level of return. Additionally, since each additional asset introduced into a portfolio further diversifies the portfolio, the optimal portfolio must comprise every asset, (assuming no trading costs) with each asset value-weighted to achieve the above (assuming that any asset is infinitely divisible).

All such optimal portfolios, i.e., one for each level of return, comprise the efficient frontier. Because the unsystematic risk is diversifiable, the total risk of a portfolio can be viewed as beta.

The Market Portfolio

An investor might choose to invest a proportion of his or her wealth in a portfolio of risky assets with the remainder in cash-earning interest at the risk free rate (or indeed may borrow money to fund his or her purchase of risky assets in which case there is a negative cash weighting).

Here, the ratio of risky assets to risk free asset does not determine overall return-this relationship is clearly linear. It is thus possible to achieve a particular return in one of two ways:

1. By investing all of one's wealth in a risky portfolio,
2. or by investing a proportion in a risky portfolio and the remainder in cash (either borrowed or invested).

For a given level of return, however, only one of these portfolios will be optimal (in the sense of lowest risk). Since the risk free asset is, by definition, uncorrelated with any other asset, option 2 will generally have the lower variance and hence be the more efficient of the two. This relationship also holds for portfolios along the efficient frontier: a higher return portfolio plus cash is more efficient than a lower return portfolio alone for that lower level of return. For a given risk free rate, there is only one optimal portfolio which can be combined with cash to achieve the lowest level of risk for any possible return. This is the market portfolio.

Assumptions of CAPM

All investors:

1. Aim to maximize economic utility.
2. Are rational and risk-averse.
3. Are broadly diversified across a range of investments.
4. Are price takers, i.e., they cannot influence prices.
5. Can lend and borrow unlimited amounts under the risk free rate of interest.
6. Trade without transaction or taxation costs.
7. Deal with securities that are all highly divisible into small parcels.
8. Assume all information is available at the same time to all investors.
9. Perfect Competitive Markets.

Shortcomings of CAPM

- The model assumes that either asset returns are (jointly) normally distributed random variables or that investors employ a quadratic form of utility. It is however frequently observed that returns in equity and other markets are not normally distributed. As a result, large swings (3 to 6 standard deviations from the mean) occur in the market more frequently than the normal distribution assumption would expect.
- The model assumes that the variance of returns is an adequate measurement of risk. This might be justified under the assumption of normally distributed returns, but for general return distributions other risk measures (like coherent risk measures) will likely reflect the investors' preferences more adequately. Indeed risk in financial investments is not variance in itself, rather it is the probability of losing: it is asymmetric in nature.
- The model assumes that all investors have access to the same information and agree about the risk and expected return of all assets (homogeneous expectations assumption).
- The model assumes that the probability beliefs of investors match the true distribution of returns. A different possibility is that investors' expectations are biased, causing market prices

to be informationally inefficient. This possibility is studied in the field of behavioural finance, which uses psychological assumptions to provide alternatives to the CAPM such as the overconfidence-based asset pricing model of Kent Daniel, David Hirshleifer, and Avanidhar Subrahmanyam (2001).

- The model does not appear to adequately explain the variation in stock returns. Empirical studies show that low beta stocks may offer higher returns than the model would predict. Some data to this effect was presented as early as a 1969 conference in Buffalo, New York in a paper by Fischer Black, Michael Jensen, and Myron Scholes. Either that fact is itself rational (which saves the efficient-market hypothesis but makes CAPM wrong), or it is irrational (which saves CAPM, but makes the EMH wrong-indeed, this possibility makes volatility arbitrage a strategy for reliably beating the market).
- The model assumes that given a certain expected return investors will prefer lower risk (lower variance) to higher risk and conversely given a certain level of risk will prefer higher returns to lower ones. It does not allow for investors who will accept lower returns for higher risk. Casino gamblers clearly pay for risk, and it is possible that some stock traders will pay for risk as well.
- The model assumes that there are no taxes or transaction costs, although this assumption may be relaxed with more complicated versions of the model.
- The market portfolio consists of all assets in all markets, where each asset is weighted by its market capitalization. This assumes no preference between markets and assets for individual investors, and that investors choose assets solely as a function of their risk-return profile. It also assumes that all assets are infinitely divisible as to the amount which may be held or transacted.
- The market portfolio should in theory include all types of assets that are held by anyone as an investment (including works of art, real estate, human capital...) In practice, such a market portfolio is unobservable and people usually substitute a stock index as a proxy for the true market portfolio. Unfortunately, it has been shown that this substitution is not innocuous and can lead to false inferences as to the validity

of the CAPM, and it has been said that due to the inobservability of the true market portfolio, the CAPM might not be empirically testable. This was presented in greater depth in a paper by Richard Roll in 1977, and is generally referred to as Roll's critique.

- The model assumes just two dates, so that there is no opportunity to consume and rebalance portfolios repeatedly over time. The basic insights of the model are extended and generalized in the intertemporal CAPM (ICAPM) of Robert Merton, and the consumption CAPM (CCAPM) of Douglas Breeden and Mark Rubinstein.
- CAPM assumes that all investors will consider all of their assets and optimize one portfolio. This is in sharp contradiction with portfolios that are held by investors: humans tend to have fragmented portfolios (or rather multiple portfolios: for each goal one portfolio-see behavioural portfolio theory and Maslowian Portfolio Theory.

Net Capital Outflow

The importance of NCO. The domestic real interest rate determined in the domestic market for loanable funds moves along the NCO curve to determine the quantity of currency available for foreign exchange. This in turn determines the real exchange rate.

Net Capital Outflow (NCO) is the net flow of funds being invested abroad by a country during a certain period of time (usually a year). A positive NCO means that the country invests outside more than the world invests in it; a negative one, that the world invests in the country more than the country invests in the world. NCO is one of two major ways of characterizing the nature of a country's financial and economic interaction with the rest of the world (the other being the balance of trade).

Explanation

NCO is linked to the market for loanable funds and the international currency exchange market in that, when graphed, the x-axis NCO is the quantity of the country's currency and the y-axis is the country's domestic real interest rate; the NCO graph has a negative slope as an increased interest rate domestically is an incentive for savers to do so at home rather than abroad.

This linkage partly determines the real exchange rate for that country's currency because one of the two determining variables of that market is the quantity of that country's currency available on the foreign exchange market—essentially, Net Capital Outflow (i.e. it is the x-axis in that market's graph). NCO serves as a perfectly inelastic supply curve for this market; thus changes in the demand for that country's currency (e.g. an increase in demand for products made in that nation) can only cause changes in the exchange rate.

NCO is always equal to Net Exports by an accounting identity, due to exports produced in one country being matched by reciprocal payments of some asset from a receiving second country.

Fluctuations in Exchange Rates

A market based exchange rate will change whenever the values of either of the two component currencies change. A currency will tend to become more valuable whenever demand for it is greater than the available supply. It will become less valuable whenever demand is less than available supply (this does not mean people no longer want money, it just means they prefer holding their wealth in some other form, possibly another currency). Increased demand for a currency is due to either an increased transaction demand for money, or an increased speculative demand for money. The transaction demand for money is highly correlated to the country's level of business activity, gross domestic product (GDP), and employment levels. The more people there are unemployed, the less the public as a whole will spend on goods and services. Central banks typically have little difficulty adjusting the available money supply to accommodate changes in the demand for money due to business transactions.

The speculative demand for money is much harder for a central bank to accommodate but they try to do this by adjusting interest rates. An investor may choose to buy a currency if the return (that is the interest rate) is high enough. The higher a country's interest rates, the greater the demand for that currency. It has been argued that currency speculation can undermine real economic growth, in particular since large currency speculators may deliberately create downward pressure on a currency in order to force that central bank to sell their currency to keep it stable (once this happens, the speculator can buy the currency back from the bank at a lower price, close out their position, and thereby take a profit).

Mundell-Fleming Model

The Mundell-Fleming model is an economic model first set forth by Robert Mundell and Marcus Fleming. The model is an extension of the IS-LM model. Whereas IS-LM deals with economy under autarky, the Mundell-Fleming model tries to describe an open economy.

Typically, the Mundell-Fleming model portrays the relationship between the nominal exchange rate and an economy's output (unlike the relationship between interest rate and the output in the IS-LM model) in the short run. The Mundell-Fleming model has been used to argue that an economy cannot simultaneously maintain a fixed exchange rate, free capital movement, and an independent monetary policy. This principle is frequently called "the Unholy Trinity," the "Irreconcilable Trinity," the "Inconsistent trinity" or the Mundell-Fleming "trilemma."

Mechanics of the Model

One important assumption is the equalization of the local interest rate to the global interest rate.

Under Flexible Exchange Rate Regime

We speak of a system of flexible exchange rates when governments (or central banks) allow the exchange rate to be determined by market forces alone.

Changes in Money Supply

An increase in money supply will shift the LM curve downward. This directly reduces the local interest rate and in turn forces the local interest rate lower than the global interest rate. This depreciates the exchange rate of local currency through capital outflow. (Hot money flows out to take advantage of higher interest rate abroad and hence currency depreciates.) The depreciation makes local goods cheaper compared to foreign goods and increases export and decreases import. Hence, net export is increased. Increased net export leads to the shifting of the IS curve (which is Y = C + I + G + NX) to the right to the point where the local interest rate will equalize with the global rate. At the same time, the BoP is supposed to shift too, as to reflect (1) depreciation of home currency and (2) an increase in current account or in other word, the increase in net export. These increases the overall income in the local economy.

A decrease in money supply will cause the exact opposite of the process.

Changes in Government Spending

An increase in government expenditure shifts the IS curve to the right. The shift will cause the local interest rate to go above the global rate. The increase in local interest will cause capital inflow and the inflow will make the local currency stronger compared to foreign currencies. Strong exchange rate also makes foreign goods cheaper compared to local goods. This encourages greater import and discourages export and hence, lower net export. As a result, the IS will return to its original location where the local interest rate is equal to the global interest rate. The level of income of the local economy stays the same. The LM curve is not at all affected.

A decrease in government expenditure will reverse the process.

Changes in Global Interest Rate

An increase in the global interest rate will cause an upward pressure on the local interest rate. The pressure will subside as the local rate closes in on the global rate. When a positive differential between the global and the local rate occurs, holding the LM curve constant, capital will flow out of the local economy. This depreciates the local currency and helps boost net export. Increasing net export shifts the IS to the right. This shift will continue to the right until the local interest rate becomes as high as the global rate. A decrease in global interest rate will cause the reverse to occur.

Under Fixed Exchange Rate Regime

We speak of a system of fixed exchange rates when governments (or central banks) announce an exchange rate (the parity rate) at which they are prepared to buy or sell any amount of domestic currency.

Changes in Money Supply

Under the fixed exchange rate system, the local central bank or any monetary authority will only change the money supply in order to maintain a level of exchange rate. If there is a pressure to appreciate the exchange rate, the local authority will buy domestic currency in order to decrease the money supply to raise the exchange rate back to its original level. If there is pressure to depreciate the exchange rate, the local authority will buy foreign currency with domestic currency in order to increase the money supply and lower the exchange rate back to its original level. A revaluation occurs when there is a permanent increase in exchange rate and hence, decrease in money supply. Devaluation is the exact opposite of revaluation.

Changes in Government Expenditure

Increased government expenditure shifts the IS curve to the right. The shift results are a rise in the interest rate and hence, an appreciation of the exchange rate. However, the exchange rate is controlled by the local monetary authority in the framework of a fixed system. In order to maintain the exchange rate and eliminate the pressure from it, the monetary authority will purchase foreign currencies with local currencies until the pressure is gone i.e. back to the original level. Such action shifts the LM curve in tandem with the direction of the IS shift. This action increases the local currency supply in the market and lowers the exchange rate—or rather, return the rate back to its original state. In the end, the exchange rate stays the same but the general income in the economy increases. The reverse is true when government expenditure decreases.

Changes in Global Interest Rate

To maintain the fixed exchange rate, the central bank must offset the capital flows (in or out) which are caused by the change of the global interest rate to the domestic rate. The central bank must restore the situation where the real domestic interest rate is equal to the real global interest rate to stop net capital flows from changing the exchange rate. If the global interest rate increases above the domestic rate, capital will flow out to take advantage of this opportunity. (Hot money flows out of the economy) This would depreciate the home currency, so the central bank may buy the home currency and sell some of its foreign currency reserves to offset this outflow. This decrease in the money supply shifts the LM curve to the left until the domestic interest rate is the global interest rate.

If the global interest rate declines below the domestic rate, the opposite occurs. Hot money flows in, the home currency appreciates, so the central bank offsets this by increasing the money supply (sell domestic currency, buy foreign currency), the LM curve shifts to the right, and the domestic interest rate becomes the global interest rate.

Differences from IS-LM

It is worth noting that some of the result from this model differs from the IS-LM because of the open economy assumption. Result for large open economy on the other hand falls within the result predicted by the IS-LM and the Mundell-Fleming models. The reason for such result is because a large open economy has both the characteristics of an autarky and a small open economy.

In the IS-LM, interest rate will be the key component in making both the money market and the good market in equilibrium. Under the Mundell-Fleming framework of small economy, interest rate is fixed and equilibrium in both market can only be achieved by a change of nominal exchange rate.

Example

A much simplified version of the Mundell-Fleming model can be illustrated by a small open economy, in which the domestic interest rate is exogenously predetermined by the *world interest rate* (r=r*).

Consider an exogenous increase in government expenditure, the IS curve will shift upward, with LM curve intact, causing the interest rate and the output to rise (partial crowding out effect) under the IS-LM model.

Nevertheless, as interest rate is predetermined in a small open economy, the LM* curve (of exchange rate and output) is vertical, which means there is exactly one output that can make the money market in the equilibrium under that interest rate. Even though the IS* curve still shift up, it will result in a higher exchange rate and same level of output (complete crowding out effect, which is different in the IS-LM model).

The example above makes an implicit assumption of flexible exchange rate. The Mundell-Fleming model can have completely different implications under different exchange rate regimes. For instance, under a fixed exchange rate system, with perfect capital mobility, monetary policy becomes ineffective. An expansionary monetary policy resulting in an outward shift of the LM curve would in turn make capital flow out of the economy. The central bank under a fixed exchange rate system would have to intervene by selling foreign money in exchange for domestic money to depreciate the foreign currency and appreciate the domestic currency. Selling foreign money and receiving domestic money would reduce real balances in the economy, until the LM curve shifts back to the left, and the interest rates come back to the world rate of interest i*.

Optimum Currency Area

In economics, an optimum currency area (OCA), also known as an optimal currency region (OCR), is a geographical region in which it would maximize economic efficiency to have the entire region share a single currency. It describes the optimal characteristics for the merger of currencies or the creation of a new currency. The theory is used often to argue whether or not a certain region is ready to become a monetary union, one of the final stages in economic integration. An optimal currency area is often larger than a country. For instance, part of the rationale behind the creation of the euro is that the individual countries of Europe do not each form an optimal currency area, but that Europe as a whole does form an optimal currency area. The creation of the euro is often cited because it provides the most modern and largest-scale case study of the engineering of an optimum currency area, and provides a comparative before-and-after model by which to test the principles of the theory.

In theory, an optimal currency area could also be smaller than a country. Some economists have argued that the United States, for example, really consists of two optimal currency areas and that the United States should have two currencies, one for the western half and one for the eastern half. The theory of the optimal currency area was pioneered by economist Robert Mundell. Credit often goes to Mundell as the originator of the idea, but others point to earlier work done in the area by Abba Lerner.

OCA with Stationary Expectations

Published by Mundell in 1961, this is the most cited by economists. Here asymmetric shocks are considered to undermine the real economy, so if they are too important and cannot be controlled, a regime with floating rates is considered better, because the global monetary policy (interest rates) will not be fine tuned for the particular situation of each constituent region.

The four often cited criteria for a successful currency union are:

- Labour mobility across the region. This includes physical ability to travel (visas, workers' rights, etc.), lack of cultural barriers to free movement (such as different languages) and institutional arrangements (such as the ability to have superannuation transferred throughout the region) (Robert A. Mundell). In the case of the Eurozone, while capital is quite mobile, labour mobility is relatively low, especially when compared to the U.S. and Japan.
- Openness with capital mobility and price and wage flexibility across the region. This is so that the market forces of supply and demand automatically distribute money and goods to where they are needed.

  In practice this does not work perfectly as there is no true wage flexibility. (Ronald McKinnon). The Eurozone members trade heavily with each other (intra-European trade is greater than international trade), and most recent empirical analyses of the 'euro effect' suggest that the single currency has increased trade by 5 to 15 percent in the euro-zone when compared to trade between non-euro countries.

- A risk sharing system such as an automatic fiscal transfer mechanism to redistribute money to areas/sectors which have been adversely affected by the first two characteristics. This usually takes the form of taxation redistribution to less developed areas of a country/region.

  This policy, though theoretically accepted, is politically difficult to implement as the better-off regions rarely give up their revenue easily. Theoretically, Europe has no bailout clause in the Stability and Growth Pact, meaning that fiscal transfers are not allowed, but it is impossible to know what will happen in practice.

- Participant counties have similar business cycles. When on country experiences a boom or recession, other countries in the union are likely to follow. This allows the shared central bank to promote growth in downturns and to contain inflation in booms.

While Europe scores well on some of the measures characterising an OCA, it has lower labour mobility than the United States and similarly cannot rely on fiscal federalism to smooth out regional economic disturbances.

Also, its Gini coefficient of 31 should have a stabilizing effect; in comparison, the USA has a Gini index of 46.9 (a lower measure indicates a more even distribution of wealth).

Additional criteria suggested are:

- Production diversification (Peter Kenen)
- Homogeneous preferences
- Commonality of destiny.

This theory has been most frequently applied in recent years to the euro and the European Union. Despite the promenience of the EU as the primary case study of a OCA, many have argued that the EU does actually not meet the criteria for an OCA. By these criteria the European Union does not constitute an Optimal Currency Area and therefore the euro should be a suboptimum union of currencies. However it is hoped that the creation of the euro will in itself help encourage the conditions enumerated by Mundell. The primary criticism of Mundell's theory is that the only area that has optimal conditions for a single currency is one that *already has* a single currency, a circular argument. Furthermore, many existing currency areas do not fulfill these requirements.

OCA with International Risk Sharing

Here Mundell tries to model how exchange rate uncertainty will interfere with the economy; this model is less often cited (publication in 1973).

Supposing that the currency is managed properly, the larger the area, the better. In contrast with the previous model, asymmetric shocks are not considered to undermine the common currency because of the existence of the common currency. This spreads the shocks in the area because all regions share claims on each other in the same currency and can use them for dumping the shock, while in a flexible exchange rate regime, the cost will be concentrated on the individual regions, since the devaluation will reduce its buying power. So despite a less fine tuned monetary policy the real economy should do better.

A harvest failure, strikes, or war, in one of the countries causes a loss of real income, but the use of a common currency (or foreign exchange reserves) allows the country to run down its currency holdings and cushion the impact of the loss, drawing on the resources of the other country until the cost of the adjustment has been efficiently spread over the future. If, on the other hand, the two countries use separate monies with flexible exchange rates, the whole loss has to be borne alone; the common currency cannot serve as a shock absorber for the nation as a whole except insofar as the dumping of inconvertible currencies on foreign markets attracts a speculative capital inflow in favour of the depreciating currency. (Mundell, 1973, *Uncommon Arguments for Common Currencies*)

Robert A. Mundell is found in both sides of the debate about the euro. Most economists cite preferentially the first (stationary expectations) and conclude against the euro, yet Mundell advocates this one, and concludes in favour of the euro. Rather than moving toward more flexibility in exchange rates within Europe the economic arguments suggest less flexibility and a closer integration of capital markets. These economic arguments are supported by social arguments as well. On every occasion when a social disturbance leads to the threat of a strike, and the strike to an increase in wages unjustified by increases in productivity and thence to devaluation, the national currency becomes threatened. Long-run costs for the nation as a whole are bartered away by governments for what they presume to be shortrun political benefits. If instead, the European currencies were bound together disturbances in the country would be cushioned, with the shock weakened by capital movements.

Criticism

Keynesian

The notion of a currency that does not accord with a state, specifically one *larger* than a state-formally, of an international monetary authority without a corresponding fiscal authority-has been criticized by Keynesian and Post-Keynesian economists, who emphasize the role of deficit spending by a government (formally, fiscal authority) in the running of an economy, and consider using an international currency without fiscal authority to be a loss of "monetary sovereignty".

Specifically, Keynesian economists argue that fiscal stimulus in the form of deficit spending may be necessary to fight unemployment, which is not possible if states in a monetary union are not allowed to run sufficient deficits. The Post-Keynesian theory of Neo-Chartalism holds that government deficit spending creates money, that ability to print money is fundamental to a state's ability to command resources, and that "money and monetary policy are intricately linked to political sovereignty and fiscal authority". Both of these critiques consider the transactional benefits of a shared currency to be minor compared to these drawbacks, and more generally place less emphasis on the *transactional* function of money (a medium of exchange) and greater emphasis on its use as a unit of account.

Austrian

Offering a contrary criticism, Austrian economists have supported the disassociation of currencies from political entities entirely. Whereas Keynesians see flaws in supranational currencies, Austrians see flaws in any centrally planned currency not determined by a free market process. This alternative approach *seeks* to limit deficit spending, as well as to increase the accountability of currency makers to their users in the same way that markets for other goods maximize the accountability of businesses to their customers. Founding Austrian economist Friedrich Hayek advocated denationalization of money reasoning that private enterprises which issued distinct currencies would have an incentive to maintain their currency's purchasing power and that customers could choose from among competing offerings. Thus, the Austrian critique of optimal currency areas does not prejudice any particular arrangement so long as it is arrived at by a fair and competitive market process. From "The Failure of OCA Analysis" (The Quarterly Journal of Austrian Economics):

Monetary unification enhances the welfare of individuals only if it springs naturally from the voluntary actions of the money users...On a free market, entrepreneurs will try to respond properly to the demands of their customers, providing goods—including money—of the type, quantity, and quality desired. Therefore, only on a free monetary market would it be possible to discover what is the "optimum" circulation of a certain currency...OCA theory fails to acknowledge this, precisely because it conflates the proper nature of money, focusing exclusively on a single type of money, namely fiat government-produced money.

Business Cycle

The term business cycle (or economic cycle) refers to economy-wide fluctuations in production or economic activity over several months or years. These fluctuations occur around a long-term growth trend, and typically involve shifts over time between periods of relatively rapid economic growth (expansion or boom), and periods of relative stagnation or decline (contraction or recession).

These fluctuations are often measured using the growth rate of real gross domestic product. Despite being termed cycles, most of these fluctuations in economic activity do not follow a mechanical or predictable periodic pattern.

History

Theory

The first systematic exposition of periodic economic crises, in opposition to the existing theory of economic equilibrium, was the 1819 *Nouveaux Principes d'economie politique* by Jean Charles Leonard de Sismondi. Prior to that point classical economics had either denied the existence of business cycles, blamed them on external factors, notably war, or only studied the long term. Sismondi found vindication in the Panic of 1825, which was the first unarguably internal economic crisis, occurring in peacetime. Sismondi and his contemporary Robert Owen, who expressed similar but less systematic thoughts in 1817 *Report to the Committee of the Association for the Relief of the Manufacturing Poor,* both identified the cause of economic cycles as overproduction and underconsumption, caused in particular to wealth inequality. They advocated government intervention and socialism, respectively, as the solution. This work did not generate interest among classical economists, though underconsumption theory developed as a heterodox branch in economics until being systematized in Keynesian economics in the 1930s.

Sismondi's theory of periodic crises was developed into a theory of alternating *cycles* by Charles Dunoyer, and similar theories, showing signs of influence by Sismondi, were developed by Johann Karl Rodbertus. Periodic crises in capitalism formed the basis of the theory of Karl Marx, who further claimed that these crises were increasing in severity and predicted communist revolution; he devoted hundreds of pages of *Das Kapital* to crises.

Classification by Periods

In 1860, French economist Clement Juglar identified the presence of economic cycles 8 to 11 years long, although he was cautious not to claim any rigid regularity. Later, Austrian economist Joseph Schumpeter argued that a Juglar cycle has four stages: (i) expansion (increase in production and prices, low interests rates); (ii) crisis (stock exchanges crash and multiple bankruptcies of firms occur); (iii) recession (drops in prices and in output, high interests rates); (iv) recovery (stocks recover because of the fall in prices and incomes). In this model, recovery and prosperity are associated with increases in productivity, consumer confidence, aggregate demand, and prices. In the mid-20th century, Schumpeter and others proposed a typology of business cycles according to their periodicity, so that a number of particular cycles were named after their discoverers or proposers:

Kitchin Cycle

Kitchin cycle is a short business cycle of about 40 months discovered in the 1920s by Joseph Kitchin.

This cycle is believed to be accounted for by time lags in information movements affecting the decision making of commercial firms. Firms react to the improvement of commercial situation through the increase in output through the full employment of the extent fixed capital assets. As a result, within a certain period of time (ranging between a few months and two years) the market gets 'flooded' with commodities whose quantity becomes gradually excessive. The demand declines, prices drop, the produced commodities get accumulated in inventories, which informs entrepreneurs of the necessity to reduce output. However, this process takes some time.

It takes some time for the information that the supply exceeds significantly the demand to get to the businessmen. Further it takes entrepreneurs some time to check this information and to make the decision to reduce production, some time is also necessary to materialize this decision (these are the time lags that generate the Kitchin cycles). Another relevant time lag is the lag between the materialization of the above mentioned decision (causing the capital assets to work well below the level of their full employment) and the decrease of the excessive amounts of commodities accumulated in inventories. Yet, after this decrease takes place one can observe the conditions for a new phase of growth of demand, prices, output, etc.

Clement Juglar

Clement Juglar (15 October 1819 in Paris – 28 February 1905 in Paris) was a French doctor and statistician.

Juglar Cycles

He was one of the first to develop an economic theory of business cycles. He identified the 7-11 year fixed investment cycle that is now associated with his name. Within the Juglar cycle one can observe oscillations of investments into fixed capital and not just changes in the level of employment of the fixed capital (and respective changes in inventories), as is observed with respect to Kitchin cycles. The recent research employing spectral analysis has confirmed the presence of Juglar cycles in the world GDP dynamics up to the present time.

Juglar's Impact

Juglar's publications led to other business cycle theories by later economists such as Joseph Schumpeter.

Publications of Clement Juglar

- "Des crises commerciales", 1856, in *Annuaire de l'economie politique.*
- *Des Crises commerciales et leur retour periodique en France, en Angleterre, et aux Etats-Unis.* Paris: Guillaumin, 1862.
- *Du Change et de la liberte d'emission,* 1868.
- *Les Banques de depot, d'escompte et d'emission,* 1884.

Kuznets Swing

Kuznets swing is a claimed medium-range economic wave with a period of 15-25 years found in 1930 by Simon Kuznets. Kuznets connected these waves with demographic processes, in particular with immigrant inflows/outflows and the changes in construction intensity that they caused, that is why he denoted them as "demographic" or "building" cycles/swings. Kuznets swings have been also interpreted as infrastructural investment cycles.

Kuznet's finding was debunked by Howrey (1968). Howrey showed that the apparent business cycle found by Kuznets was an artifact of the filter Kuznets used. Howrey showed that the same cyclical pattern could be found in white noise series when the Kuznets filter was applied.

Kondratiev Wave

Kondratiev waves—also called Supercycles, surges, long waves or K-waves—are described as regular, sinusoidal-like cycles in the modern (capitalist) world economy. Averaging fifty and ranging from approximately forty to sixty years in length, the cycles consist of alternating periods between high sectoral growth and periods of relatively slow growth. Unlike the short-term business cycle which in various forms has been familiar since the nineteenth century, the long wave of this theory does not belong within current orthodox economics and is sometimes categorized as part of heterodox economics (a catch-all term for alternative ideas to economic ideologies in force).

The Russian economist Nikolai Kondratiev (also written Kondratieff) was the first to bring these observations to international attention in his book *The Major Economic Cycles* (1925) alongside other works written in the same decade. Two Dutch economists, Jacob van Gelderen and Samuel de Wolff, had previously argued for the existence of 50 to 60 year cycles in 1913. However, the work of de Wolff and van Gelderen has only recently been translated from Dutch to reach a wider audience.

Kondratiev was a Soviet economist, but his economic conclusions were disliked by the Soviet leadership and upon their release he was quickly dismissed from his post as director of the Institute for the Study of Business Activity in the Soviet Union in 1928. His conclusions were seen as a criticism of Stalin's intentions for the Soviet economy: as a result he was sentenced to the Soviet Gulag and later received the death penalty in 1938.

Later, in *Business Cycles* (1939), Joseph Schumpeter suggested naming the cycles, "Kondratieff waves", in honour of the economist who first noticed them. In the 1950s, French economist Francois Simiand proposed naming the ascendant period of the cycle "Phase A" and the downward period "Phase B". Some market commentators divide the Kondratiev wave into four 'seasons', namely, the Kondratiev Spring (improvement or plateau) and Summer (acceleration or prosperity) of the ascendant period and the Kondratiev Fall (recession or plateau) and Winter (acceleration or depression) of the downward period.

Characteristics of the Cycle

The cycle is supposedly more visible in international production data than in individual national economies. It affects all the sectors of an economy, and concerns mainly output rather than prices (although Kondratieff had made observations focusing more on prices, inflation and interest rates). According to Kondratieff, the ascendant phase is characterized by an increase in prices and low interest rates, while the other phase consists of a decrease in prices and high interest rates.

Kondratieff identified three phases in the cycle: expansion, stagnation, recession. More common today is the division into four periods with a turning point (collapse) between the first and second phases. Writing in the 1920s, Kondratieff proposed to apply the theory to the 19th century:

- 1790 – 1849 with a turning point in 1815.
- 1850 – 1896 with a turning point in 1873.
- Kondratieff supposed that in 1896, a new cycle had started.

The phases of Kondratieff's waves also carry with them social shifts and changes in the public mood. The first stage of expansion and growth, the "Spring" stage, encompasses a social shift in which the wealth, capital accumulation, and innovation that are present in this first period of the cycle create upheavals and displacements in society. The economic changes result in redefining work and the role of participants in society. In the next phase, the "Summer" stagflation, there is a mood of affluence from the previous growth stage that change the attitude towards work in society, creating inefficiencies. After this stage comes the season of deflationary growth, or the plateau period. The popular mood changes during this period as well. It shifts toward stability, normalcy, and isolationism after the policies and economics during unpopular excesses of war. Finally, the "Winter" stage, that of severe depression, includes the integration of previous social shifts and changes into the social fabric of society, supported by the shifts in innovation and technology.

A fourth cycle may have roughly coincided with the Cold War: beginning in 1949, turning with the economic peak of the mid-1960s and the Vietnam War escalation, hitting a trough in 1982 amidst growing predictions in the United States of worldwide Soviet domination and ending with the fall of the Berlin Wall in 1989. The current cycle most likely peaked in 1999 with a possible winter phase beginning in late 2008. The Austrian-school economists point out that extreme price inflation in the absence of economic growth is a form of capital destruction, allowing either stagflation (as in the 1970s and much of the 2000s during the gold and oil price run-ups) or deflation (as in the 1930s and possibly following the crash in commodity prices beginning in 2008) to represent a recession or depression phase of the Kondratieff theory.

Tentative Explanations of the Cycle

Early on, four schools of thought emerged as to why capitalist economies have these long waves. These schools of thought centered on innovations, capital investment, war and capitalist crisis. According to the innovation theory, these waves arise from the bunching of basic innovations that launch technological revolutions that in turn create leading industrial or commercial sectors. Kondratiev's ideas were taken up by Joseph Schumpeter in the 1930s. The theory hypothesized the existence of very long-run macroeconomic and price cycles, originally estimated to last 50–54 years.

A rough schematic drawing showing the "World Economy" over time according to the Kondratiev theory

Since the inception of the theories, various studies have expanded the range of possible cycles, finding longer or shorter cycles in the data. The Marxist scholar Ernest Mandel revived interest in long wave theory with his 1964 essay predicting the end of the long boom after five years and in his Alfred Marshall lectures in 1979. However, in Mandel's theory, there are no long "cycles", only distinct epochs of faster and slower growth spanning 20–25 years. More recently, investment theorist Ian Gordon has advocated a 4 season Kondratiev model in which spring is moderate growth from a stock market and inflationary bottom, summer is characterized by accelerating growth and high inflation, autumn is characterized by declining inflation and asset bubbles, and winter involves the collapse of the asset bubbles.

Long wave theory is not accepted by most academic economists, but it is one of the bases of innovation-based, development, and evolutionary economics, i.e. the main heterodox stream in economics. Among economists who accept it, there has been no universal agreement about the start and the end years of particular waves. This points to another criticism of the theory: that it amounts to seeing patterns in a mass of statistics that aren't really there.

Moreover, there is a lack of agreement over the cause of this phenomenon. How much this matters is disputed: some scientific patterns have in the past been identified before an explanation could be advanced. (The best known example is that of the precursors to the periodic table, which were in fact rejected by many scientists precisely on the grounds of lack of explanation.)

There is controversy over the validity of Kondratiev's theory among many scholars. Some believe that not enough is attributed to actual human errors that have created some of the economic situations of history, and too much to the inevitability of the characteristics of the phases of the waves. They claim that many of the situations were entirely avoidable, not the consequences of an unstoppable wave pattern. Others doubt the legitimacy of Kondratiev's waves because they believe that every wave is a structural cycle that has unique characteristics and cannot be repeated. There is also controversy over Kondratiev's research—many believe that the conclusions and results of his research are biased because he highlighted and used only certain events to reach his conclusions and left out other important data and events that could have affected his outcomes.

Modern Modifications of Kondratiev Theory

Most cycle theorists agree, however, with the "Schumpeter-Freeman-Perez" paradigm of five waves so far since the industrial revolution, and the sixth one to come. These five cycles are:

- The Industrial Revolution—1771
- The Age of Steam and Railways—1829
- The Age of Steel, Electricity and Heavy Engineering—1875
- The Age of Oil, the Automobile and Mass Production—1908
- The Age of Information and Telecommunications—1971.

According to this theory, we are currently at the turning-point of the 5th Kondratiev. Some scholars, particularly Immanuel Wallerstein, argue that cycles of global war are tied to Capitalist Long Waves. Major, highly-destructive wars tend to begin just prior to an output upswing.

Independently, the economists/physicists Cesare Marchetti and Theodore Modis have evidenced the cyclical Kondratiev pattern from physical variables such as energy consumption, the use of horsepower, the appearance of basic innovations, the discovery of stable elements, bank failures, homicides, and one-mile-run records.

The historian Eric Hobsbawm wrote of the theory: "That good predictions have proved possible on the basis of Kondratiev Long Waves—this is not very common in economics—has convinced many historians and even some economists that there is something in them, even if we don't know what." More recently the physicist and systems scientist Tessaleno Devezas advanced a causal model for the long wave phenomenon based on a generation-learning model and a nonlinear dynamic behaviour of information systems.

In both works a complete theory is presented containing not only the explanation for the existence of K-Waves, but also and for the first time an explanation for the timing of a K-Wave (~60 years = 2 generations).

A specific modification of the theory of Kondratiev cycles was developed by Daniel Smihula.. For the era of the modern society and capitalistic economy he defined 6 long economic waves (cycles) and each of them was initiated by a specific technological revolution:

- (1600-1780) The wave of the Financial-agricultural revolution
- (1780-1880) The wave of the Industrial revolution
- (1880-1940) The wave of the Technical revolution
- (1940–1985) The wave of the Scientific-technical revolution
- (1985-2015) The wave of the Information and telecommunications revolution
- (2015-2035?) The hypothetical wave of the post-informational technological revolution.

Unlike original Kondratiev's and Schumpeter's views in Smihula's conception each new "wave" (due to acceleration of scientific and technological progress) is shorter then a previous one. The main stress is put on *technological progress* and new technologies as decisive factors of any longtime economic development. Each of these waves has its *innovation phase* (there occur innovations in a form applicable in practical life and also their first real application) which is described as a technological revolution and an *application phase* in which the number of revolutionary innovations falls and attention focuses on exploiting and extending existing innovations.

(As soon as an innovation or a "chain of innovations" becomes available, it becomes more efficient to invest in its adoption, extension and use than in creating new innovations.) Each wave (each cycle) of technological innovations can be characterized by the area in which the most revolutionary changes took place ("*leading sectors*"). Every wave of innovations lasts approximately until the profits from the new innovation or sector falls to the level of other, older, more traditional sectors.

It is a situation when the new technology, which originally increased a capacity to utilize new sources from nature, reached its limits and it is not possible to overcome this limit without an application of another new technology. For the end of an application phase of any wave there are typical an economic crisis and stagnation. The crisis in 2007-2010 is a result of the coming end of the "wave of the Information and telecommunications technological revolution". Interest in these different typologies of cycles has waned since the development of modern macroeconomics, which gives little support to the idea of regular periodic cycles.

Occurrence

There were frequent crises in Europe and America in the 19th and first half of the 20th century, specifically the period 1815–1939, starting from the end of the Napoleonic wars in 1815, which was immediately followed by the Post-Napoleonic depression in the United Kingdom (1815–30), and culminating in the Great Depression of 1929–39, which lead into World War II.

Business cycles in the OECD after World War II were generally more restrained than the earlier business cycles, particularly during the Golden Age of Capitalism (1945/50–1970s), and the period 1945–2008 did not experience a global downturn until the Late-2000s recession. Economic stabilization policy using fiscal policy and monetary policy appeared to have dampened the worst excesses of business cycles, and automatic stabilization due to the aspects of the government's budget also helped mitigate the cycle even without conscious action by Policymaking.

In this period the economic cycle – at least the problem of depressions – was twice declared dead; first in the late 1960s, when Phillips curve was seen as being able to steer the economy – which was followed by stagflation in the 1970s, which discredited the theory, secondly in the early 2000s, following the stability and growth in the 1980s and 1990s in what came to be known as The Great Moderation – which was followed by the Late-2000s recession. Notably, in 2003, Robert Lucas, in his presidential address to the American Economic Association, declared that the "central problem of depression-prevention [has] been solved, for all practical purposes."

Note however that various regions have experienced prolonged depressions, most dramatically the economic crisis in former Eastern Bloc countries following the end of the Soviet Union in 1989; for several of these countries the period 1989–2010 has been an ongoing depression, with real income still lower than in 1989.

Identifying

In 1946, economists Arthur F. Burns and Wesley C. Mitchell provided the now standard definition of business cycles in their book *Measuring Business Cycles*:

Business cycles are a type of fluctuation found in the aggregate economic activity of nations that organize their work mainly in business enterprises: a cycle consists of expansions occurring at about the same time in many economic activities, followed by similarly general recessions, contractions, and revivals which merge into the expansion phase of the next cycle; in duration, business cycles vary from more than one year to ten or twelve years; they are not divisible into shorter cycles of similar characteristics with amplitudes approximating their own.

According to A. F. Burns: Business cycles are not merely fluctuations in aggregate economic activity. The critical feature that distinguishes them from the commercial convulsions of earlier centuries or from the seasonal and other short term variations of our own age is that the fluctuations are widely diffused over the economy—its industry, its commercial dealings, and its tangles of finance. The economy of the western world is a system of closely interrelated parts. He who would understand business cycles must master the workings of an economic system organized largely in a network of free enterprises searching for profit. The problem of how business cycles come about is therefore inseparable from the problem of how a capitalist economy functions.

In the United States, it is generally accepted that the National Bureau of Economic Research (NBER) is the final arbiter of the dates of the peaks and troughs of the business cycle. An expansion is the period from a trough to a peak, and a recession as the period from a peak to a trough. The NBER identifies a recession as "a significant decline in economic activity spread across the economy, lasting more than a few months, normally visible in real GDP, real income, employment, industrial production".

9

Financial Statements and the Framework of Accounting

Financial Accounting

Accounting provides an account – an explanation or report in financial terms – about the transactions of an organisation. Accounting enables managers to satisfy the stakeholders in the organisation (owners, government, financiers, suppliers, customers, employees etc.) that they have acted in the best interests of stakeholders rather than themselves. These explanations are provided to stakeholders through financial statements or reports, often referred to as the company's 'accounts'. The main financial reports are the Profit and Loss account, the Balance Sheet and the Cash Flow statement. There is a legal requirement for the financial statements of companies (other than very small ones) to be audited. Auditors are professionally qualified accountants who have to conduct an audit – an independent examination of the financial statements – and form an opinion as to whether the financial statements form a true and fair view and have been prepared in accordance with the Companies Act. Although the requirement for a true and fair view is subjective and has never been tested at law, it takes precedence over accounting standards. Accounting standards are principles to which accounting reports should conform. They are aimed at:

- achieving comparability between companies, through reducing the variety of accounting practice;
- providing full disclosure of material (i.e. significant) factors through the judgements made by the preparers of those financial reports; and

- ensuring that the information provided is meaningful for the users of financial reports.

However, a criticism of the standards is that they are set by the preparers (professional accountants) rather than the users (shareholders and financiers) of financial reports. Financial Reporting Standards (FRSs) are issued by the Accounting Standards Board (ASB) and Statements of Standard Accounting Practice (SSAPs) were issued by the Accounting Standards Committee, which preceded the ASB. FRSs and SSAPs govern many aspects of the presentation of financial statements and the disclosure of information.

A Financial Reporting Review Panel has the power to seek revision of a company's accounts where those accounts do not comply with the standards and if necessary to seek a court order to ensure compliance. Interestingly, the US equivalent of the true and fair view is for financial statements to be presented fairly and in accordance with Generally Accepted Accounting Principles (or GAAP).

There is a move towards the harmonization of accounting standards between countries through the work of the International Accounting Standards Board (IASB). This has been a consequence of the globalization of capital markets, with the consequent need for accounting rules that can be understood by international investors.

The dominance of multinational corporations and the desire of companies to be listed on several stock exchanges have led to the need to rationalize different reporting practices in different countries. In Europe, all listed companies of member states of the European Union have to comply with IASB standards by 2005.

Reporting Profitability

Businesses exist to make a profit. Thus, the basic accounting concept is that:

profit = income “ expenses

However, business profitability is determined by the matching principle – matching income earned with the expenses incurred in earning that income. Income is the value of sales of goods or services produced by the business. Expenses are all the costs incurred in buying, making or providing those goods or services and all the marketing and selling, production, logistics, human resource, IT, financing, administration and management costs involved in operating the business. The profit (or loss) of a business for a financial period is reported in a Profit and Loss account.

The turnover is the business income or sales of goods and services. The cost of sales is either:

- the cost of providing a service; or
- the cost of buying goods sold by a retailer; or
- the cost of raw materials and production costs for a product manufacturer.

However, not all the goods bought by a retailer or used in production will have been sold in the same period as the sales are made. The matching principle requires that the business adjusts for increases or decreases in inventory – the stock of goods bought or produced for resale but not yet sold. Therefore, the cost of sales in the accounts is more properly described as the cost of goods sold, not the cost of goods produced. Because the production and sale of services are simultaneous, the cost of services produced always equals the cost of services sold (there is no such thing as an inventory of services). The distinction between cost of sales and expenses leads to two types of profit being reported: gross profit and operating profit. Gross profit is the difference between the selling price and the purchase (or production) cost of the goods or services sold. Using a simple example, a retailer selling baked beans may buy each tin for 5p and sell it for 9p. The gross profit is 4p per tin.

gross profit = sales " cost of sales

Expenses will include all the other (selling, administration, finance etc.) costs of the business, that is those not directly concerned with buying, making or providing goods or services, but supporting that activity. The same retailer may treat the rent of the store, salaries of employees, distribution and computer costs and so on as expenses in order to determine the operating profit.

operating profit = gross profit " expenses

The operating profit is one of the most significant figures because it represents the profit generated from the ordinary operations of the business. It is also called net profit, profit before interest and taxes (PBIT) or earnings before interest and taxes (EBIT). The distinction between cost of sales and expenses can vary between industries and organisations. A single store may treat only the product cost as the cost of sales and salaries and rent as expenses. A large retail chain may include the salaries of staff and the store rental as cost of sales with expenses covering the head office, corporate costs. For any particular business, it is important to determine the demarcation between cost of sales and expenses. From operating profit, a company must pay interest to its lenders, income tax to the government and a dividend to shareholders (for their share of the profits as they – unlike lenders – do not receive an interest rate for their investment). The remaining profit is retained by the business as part of its capital.

Reporting Financial Position

Not all business transactions appear in the Profit and Loss account. The second financial statement is the Balance Sheet. This shows the financial position of the business – its assets, liabilities and capital – at the end of a financial period. Some business payments are to acquire assets. Fixed assets are things that the business owns and uses as part of its infrastructure. There are two types of fixed assets: tangible and intangible. Tangible fixed assets comprise those physical assets that can be seen and touched, such as buildings, machinery, vehicles, computers etc. Intangible fixed assets comprise non-physical assets such as the customer goodwill of a business or its intellectual property, e.g. its ownership of patents and trademarks.

Current assets include money in the bank, debtors (the sales to customers on credit, but unpaid) and inventory (the stock of goods bought or manufactured, but unsold). The word current in accounting means 12 months, so current assets are those that will change their form during the next year.

Sometimes assets are acquired or expenses incurred without paying for them immediately. In doing so, the business incurs liabilities. Liabilities are debts that the business owes. Liabilities – called creditors in the Balance Sheet – may be current liabilities such as bank overdrafts, trade creditors (purchases of goods on credit, but unpaid) and amounts due for taxes etc. As for assets, the word current means that the liabilities will be repaid within 12 months. Current liabilities also form part of working capital.

Long-term liabilities or creditors due after more than one year cover loans to finance the business that are repayable after 12 months and certain kinds of provisions. Capital is a particular kind of liability, as it is the money invested by the owners in the business. As mentioned above, capital is increased by the retained profits of the business (the profit after paying interest, tax and dividends).

In the Balance Sheet, the assets must agree with the total of liabilities and capital, because what the business owns is represented by what it owes to outsiders (liabilities) and to the owners (capital). This is called the accounting equation:

assets = liabilities + capital

or

assets “ liabilities = capital

However, the capital of the business does not represent the value of the business – it is the result of the application of a number of accounting principles. In addition to the Financial Reporting Standards and Statements of Standard Accounting Practice referred to earlier, there are some basic accounting principles that are generally accepted by the accounting profession as being important in preparing accounting reports. However, an important principle that is particularly relevant to the interpretation of accounting reports is the matching principle.

The matching (or accruals) principle recognizes income when it is earned and recognizes expenses when they are incurred (accrual accounting), not when money is received or paid out (cash accounting). While cash is very important in business, the accruals method provides a more meaningful picture of the financial performance of a business from year to year.

Accruals Accounting

Unlike a system of cash accounting, where receipts are treated as income and payments as expenses (which is common in not-for-profit organisations), the matching principle requires a system of accrual accounting, which takes account of the timing differences between receipts and payments and when those cash flows are treated as income earned and expenses incurred for the calculation of profit. Accruals accounting makes adjustments for:

- prepayments;
- accruals; and
- provisions.

The matching principle requires that certain cash payments made in advance are treated as prepayments, i.e. made in advance of when they are treated as an expense for profit purposes. Other expenses are accrued, i.e. treated as expenses for profit purposes even though no cash payment has yet been made. A good example of a prepayment is insurance, which is paid 12 months in advance. Assume that a business which has a financial year ending 31 March pays its 12 months insurance premium of £12,000 in advance on 1 January. At its year end, the business will only treat £3,000 (3/12 of £12,000) as an expense and will treat the remaining £9,000 as a prepayment (a current asset in the Balance Sheet). A good example of an accrual is electricity, which like most utilities is paid (often quarterly) in arrears. If the same business usually receives its electricity bill in May (covering the period March to May) it will need to accrue an expense for the month of March, even if the bill has not yet been received. If the prior year's bill was £2,400 for the same quarter (allowing for seasonal fluctuations in usage) then the business will accrue £800 (1/3 of £2,400).

A further example of the matching principle is in the creation of provisions. Provisions are estimates of possible liabilities that may arise. An example of a possible future liability is a provision for warranty claims that may be payable on sales of products. The estimate will be based on the likely costs to be incurred in the future.

Other types of provisions cover reductions in asset values. The main examples are:

- Doubtful debts: customers may experience difficulty in paying their accounts and a provision may be made based on experience that a proportion of debtors will never pay.
- Inventory: some stock may be obsolete but still held in the store. A provision reduces the value of the obsolete stock to its sale or scrap value (if any).
- Depreciation: this is a charge against profits, intended to write off the value of each fixed asset over its useful life.

Provisions for likely future liabilities are shown in the Balance Sheet as liabilities, while provisions that reduce asset values are shown as deductions from the cost of the asset. The most important provision, because it typically involves a large amount of money, is for depreciation.

Depreciation

Fixed assets are capitalized in the Balance Sheet so that the purchase of fixed assets does not affect profit. However, depreciation is an expense that spreads the cost of the asset over its useful life. The following example illustrates the matching principle in relation to depreciation. An asset costs £100,000. It is expected to have a life of four years and have a resale value of £20,000 at the end of that time.

It is important to recognize that the cash outflow of £100,000 occurs when the asset is bought. The depreciation charge of £20,000 per annum is a non-cash expense each year.

If the asset is then sold, any profit or loss on sale is treated as a separate item in the Profit and Loss account. Alternatively, the asset can be depreciated to a nil value in the Balance Sheet even though it is still in use. A type of depreciation used for certain assets, such as goodwill or leasehold property improvements, is called amortization, which has the same meaning and is calculated in the same way as depreciation. In reporting profits, some companies show the profit before depreciation (or amortization) is deducted, because it can be a substantial cost, but one that does not result in any cash flow. A variation of EBIT is EBITDA: earnings before interest, taxes, depreciation and amortization. Reporting cash flow The third financial statement is the cash flow. The Cash Flow statement shows the movement in cash for the business during a financial period. It includes:

- cash flow from operations;
- interest receipts and payments;
- income taxes paid;
- capital expenditure (i.e. the purchase of new fixed assets);
- dividends paid to shareholders;
- new borrowings or repayment of borrowings.

The cash flow from operations differs from the operating profit because of:

- depreciation, which as a non-cash expense is added back to profit (since operating profit is the result after depreciation is deducted);
- increases (or decreases) in working capital (e.g. debtors, inventory, prepayments, creditors and accruals), which reduce (or increase) available cash.

The management of working capital is a crucial element of cash management.

Working Capital

Working capital is the difference between current assets and current liabilities (or creditors). In practical terms, we are primarily concerned with stock and debtors, although prepayments are a further element of current assets. Current liabilities comprise creditors and accruals. The other element of working capital is bank, representing either surplus cash (a current asset) or short-term borrowing through a bank overdraft facility (a creditor).

Money tied up in debtors and stock puts pressure on the firm, either to reduce the level of that investment or to seek additional borrowings. Alternatively, cash surpluses can be invested to generate additional income through interest earned.

Managing working capital is essential for success, as the ability to avoid a cash

crisis and pay debts as they fall due depends on:

- managing debtors through effective credit approval, invoicing and collection activity;
- managing stock through effective ordering, storage and identification of stock;
- managing trade creditors by negotiation of trade terms and through taking advantage of settlement discounts; and
- managing cash by effective forecasting, short-term borrowing and/or investment of surplus cash where possible.

Managing Debtors

The main measure of how effectively debtors are managed is the number of days' sales outstanding.

The target number of days' sales outstanding will be a function of the industry, the credit terms offered by the firm and its efficiency in both credit approval and collection activity. Management of debtors will aim to reduce days' sales outstanding over time and minimize bad debts. Acceptance policies will aim to determine the creditworthiness of new customers before sales are made. This can be achieved by checking trade and bank references, searching company accounts and consulting a credit bureau for any adverse reports. Credit limits can be set for each customer.

Collection policy should ensure that invoices and statements are issued quickly and accurately, that any queries are investigated as soon as they are identified and that continual follow-up (by telephone and post) of late-paying customers should take place. Discounts may be offered for settlement within credit terms. Bad debts may occur because a customer's business fails. For this reason, firms establish a provision to cover the likelihood of customers not being able to pay their debts.

Managing Stock

Sound management of stock requires an accurate and up-to-date stock control system. Often in stock control the Pareto principle (also called the 80/20 rule) applies. This recognizes that a small proportion (often about 20 per cent) of the number of stock items accounts for a relatively large proportion (say 80 per cent) of the total value. In stock control, ABC analysis takes the approach that, rather than attempt to manage all stock items equally, efforts should be made to prioritize the 'A' items that account for most value, then 'B' items and only if time permits the many smaller-value 'C' items. Some businesses adopt just-in-time (JIT) methods to minimize stockholding, treating any stock as a wasted resource. JIT requires sophisticated production planning, inventory control and supply chain management so that stock is only received as it is required for production or sale. Stock may be written off because of stock losses, obsolescence or damage. For this reason, firms establish a provision to cover the likelihood of writing off part of the value of stock.

Managing Creditors

Just as it is important to collect debts from customers, it is also essential to ensure that suppliers are paid within their credit terms. As for debtors, the main measure of how effectively creditors are managed is the number of days' purchases outstanding.

The number of days' purchases outstanding will reflect credit terms offered by the supplier, any discounts that may be obtained for prompt payment and the collection action taken by the supplier. Failure to pay creditors may result in the loss or stoppage of supply, which can then affect the ability of a business to satisfy its customers' orders.

A Theoretical Perspective on Financial Statements

A necessary ingredient for shareholder value, given the separation of ownership from control in most large business organisations, is the control of what managers actually do. Control is considered in the rational-economic paradigm through the notion of contract, in which the role of control is to measure and reward performance such that there will be greater goal congruence, i.e. that individuals pursuing their own self-interest will also pursue the collective interest. There are two main versions of contractual theory: agency theory and transaction cost economics. Agency theory sees the economy as a network of interlocking contracts. The transaction cost approach sees the economy as a mixture of markets and hierarchies.

Agency Theory

Agency theory is concerned with contractual relationships within the firm, between a principal and an agent, whose rights and duties are specified by a contract of employment. This model recognizes the behaviour of an agent (the manager), whose actions the management accounting and control system seeks to influence and control. Both are assumed to be rational-economic persons motivated solely by self-interest, although they may differ with respect to their preferences, beliefs and information.

The principal wishes to influence what the agent does, but delegates tasks to the agent in an uncertain environment. The agent expends effort in the performance of these tasks. The outcome depends on both environmental factors and the effort expended by the agent. Under the sharing rule, the agent usually receives a reward, being a share of the outcome. The reward will depend on the information system used to measure the outcome. Consequently, financial reports play an important role in regulating the actions of agents. The assumption of agency theory is that the agent obtains utility (a benefit) from the reward but disutility from expending effort. Both principal and agent are assumed to be risk averse and utility maximizers.

The agency model involves seeking an employment contract that specifies the sharing rule and the information system. An accounting system can provide output measures from which an agent's efforts can be inferred, but the measures may not accurately reflect the effort expended. This leads to uncertainty about the relationship between the accounting measure and the agent's effort. If the principal cannot observe the agent's effort, or infer it from measured output, the agent may have an incentive to act in a manner different to the employment contract – this is called moral hazard. A principal who can observe the agent's effort but does not have access to all the information held by the agent does not know whether the effort expended has been based on the agent's information or whether the agent has 'shirked'. This is called adverse selection. Moral hazard and adverse selection are a consequence of information asymmetry. This happens because principal and agent have different amounts of information. A function of accounting under agency theory is to improve efficiency by minimizing the losses caused through moral hazard and adverse selection.

Seal gives the example of renting a holiday home that is used by the owner only a few weeks of the year. The owner (the principal) may appoint a local agent to let out the home. The agency problem is how to motivate and monitor the agent in return for the commission earned by the agent. The owner will expect regular accounts of income and expenditure. Agency theorists use this reasoning to explain the development of financial accounting and auditing in more complex agency relationships. There are problems with agency theory, however. It ignores the effect of capital markets by assuming a single owner rather than a group of owners. The model focuses on single-period behaviour; many individuals violate the assumptions of rational self-interested behaviour and the agency perspective is narrow because there is no regard given to power, trust, ethical issues or equity, all of which may affect behaviour.

Interpreting Financial Statements and Alternative Theoretical Perspectives

Interpreting Financial Statements

Financial statements are an important part of a company's Annual Report, which is required for all companies listed on the Stock Exchange. For companies not listed, the Companies Act requires the preparation of financial statements. The process of interpreting financial statements begins with a consideration of the wider context: economic conditions; changes in the industry (e.g. regulation, technology); and the competitive advantage (e.g. marketing, operations, distribution etc.) held by the business. Within this context, often gained through the financial press and trade periodicals, the Annual Report itself can be considered. The Annual Report for a listed company typically contains:

1. A financial summary – the key financial information.
2. The chairman's or directors' report. This provides a useful summary of the key factors affecting the company's performance over the past year and its prospects for the future. It is important to read this information as it provides a background to the financial statements, in particular the company's products and major market segments. It is important to 'read between the lines' in this report, since the intention of the Annual Report is to paint a 'glossy' picture of the business. However, as competitors will also read the Annual Report, the company takes care not to disclose more than is necessary.
3. The statutory reports (i.e. those required by the Companies Act) by the directors and auditors. These will help to identify any key issues that may be found in the accounts themselves.
4. The financial statements: Profit and Loss account, Balance Sheet and Cash Flow statement. The consolidated figures should be used, as these are the total figures for the group of companies that comprise the whole business.
5. Notes to the accounts, which provide detailed figures and explanations to the accounts. These often run to many pages.
6. A five-year summary of key financial information.

The Accounting Standards Board recommends that listed companies include an operating and financial review that provides 'a framework for the directors to discuss and analyse the business's performance and the factors underlying its results and financial position, in order to assist users to assess for themselves the future potential of the business'. The operating and financial review would replace much of the information contained in the chairman's or directors' reports (item 2 above). The Profit and Loss account, Balance Sheet and Cash Flow statement can be studied using ratios. Ratios are typically two numbers, with one being expressed as a percentage of the other. Ratio analysis can be used to help interpret trends in performance year on year and by benchmarking to industry averages or to the performance of individual competitors. Ratio analysis can be used to interpret performance against five criteria:

- the rate of profitability;
- liquidity, i.e. cash flow;
- gearing, i.e. the proportion of borrowings to shareholders' investment;
- how efficiently assets are utilized; and
- the returns to shareholders.

Ratio Analysis

There are different definitions that can be used for each ratio. However, it is important that whatever ratios are used, they are meaningful to the business and applied consistently. The most common ratios follow.

Profitability

Each of the profitability ratios provides a different method of interpreting profitability. Satisfactory business performance requires an adequate return on shareholders' funds and total capital employed in the business (the total of the investment by shareholders and lenders). Profit must also be achieved as a percentage of sales, which must itself grow year on year. The operating profit and gross profit margins emphasize different elements of business performance.

A business that has an acid test of less than 100 per cent may experience difficulty in paying its debts as they fall due. On the other hand, a company with too high a working capital ratio may not be utilizing its assets effectively. The higher the gearing, the higher the risk of repaying debt and interest. The lower the interest cover, the more pressure there is on profits to fund interest charges. However, because external funds are being used, the rate of profit earned by shareholders is higher where external funds are used. The relationship between risk and return is an important feature of interpreting business performance.

While in the above example the return on capital employed is a constant 20 per cent (an operating profit of £20,000 on capital employed of £100,000), the return on shareholders' funds increases as debt replaces equity.

This improvement to the return to shareholders carries a risk, which increases as the proportion of profits taken by the interest charge increases (and is reflected in the interest cover ratio). If profits turn down, there are substantially more risks carried by the highly geared business. This is a measure of how efficiently assets are utilized to generate sales. Investment in assets has as its principal purpose the generation of sales. Three other efficiency ratios are those concerning debtors' collections, stock turnover and creditors' payments.

The shareholder ratios are measures of returns to shareholders on their investment in the business. The dividend and earnings ratios reflect the annual return to shareholders, while the P/E ratio measures the number of years over which the investment in shares will be recovered through earnings.

Interpreting Financial Information using Ratios

The interpretation of any ratio depends on the industry. In particular, the ratio needs to be interpreted as a trend over time, or by comparison to industry averages of competitor ratios. These comparisons help determine whether performance is improving and where improvement maybe necessary. Based on the understanding of the business context and competitive conditions and the information provided by ratio analysis, users of financial statements can make judgements about the pattern of past performance and prospects for a company and its financial strength. Broadly speaking, businesses seek:

- increasing rates of profit on shareholders' funds, capital employed and sales;
- adequate liquidity (a ratio of current assets to liabilities of not less than 100 per cent) to ensure that debts can be paid as they fall due, but not an excessive rate to suggest that funds are inefficiently used;
- a level of debt commensurate with the business risk taken;
- high efficiency as a result of maximizing sales from the business's investments; and
- a satisfactory return on the investment made by shareholders.

When considering the movement in a ratio over two or more years, it is important to look at possible causes for the movement. These can be gained by understanding that either the numerator (top number in the ratio) or denominator (bottom number in the ratio) or both can influence the change. Some of the possible explanations behind changes in ratios are described below.

Profitability

Improvements in the returns on shareholders' funds (ROI) and capital employed (ROCE) may either be because profits have increased and/or because the capital used to generate those profits has altered. When businesses are taken over by others, one way of improving ROI or ROCE is to increase profits by reducing costs (often as a result of economies of scale), but another is to maintain profits while reducing assets and repaying debt. Improvements in operating profitability as a proportion of sales (PBIT or EBIT) are the result of profitability growing at a faster rate than sales growth, a result either of a higher gross margin or lower expenses. Note that sales growth may result in a higher profit but not necessarily in a higher rate of profit as a percentage of sales. Improvement in the rate of gross profit may be the result of higher selling prices, lower cost of sales, or changes in the mix of product/services sold or different market segments in which they are sold, which may reflect differential profitability. Naturally, the opposite explanations hold true for deterioration in profitability.

Liquidity

Improvements in the working capital and acid test ratios are the result of changing the balance between current assets and current liabilities. Money changes form between debtors, stock, bank and creditors. Borrowing over the long term in order to fund current assets will improve this ratio, as will profits that generate cash flow. By contrast, using liquid funds to repay long-term loans or incurring losses will reduce the working capital used to repay creditors.

Gearing

The gearing ratio reflects the balance between long-term debt and shareholders' equity. It changes as a result of changes in either shareholders' funds (more shares may be issued), raising new borrowings or repayments of debt. As debt increases in proportion to shareholders' funds, the gearing ratio will increase. Interest cover may increase as a result of higher profits or lower borrowings (and reduce as a result of lower profits or higher borrowings), but even with constant borrowings changes in the interest rate paid will also influence this ratio.

Activity/efficiency

Asset turnover improves either because sales increase or the total assets used reduce, a similar situation to that described above for ROCE. The efficiency with which debtors are collected, inventory is managed and creditors paid is also an important measure.

Shareholder return

Decisions made by directors influence both the dividend per share and the dividend payout ratio. Dividends are a decision made by directors on the basis of the proportion of profits they want to distribute and the capital needed to be retained in the business to fund growth. Often, shareholder value considerations will dictate the level of dividends, which businesses do not like to reduce on a per share basis. This is sometimes at the cost of retaining fewer profits and then having to borrow additional funds to support growth strategies. However, the number of shares issued also affects this ratio, as share issues will result in a lower dividend per share unless the total dividend is increased.

As companies have little influence over their share price, which is a result of market expectations as much as past performance, dividend yield, while influenced by the dividend paid per share, is more readily influenced by changes in the market price of the shares. Earnings per share is influenced, as for profitability, by the profit but also (like dividends) by the number of shares issued. As for the dividend yield, the price/earnings (P/E) ratio is often more a result of changes in the share price than in the profits reflected in the earnings per share.

Social and Environmental Reporting

The concern with stakeholders rather than shareholders began in the 1970s and is generally associated with the publication in 1975 of The Corporate Report, a publication by the Accounting Standards Steering Committee. Accounting academics began to question profit as the sole measure of business performance and suggested a wider social responsibility for business and social accounting. Concepts of corporate social accounting and socially responsible accounting – most recently corporate social and environmental reporting (CSR) – attempt to highlight the impact of organisations on society.

Jones suggested three reasons for this:

1. A moral imperative that business organisations were insufficiently aware of the social consequences of their activities.
2. External pressure from government and pressure groups and the demand by some institutional investors for ethical investments.

This was linked to the role of accounting in demonstrating how well organisations were fulfilling their social contract, the implied contract between an organisation and society.

3. Internal change taking place within organisations as a result of education etc. However, there has been little support for broader social accounting because accountants and managers have generally seen themselves as the agents of owners. Social reporting could be seen as undermining the power of shareholders and the foundation of the capitalist economic system. There are also technical difficulties associated with social reporting and a dominant belief among business leaders that government and not business had the responsibility to determine what was reported.

During the 1980s and 1990s environmental accounting focused on responsibility for the natural environment and in particular on sustainability as a result of concerns about ozone depletion, the greenhouse effect and global warming. These concerns were associated with the growth of pressure groups such as Greenpeace and Friends of the Earth. Part of the appeal of environmental accounting was that issues of energy efficiency, recycling and reductions in packaging had cost-saving potential and therefore profits and social responsibility came to be seen as not necessarily mutually exclusive.

Zadek argued that social and ethical accounting, auditing and reporting together provide one of the few practical mechanisms for companies to integrate new patterns of civil accountability and governance with a business success model focused on stakeholders and core non-financial as well as financial values.

Socially responsible businesses: find the spaces in the pipeline between investors and consumers where some choice in behaviour is possible... [and] a far more ambitious agenda of shifting the basic boundaries by raising public awareness towards social and environmental agendas and supporting the emergence of new forms of investors that take non-financial criteria into account. A further example of how the boundaries of accounting are set in arguably inappropriate ways by the rational-economic paradigm is in the exclusion of intellectual capital from financial statements.

Intellectual Capital

Edvinsson and Malone defined intellectual capital as 'the hidden dynamic factors that underlie the visible company'. Stewart defined intellectual capital as 'formalized, captured and leveraged knowledge'.

Intellectual capital is of particular interest to accountants in increasingly knowledge-based economies in which the limitations of traditional financial statements erode their value as a tool supporting meaningful decision-making. Three dimensions of intellectual capital have been identified in the literature: human (developing and leveraging individual knowledge and skills); organisational (internal structures, systems and procedures); and customer (loyalty, brand, image etc.). The disclosure of information about intellectual capital as an extension to financial reporting has been proposed by various accounting academics. The most publicized example is the Skandia Navigator.

While most businesses espouse a commitment to employees and the value of their knowledge, as well as to some form of social or environmental responsibility, this is often merely rhetoric, a facade to appease the interest groups of stakeholders. The institutional setting of organisations provides another perspective from which to view accounting and reporting.

Institutional Theory

Institutional theory is valuable because it locates the organisation within its historical and contextual setting. It is predicated on the need for legitimation and on isomorphic processes. Scott describes legitimation as the result of organisations being dependent, to a greater or lesser extent, on support from the environment for their survival and continued operation. Organisations need the support of governmental institutions where their operations are regulated (and few organisations are not regulated in some form or other). Organisations are also dependent on the acquisition of resources (labour, finance, technology etc.) for their purposes. If an organisation is not legitimated, it may incur sanctions of a legal, economic or social nature.

The second significant aspect of institutional power is the operation of isomorphism, the tendency for different organisations to adopt similar characteristics. DiMaggio and Powell identified three forms of isomorphism: coercive, as a result of political influence and the need to gain legitimacy; mimetic, following from standard responses to uncertainty; and normative, associated with professionalization. They held that isomorphic tendencies between organisations were a result of wider belief systems and cultural frames of reference.

Processes of education, inter-organisational movement of personnel and professionalization emphasize these belief systems and cultural values at an institutional level and facilitate the mimetic processes that result in organisations imitating each other. Isomorphic tendencies exist because 'organisations compete not just for resources and customers, but for political power and institutional legitimacy, for social as well as economic fitness'.

These legitimating and isomorphic processes become taken for granted by organisations as they strive to satisfy the demands of external regulators, resource suppliers and professional groups. These taken-for-granted processes themselves become institutionalized in the systems and processes – including accounting and reporting – adopted by organisations. Meyer argued that accounting arises 'in response to the demands made by powerful elements in the environment on which organisations are dependent'. Each of these theoretical perspectives provides a different view of the role of preparers and the needs of users of financial statements. This perspective also follows through to the users of management accounting information. However, as we have suggested earlier accounting is not without its limitations.

Creative Accounting and Ethics

Accounting choices, according to Francis, are moral choices:

Accounting is important precisely to the extent the accountant can transform the world, can influence the lived experience of others in ways which cause that experience to differ from what it would be in the absence of accounting, or in the presence of an alternative kind of accounting. Creative accounting practices have been justified by managers for reasons of income smoothing, to bring profits closer to forecasts; changing accounting policies to distract attention from poor performance; or maintaining or boosting share prices. Despite the role of accounting standards and other regulations, creative accounting has always played a part in the efforts made by a few companies to present their performance in a better light.

Griffiths commented on the power of financial analysts and investment advisers in the City (of London) and the aim of company directors to present the business as having steady growth in income and profits. This desire for a smoothing effect can be achieved by practices such as accruals, stock valuation, creating or reducing provisions, capitalizing or expensing costs and off-Balance Sheet financing (which was the main factor in Enron's downfall in the United States). While creative accounting has been frowned on, earnings management has not.

Under earnings management, directors aim to satisfy the market expectations influenced by stock analysts. Smith described the techniques adopted by companies and claimed that 'much of the apparent growth in profits which had occurred in the 1980s was the result of accounting sleight of hand rather than genuine economic growth'. However, although accounting standards continually improve, there are always loopholes that accountants seem to find as quickly as standards are produced. Richardson and Richardson emphasized the role of accountants in organisations.

They occupy special positions that privilege them to information that has the potential to reveal deviant top management behaviour, which can lead to social and emotional costs for innocent stakeholders and to corporate failures. As these conflicts are unlikely to be resolved internally, the authors argue for the ability to 'blow the whistle'. However, as things stand, it is more likely that the accountant will simply leave the organisation. The problem with whistle blowing, the authors comment, is that to some it is an act of subversion, while to others it is an act of citizenship. To the organisation, it is an act of disloyalty.

10

The Role of Management Accounting

The advent of mechanized production following the Industrial Revolution increased the size and complexity of production processes, which employed more people and required larger sums of capital to finance machinery. Accounting historians suggest that the increase in the number of limited companies that led to the separation of ownership from control caused the attention of cost accounting to shift from determining cost to exercising control by absent owners over their managers. The predecessor of management accounting, 'cost accounting', was reflected in the earlier title of management accountants as cost or works accountants. Typically situated in factories, these accountants tended to know the business and advise non-financial managers in relation to operational decisions. Cost accounting was concerned with determining the cost of an object, whether a product, an activity, a division of the organisation or market segment. The first book on cost accounting is believed to be Garcke and Fell's Factory Accounts, which was published in 1897. Historians have argued that the new corporate structures that were developed in the twentieth century – multidivisional organisations, conglomerates and multinationals – placed increased demands on accounting. These demands included divisional performance evaluation and budgeting. It has also been suggested that developments in cost accounting were driven by government demands for cost information during both World Wars. It appears that 'management accounting' is a term used only after the Second World War.

In their acclaimed book Relevance Lost, Johnson and Kaplan traced the development of management accounting from its origins in the Industrial Revolution supporting process-type industries such as textile and steel conversion, transportation and distribution. These systems were concerned with evaluating the efficiency of internal processes, rather than measuring organisational profitability. Financial reports were produced using a separate transactions-based system that reported financial performance. Johnson and Kaplan argued that by 1925 'virtually all management accounting practices used today had been developed'. They also described how the early manufacturing firms attempted to improve performance via economies of scale by reducing unit cost through increasing the volume of output. This led to a concern with measuring the efficiency of the production process. Calculating the cost of different products was unnecessary because the product range was homogeneous. Over time, the product range expanded and businesses sought economies of scope through producing two or more products in a single facility. This led to the need for better information about how the mix of products could improve total profits. However, after 1900 the production of accounting information was largely for external reporting to shareholders and not to assist managerial decision-making. Johnson and Kaplan described how a management accounting system must provide timely and accurate information to facilitate efforts to control costs, to measure and improve productivity and to devise improved production processes. The management accounting system must also report accurate product costs so that pricing decisions, introduction of new products, abandonment of obsolete products and response to rival products can be made.

The Chartered Institute of Management Accountants' definition of the core activities of management accounting includes:

- participation in the planning process at both strategic and operational levels, involving the establishment of policies and the formulation of budgets;
- the initiation of and provision of guidance for management decisions, involving the generation, analysis, presentation and interpretation of relevant information;
- contributing to the monitoring and control of performance through the provision of reports including comparisons of actual with budgeted performance and their analysis and interpretation.

One of the earliest writers on management accounting described 'different costs for different purposes'. This theme was developed by one of the earliest texts on management accounting. Vatter distinguished the information needs of managers from those of external shareholders and emphasized that it was preferable to get less precise data to managers quickly than complete information too late to influence decision-making. Johnson and Kaplan commented that even today, organisations with access to far more computational power... rarely distinguish between information needed promptly for managerial control and information provided periodically for summary financial statements. They argued that the developments in accounting theory in the first decades of the twentieth century came about by academics who emphasized simple decision-making models in highly simplified firms – those producing one or only a few products, usually in a onstage production process. The academics developed their ideas by logic and deductive reasoning. They did not attempt to study the problems actually faced by managers of organisations producing hundreds or thousands of products in complex production processes.

They concluded: Not surprisingly, in this situation actual management accounting systems provided few benefits to organisations. In some instances, the information reported by existing management accounting systems not only inhibited good decision-making by managers, it might actually have encouraged bad decisions.

Johnson and Kaplan described how the global competition that has taken place since the 1980s has left management accounting behind in terms of its decision usefulness. Developments such as total quality management, just-in-time inventory, computer-integrated manufacturing, shorter product life cycles and the decline of manufacturing and rise of service industries have led to the need for 'accurate knowledge of product costs, excellent cost control and coherent performance measurement'. And 'the challenge for today's competitive environment is to develop new and more flexible approaches to the design of effective cost accounting, management control and performance measurement systems'.

Recent Developments in Management Accounting

Partly as a result of the stimulus of Relevance Lost but perhaps more so as a consequence of rapidly changing business conditions, management accounting has moved beyond its traditional concern with a narrow range of numbers to incorporate wider issues of performance measurement and management. Management accounting is now implicated, to greater or lesser degrees in different organisations, with:

- value-based management;
- non-financial performance measurement systems;
- quality management approaches;
- activity-based management; and
- strategic management accounting.

Value-based management is in brief a concern with improving the value of the business to its shareholders. Management accounting is implicated in this, as a fundamental role of non-financial managers is to make decisions that contribute to increasing the value of the business.

The limitations of accounting information, particularly as a lagging indicator of performance, have led to an increasing emphasis on non-financial performance measures. Non-financial measures are a major concern of both accountants and non-financial managers, as they tend to be leading indicators of the financial performance that will be reported at some future time.

Improving the quality of products and services is also a major concern, since advances in production technology and the need to improve performance by reducing waste have led to management tools such as total quality management (TQM), just-in-time (JIT), business process re-engineering (BPR) and continuous improvement processes such as Six Sigma and the Business Excellence model. Management accounting has a role to play in these techniques and non-financial managers need to understand the relationships between accounting and new management techniques.

Activity-based management is an approach that emphasizes the underlying business processes that are required to produce goods and services and the need to identify the drivers or causes of those activities in order to be able to budget for and control costs more effectively.

Strategic management accounting, is an attempt to shift the perceptions of accountants and non-financial managers from an inward-looking to an outward-looking one, recognizing the need to look beyond the business along the value chain to its suppliers and customers and to seek ways of achieving and maintaining competitive advantage.

These changes to the narrow view of accountants, from 'bean-counters' to more active participants in formulating and implementing business strategy, have been accompanied by a shift in the collection, reporting and analysis of routine financial information from accountants to non-financial line managers. This decentring of accounting is evidenced by the delegation of responsibility for budgets and cost control to line managers and is the underlying reason that non-financial managers need a better understanding of accounting information and how that information can be used in decision-making.

A Critical Perspective

Although the concepts and assumptions underlying accounting are yet to be introduced, having begun this book with an introduction to accounting history it is worthwhile considering a contrasting viewpoint. While this viewpoint is one that may not be accepted by many practising managers, it is worth knowing, because it does lie at the very basis of the capitalist economic system in which we live and in which accounting plays such an important role.

The Marxist historian Hobsbawm argued that colonialism had been created by the cotton industry that dominated the UK economy and this resulted in a shift from domestic production to factory production. Sales increased but profits shrank, so labour (which was three times the cost of materials) was replaced by mechanization during the Industrial Revolution. Entrepreneurs started with borrowings and small items of machinery and growth was largely financed by borrowings. The Industrial Revolution produced 'such vast quantities and at such rapidly diminishing cost, as to be no longer dependent on existing demand, but to create its own market'.

Advances in mass production followed the development of the assembly line, supported by railways and shipping to transport goods and communications through the electric telegraph. At the same time, agriculture diminished in importance. Due to the appetite of the railways for iron and steel, coal, heavy machinery, labour and capital investment, 'the comfortable and rich classes accumulated income so fast and in such vast quantities as to exceed all available possibilities of spending and investment'.

While the rich accumulated profits, labour was exploited with wages at subsistence levels. Labour had to learn how to work, unlike agriculture or craft industries, in a manner suited to industry and the result was a draconian master/servant relationship. In the 1840s a depression led to unemployment and high food prices and 1848 saw the rise of the labouring poor in European cities, who threatened both the weak and obsolete regimes and the rich.

This resulted in a clash between the political and industrial revolutions, the 'triumph of bourgeois-liberal capitalism' and the domination of the globe by a few western regimes, especially the British in the mid-nineteenth century, which became a 'world hegemony'.

This 'global triumph' of capitalism in the 1850s was a consequence of the combination of cheap capital and rising prices. Stability and prosperity overtook political questions about the legitimacy of existing dynasties and technology cheapened manufactured products. There was high demand but the cost of living did not fall, so labour became dominated by the interests of the new owners of the means of production. 'Economic liberalism' became the recipe for economic growth as the market ruled labour and helped national economic expansion. Industrialization made wealth and industrial capacity decisive in international power, especially in the US, Japan and Germany.

This 'British' capitalist system was exported throughout the world, not least with the support of a colonial expansionist Empire that lent large sums of money in return for adopting the British system. This system has since been taken over by multinational corporations, largely based in the United States. Armstrong traced the historical factors behind the comparative (in relation to other professions) pre-eminence of accountants in British management hierarchies and the emphasis on financial control. He concluded that accounting controls were installed by accountants as a result of their power base in global capital markets, which was achieved through their role in the allocation of the profit surplus to shareholders.

Armstrong argued that mergers led to control problems that were tackled by American management consultants who tended to recommend the multidivisional form of organisation... [which] entirely divorce headquarters management from operations. Functional departments and their managers are subjected to a battery of financial indicators and budgetary controls... [and] a subordination of operational to financial decision-making and a major influx of accountants into senior management positions. Roberts suggested that organisational accounting embodies the separation of instrumental and moral consequences, which is questionable. He argued:

The mystification of accounting information helps to fix, elevate and then impose upon others its own particular instrumental interests, without regard to the wider social and environmental consequences of the pursuit of such interests. Accounting thus serves as a vehicle whereby others are called to account, while the interests it embodies escape such accountability. This is a more critical perspective than that associated with the traditional notion of accounting as a report to shareholders and managers, which is a result of the historical development of capitalism in the West.

While this book is designed to help non-financial managers understand the tools and techniques of accounting, it is also intended to make readers think critically about the role of accounting and the limitations of accounting, some of which have been historically defined.

One intention is to reinforce to readers that: accounting information provides a window through which the real activities of the organisation may be monitored, but it should be noted also that other windows are used that do not rely upon accounting information.

Shareholder Valu and Business Structure

Capital and Product Markets

Since the seventeenth century, companies have been formed by shareholders in order to consolidate resources and invest in opportunities. Shareholders had limited liability through which their personal liability in the event of business failure was limited to their investment in shares.

Shareholders appointed directors to manage the business, who in turn employed managers. Shareholders have few direct rights in relation to the conduct of the business. Their main powers are to elect the directors and appoint the auditors in an annual general meeting of shareholders. They are also entitled to an annual report containing details of the company's financial performance.

The market in which investors buy and sell the shares of companies is called the capital market, which is normally associated with the Stock Exchange. Companies obtain funds raised from shareholders (equity) and borrowings from financiers (debt). Both of these constitute the capital employed in the business.

The cost of capital represents the cost incurred by the organisation to fund all its investments, comprising the cost of equity and the cost of debt weighted by the mix of debt and equity. The cost of debt is interest, which is the price charged by the lender.

The cost of equity is partly dividend and partly capital growth, because most shareholders expect both regular income from profits (the dividend) and an increase in the value of their shares over time in the capital market. Thus the different costs of each form of capital, weighted by the proportions of different forms of debt and equity, constitute the weighted average cost of capital. The management of the business relationship with capital markets is called financial management or corporate finance.

Companies use their capital to invest in technologies, people and materials in order to make, buy and sell products or services to customers. This is called the product market. The focus of shareholder wealth, according to Rappaport, is to obtain funds at competitive rates from capital markets and invest those funds to exploit imperfections in product markets. Where this takes place, shareholder wealth is increased through dividends and increases in the share price. The 1990s saw a growing concern with the role of accounting in improving shareholder wealth.

Value-based Management

Since the mid-1980s, there has been more and more emphasis on increasing the value of the business to its shareholders. Traditionally, business performance has been measured through accounting ratios such as return on capital employed (ROCE), return on investment (ROI), earnings per share and so on. However, it has been argued that these are historical rather than current measures and they vary between companies as a result of different accounting treatments.

Rappaport described how companies with strong cash flows diversified in the mid-twentieth century, often into uneconomic businesses, which led to the 'value gap' – the difference between the market value of the shares and the value of the business if it had been managed to maximize shareholder value. The consequence was the takeover movement and subsequent asset stripping of the 1980s, which provided a powerful incentive for managers to focus on creating value for shareholders. The takeover movement itself led to problems as high acquisition premiums (the excess paid over and above the calculated value of the business, i.e. the goodwill) were paid to the owners and financed by high levels of debt. During the 1990s institutional investors (pension funds, insurance companies, investment trusts etc.), through their dominance of share ownership, increased their pressure on management to improve the financial performance of companies.

Value-based management (VBM) emphasizes shareholder value, on the assumption that this is the primary goal of every business. VBM approaches include total shareholder return, market value added, shareholder value added and economic value added. Recent research into the use of value-based management approaches by UK companies is covered by Cooper et al. Total shareholder return (TSR) compares the dividends received by shareholders and the increase in the share price with the original shareholder investment, expressing the TSR as a percentage of the initial investment. Market value added (MVA) is the difference between total market capitalization (number of shares issued times share price plus the market value of debt) and the total capital invested in the business by debt and equity providers. This is a measure of the value generated by managers for shareholders.

Rappaport coined shareholder value added (SVA) to refer to the increase in shareholder value over time. He defines shareholder value as the economic value of an investment, which can be calculated by using the cost of capital to discount forecast future cash flows (which he called free cash flows) into present values.

The business must generate profits in product markets that exceed the cost of capital in the capital market for value to be created (if not, shareholder value is eroded). Rappaport developed a shareholder value network.

Through this diagram, he identified seven drivers of shareholder value: sales growth rate, operating profit margin, income tax rate, working capital investment, fixed capital investment, cost of capital and forecast duration. Managers make three types of decisions that influence these value drivers and lead to shareholder value:

- Operating decisions – product mix, pricing, promotion, customer service etc., which are then reflected in the sales growth rate, operating profit margin and income tax rate.
- Investment decisions – in both inventory and capacity, which are then reflected in both working capital and fixed capital investment.
- Financing decisions – the mix of debt and equity and the choice of financial instrument determine the cost of capital, which is assessed by capital markets in terms of business risk.

The value growth duration is the estimated number of years over which the return from investments is expected to exceed the cost of capital.

The seven value drivers determine the cash flow from operations, the level of debt and the cost of capital, all of which determine shareholder value. A detrimental consequence of the emphasis on shareholder value is that it has led to a continued focus on short-term financial performance at the expense of longer-term strategy.

Economic Value Added (EVA) is a financial performance measure developed by consultants Stern Stewart & Co. It claims to capture the economic profit of a business that leads to shareholder value creation. In simple terms, EVA is net operating profit after deducting a charge to cover the opportunity cost of the capital invested in the business. EVA's 'economic profit' is the amount by which earnings exceed (or fall short of) the minimum rate of return that shareholders and financiers could get by investing in other securities with a comparable risk.

EVA accepts the assumption that the primary financial objective of any business is to maximize the wealth of its shareholders. The value of the business depends on the extent to which investors expect future profits to be greater or less than the cost of capital. Returns over and above the cost of capital increase shareholder wealth, while returns below the cost of capital erode shareholder wealth. Stern Stewart argues that managers understand this measure because it is based on operating profits. By introducing a notional charge based on assets held by the business, managers (whether at a corporate or divisional level) manage those assets as well as the profit generated.

EVA also has its critics. For example, the calculation of EVA allows up to 164 adjustments to reported accounting profits in order to remove distortions caused by arbitrary accounting rules and estimates the risk-adjusted cost of capital, both of which can be argued as subjective, although Stern Stewart argues that most organisations need only about a dozen of these. The increase in shareholder value is reflected in compensation strategies for managers whose goals, argues Stern Stewart, are aligned to increasing shareholder wealth through bonus and share option schemes that are paid over a period of time to ensure consistent future performance.

Accounting and Strategy

This book treats accounting as part of the broader business context of strategy, marketing, operations and human resources. The focus of accounting in business organisations is shareholder value – increasing the value of the business to its shareholders – through dividends from profits and/or through capital growth. Strategy both influences and is influenced by shareholder value. Strategy is reflected in the functional business areas of marketing, operations and human resources, through the actions the business wants to take to achieve, maintain and improve competitive advantage.

Financial management is concerned with raising funds from shareholders or financiers to provide the capital the business needs to sell and produce goods and services. Financial accounting represents the stewardship function, that managers are accountable to those with a financial interest in the business and produce financial reports to satisfy that accountability. Management accounting provides the information for planning, decision-making and control. Therefore, the main content of this book is the interaction between the functional areas of marketing, operations and human resources – driven by strategy – and how accounting provides a set of tools and techniques to assist functional managers. Management accounting both influences and is influenced by the functional areas and by business strategy.

The importance of strategy for management accounting and the information it provides is that a strategic perspective involves taking a longer-term view about the business than is usually provided by traditional accounting reports. Management accounting comprises a set of tools and techniques to support planning, decisionmaking and control in business organisations. Accounting is – or at least should be – integrated with business strategy. However, these same accounting tools and techniques can be used to help evaluate the performance of customers, suppliers and competitors in order to improve competitive advantage. Accounting should also extend beyond a narrow concern with financial measurement and encompass non-financial performance measurement, a subject of steadily increasing importance for those managers who are responsible for achieving performance targets, as well as for accountants.

Strategy is concerned with long-term direction, achieving and maintaining competitive advantage, identifying the scope and boundaries of the organisation and matching the activities of the organisation to its environment. Strategy is also about building on resources and competences to create new opportunities and take advantage of those opportunities and manage change within the organisation. There is also a link between strategy and operational decisions in order to turn strategy formulation into strategy implementation.

An economic perspective is added by Grant, who saw the value created by firms distributed among customers, suppliers and equity risk-takers. In order to provide this value, business firms establish profit as the single dominant objective. The purpose of strategy 'is to pursue profit over the long term'. Strategy is thus linked to performance by setting performance targets for the business as a whole and for individual business units and then measuring performance against those targets. It is to the divisionalized organisational form that we now turn.

Structure of Business Organisations

Organisations are typically considered to be of three types:

- the private sector, comprising businesses whose prime goal is profit;
- the public sector, which is government funded (through various kinds of taxation), providing services for the public, such as in health, education, law and order etc.; and

- the 'third sector' of not-for-profit organisations, providing a range of charitable or social services, funded by donations, lottery grants etc.

The accounting described in this book is primarily concerned with for-profit businesses, although many of the concepts are equally applicable to the other two sectors. Business organisations can be further subdivided into a number of major types:

- agriculture, or primary production;
- manufacturing, or secondary production;
- services, or tertiary production.

Again, our concern is with all businesses other than agriculture as the means of production and the accounting requirements of that type of business are significantly different from the latter two, which in any event dominate the economy. Manufacturing and service businesses are concerned with satisfying customer demand for products or services. Businesses produce products/services through a variety of organisational forms, but predominantly through either a functional structure or a divisionalized structure.

The functional structure locates decision-making at the top of the corporate hierarchy, with functional responsibilities for marketing, operations, human resources, finance and so on allocated to departments. In the functional structure, accounting provides a staff function to the line functions, simplified here as marketing, operations and human resources. Accounting knowledge tends to be centralized in the accounting department, which collects, produces, reports and analyses accounting information on behalf of its (internal) customer departments. The functional structure may be suitable for smaller organisations with a narrow geographic spread and a limited product/service range, but it is not generally suitable for larger organisations.

The divisional structure is based on a head office with corporate specialists supporting the chief executive, with divisions established for major elements of the business. These divisions may be based on geographic territories or different products/services and each division will typically have responsibility for all the functional areas: marketing, operations, human resources and accounting.

The advantage of the divisional structure is that while planning is centrally coordinated, the implementation of plans, decision-making and control is devolved to local management who should have a better understanding of their local operations. The divisions are often referred to as strategic business units (SBUs) to describe their devolved responsibility for a segment of the business. These SBUs are, in accounting, termed responsibility centres. Responsibility centres, through their managers, are held responsible for achieving certain standards of performance. There are three types of responsibility centres:

- cost centres, which are responsible for controlling costs;
- profit centres, which are responsible for achieving profit targets; and
- investment centres, which are responsible for achieving an adequate return on the capital invested in the division.

Management within divisions will carry out a significant function in analyzing and interpreting financial information as part of their local management responsibilities, typically supported by locally based accounting support staff. Accounting influences and is influenced by the structure adopted and the extent of managerial responsibility for business unit performance, which considers how the performance of business units and their managers can be evaluated.

Emmanuel et al. described organisational structure as: a potent form of control because, by arranging people in a hierarchy with defined patterns of authority and responsibility, a great deal of their behaviour can be influenced or even pre-determined.

Child defined organisation structure as 'the formal allocation of work roles and the administrative mechanisms to control and integrate work activities', emphasizing that structure depends on the decision-makers' evaluation of environmental impacts, the standard of required performance and the level of performance actually achieved. This stresses the role of decision-makers, defined as the 'power-holding group'.

Galbraith and Nathanson suggested that the choice of organisational form was the result of choices about five design variables: task, people, structure, reward systems and information and decision processes. These choices should be consistent with the firm's product-market strategy, i.e. there should be 'fit' or 'congruence'. Galbraith and Nathanson applied Chandler's four growth strategies – expansion of volume, geographic dispersion, vertical integration and product diversification – to see how each affects the form of organisational structure, based on Chandler's thesis that structure follows strategy. They argued: Variation in strategy should be matched with variation in processes and systems as well as in structure, in order for organisations to implement strategies successfully.

Galbraith and Nathanson further built on Chandler's research, adding that diversification leads to multidivisional forms, with competition as an important variable.

A Critical Perspective

The shareholder value movement has subsumed much consideration of the wider accountability of business to other stakeholders. Shareholders' interests dominate business and accountants occupy a privileged position as those who establish the rules and report business performance. This can be seen as a historical development.

Stakeholder theory looks beyond shareholders to those groups who influence, or are influenced by, the organisation. Shareholders are not representative of society and stakes are held in the organisation by employees, customers, suppliers, government and the community. Stakeholder theory is concerned with how the power of stakeholders, with their competing interests, is managed by the organisation in terms of its broader accountability. Dermer suggested a broader view of organisations with interdependent but conflicting stakeholders, arguing: Cognitive and/or political models view organisations as non-goal-oriented, non-instrumental social systems, enmeshed in broader socio-political contexts.

Dermer contrasted the presumption of managerial authority and unitary purpose with a pluralistic governance model comprising four elements: leadership (management); citizenship (stakeholders); institutions (formal and informal patterns of relating); and ideologies (patterns of belief).

Given that accountability is the duty to provide an explanation – an account – of the actions for which an organisation is responsible, this implies a social accounting and a right to information by various stakeholder groups in a democracy. Strategy is also open to criticism. Mintzberg was critical of strategic planning because it is a 'calculating style of management' resulting in strategies that are extrapolated from the past or copied from others. Rather, Mintzberg saw some strategy as deliberate but other strategy as an emergent process, which should lead to learning. He argued:

Strategic planning often spoils strategic thinking, causing managers to confuse real vision with the manipulation of numbers. A critical stance can also be applied to the divisionalized form of organisation. Roberts and Scapens argued that in a divisionalized company there is distance between the division and the head office, such that 'the context within which accounting information is gathered will typically be quite different from the context in which it is interpreted'. This may result in manipulating the appearance of accounting reports. Roberts and Scapens concluded: The image of an organisation which is given through Accounts will be from a particular point of view, at a particular point in time and will be selective in its focus. Events, actions, etc. which are significant for the organisation may be out of focus, or not in the picture at all... the image conveyed by the Accounts may misrepresent the actual flow of events and practices that it is intended to record.

The separation of management from control, the creation of decentralized business units and the pursuit of shareholder value imply a particular goal-oriented, economic and rational theory of management behaviour and organisational action.

11

Stocks and Stock Investing

What Are the Components of the Stock Market?

To a lot of people, the Dow is the stock market. However, the Dow, which is the nickname for the Dow Jones *Industrial* Average, is just one component among many.

There is also the Dow Jones *Transportation* Average and the Dow Jones *Utilities* Average. The stocks that make up these averages are traded on the world's exchanges, two of which include the New York Stock Exchange and the NASDAQ.

What Are Mutual Funds?

Mutual funds give you the ability to buy a lot of stocks at once. In a way this makes them an easier tool to invest in than individual stocks. By reducing stock market volatility, they have also had a calming effect on the U.S. economy. Despite their benefits, you still need to learn how to select a good mutual fund.

What is the Bond Market?

Generally, when stocks go up, bonds go down. However, there are many different types of bonds, including Treasury Bonds, corporate bonds, and municipal bonds. Bonds also provide some of the liquidity that helps keep the U.S. economy lubricated. Their most important effect is on mortgage interest rates.

What are Commodities?

The most important commodity to the U.S. economy is oil, and its price is determined in the commodities futures market. What are futures? They are a way to pay for something today that is delivered tomorrow, which helps to remove some of the volatility in the U.S. economy. However, futures also increase the trader's leverage by allowing him to borrow the money to purchase the commodity. This can have a huge impact on the stock market, and the U.S. economy, if the trader guesses wrong.

What are Hedge Funds?

Recently, hedge funds have increased in popularity due to their supposed higher returns for high-end investors. Since hedge funds invest heavily in futures, some have argued they have decreased the volatility of the stock market and therefore the U.S. economy. However, in 1997 the world's largest hedge fund at the time, Long Term Capital Management, practically brought down the U.S. economy.

Indian Financial System and Capital Market

Overview of Indian Financial System

The Indian financial system comprises a set of financial institutions, financial markets and financial infrastructure. The financial institutions mainly consist of commercial and cooperative banks, regional rural banks (RRBs), all-India financial institutions (AIFIs) and non-banking financial companies (NBFCs). The banking sector which forms the bedrock of the Indian financial system, falls under the regulatory ambit of the Reserve Bank of India under the provisions of the Banking Regulation Act, 1949 and the Reserve Bank of India Act, 1934. The Reserve Bank also regulates select AIFIs. Consequent upon amendments to the Reserve Bank of India (Amendment) Act in 1997, a comprehensive regulatory framework in respect of NBFCs was put in place in January 1997.

The financial market in India comprises the money market, the Government securities market, the foreign exchange market and the capital market. A holistic approach has been adopted in India towards designing and development of a modern, robust, efficient, secure and integrated payment and settlement system. The Reserve Bank set up the Institute for Development and Research in Banking Technology (IDRBT) in 1996, which is an autonomous centre for technology capacity building for banks and providing core IT services.

Financial Institutions

Scheduled commercial banks (SCBs) occupy a predominant position in the financial system accounting for around three fourths of the total assets in the financial system. While the public sector banks (PSBs), consisting of eight banks in the State Bank group and 19 nationalised banks, constitute almost three fourths of the total assets of SCBs, the private sector banks, 30 in number, constitute less than one-fifth of the total assets. The 33 foreign banks operating in India account for about 6-7 per cent of the assets of SCBs. The 196 RRBs play a critical role in extending credit to the poorer sections of the rural society. The ownership of RRBs jointly vests with the Central Government, the State Governments and the sponsor banks. The cooperative banking system, with two broad segments of urban and rural cooperatives, forms an integral part of the Indian financial system. While the urban cooperative banking system has a single tier comprising the Primary Cooperative Banks (commonly known as [1]urban cooperative banks – UCBs), the rural cooperative credit system is divided into long-term and short-term cooperative credit institutions which have a multi-tier structure.

The term-lending institutions are mostly Government-owned and have been the traditional providers of long-term project loans. Non-Banking Financial Companies (NBFCs) encompass an extremely heterogeneous group of intermediaries and provide a gamut of financial services. Primary Dealers (PDs) in the Government securities market constitutes a systemically important segment of the NBFCs. At present, there are a total of 17 PDs playing active role in the Government securities market. A majority of them are promoted by banks.

Apart from this, India has a well-established and vibrant insurance sector within the financial system. The Insurance Regulatory and Development Agency (IRDA) has been established to regulate and supervise the insurance sector.

Pre-reforms Phase

Until the early 1990s, the role of the financial system in India was primarily restricted to the function of channelling resources from the surplus to deficit sectors. Whereas the financial system performed this role reasonably well, its operations came to be marked by some serious deficiencies over the years.

The banking sector suffered from lack of competition, low capital base, low productivity and high intermediation cost. After the nationalisation of large banks in 1969 and 1980, the Government-owned banks dominated the banking sector. The role of technology was minimal and the quality of service was not given adequate importance. Banks also did not follow proper risk management systems and the prudential standards were weak. All these resulted in poor asset quality and low profitability. Among non-banking financial intermediaries, development finance institutions (DFIs) operated in an overprotected environment with most of the funding coming from assured sources at concessional terms. In the insurance sector, there was little competition. The mutual fund industry also suffered from lack of competition and was dominated for long by one institution, viz., the Unit Trust of India. Non-banking financial companies (NBFCs) grew rapidly, but there was no regulation of their asset side.

Financial markets were characterised by control over pricing of financial assets, barriers to entry, high transaction costs and restrictions on movement of funds/participants between the market segments. This apart from inhibiting the development of the markets also affected their efficiency.

Financial Sector Reforms in India

It was in this backdrop that wide-ranging financial sector reforms in India were introduced as an integral part of the economic reforms initiated in the early 1990s with a view to improving the macroeconomic performance of the economy. The reforms in the financial sector focussed on creating efficient and stable financial institutions and markets. The approach to financial sector reforms in India was one of gradual and non-disruptive progress through a consultative process. The Reserve Bank has been consistently working towards setting an enabling regulatory framework with prompt and effective supervision, development of technological and institutional infrastructure, as well as changing the interface with the market participants through a consultative process. Persistent efforts have been made towards adoption of international benchmarks as appropriate to Indian conditions. While certain changes in the legal infrastructure are yet to be effected, the developments so far have brought the Indian financial system closer to global standards.

The reform of the interest regime constitutes an integral part of the financial sector reform. With the onset of financial sector reforms, the interest rate regime has been largely deregulated with a view towards better price discovery and efficient resource allocation. Initially, steps were taken to develop the domestic money market and freeing of the money market rates. The interest rates offered on Government securities were progressively raised so that the Government borrowing could be carried out at market-related rates. In respect of banks, a major effort was undertaken to simplify the administered structure of interest rates. Banks now have sufficient flexibility to decide their deposit and lending rate structures and manage their assets and liabilities accordingly. At present, apart from savings account and NRE deposit on the deposit side and export credit and small loans on the lending side, all other interest rates are deregulated.

Indian banking system operated for a long time with high reserve requirements both in the form of Cash Reserve Ratio (CRR) and Statutory Liquidity Ratio (SLR). This was a consequence of the high fiscal deficit and a high degree of monetisation of fiscal deficit. The efforts in the recent period have been to lower both the CRR and SLR. The statutory minimum of 25 per cent for SLR has already been reached, and while the Reserve Bank continues to pursue its medium-term objective of reducing the CRR to the statutory minimum level of 3.0 per cent, the CRR of SCBs is currently placed at 5.0 per cent of NDTL.

As part of the reforms programme, due attention has been given to diversification of ownership leading to greater market accountability and improved efficiency. Initially, there was infusion of capital by the Government in public sector banks, which was followed by expanding the capital base with equity participation by the private investors.

This was followed by a reduction in the Government shareholding in public sector banks to 51 per cent. Consequently, the share of the public sector banks in the aggregate assets of the banking sector has come down from 90 per cent in 1991 to around 75 per cent in 2004. With a view to enhancing efficiency and productivity through competition, guidelines were laid down for establishment of new banks in the private sector and the foreign banks have been allowed more liberal entry. Since 1993, twelve new private sector banks have been set up. As a major step towards enhancing competition in the banking sector, foreign direct investment in the private sector banks is now allowed up to 74 per cent, subject to conformity with the guidelines issued from time to time.

As a part of the financial sector reforms, the regulatory framework and supervisory practices have almost converged with the best practices elsewhere in the world. The minimum capital to risk assets ratio (CRAR) has been kept at nine per cent which is one percentage point above the international norm; and additionally, banks are required to maintain a separate Investment Fluctuation Reserve (IFR) out of profits, towards interest rate risk. Impressive institutional and legal reforms have been undertaken in relation to the banking sector. There have been a number of measures for enhancing the transparency and disclosures standards. The regulatory framework in India, in addition to prescribing prudential guidelines and encouraging market discipline, is increasingly focusing on ensuring good governance through "fit and proper" owners, directors and senior managers of the banks. Transfer of shareholding of five per cent and above requires acknowledgement from the Reserve Bank and such significant shareholders are put through a 'fit and proper' test. Banks have also been asked to ensure that the nominated and elected directors are screened by a nomination committee to satisfy 'fit and proper' criteria. Directors are also required to sign a covenant indicating their roles and responsibilities. The Reserve Bank has recently issued detailed guidelines on ownership and governance in private sector banks emphasizing diversified ownership.

In 1994, a Board for Financial Supervision (BFS) was constituted comprising select members of the Reserve Bank Board with a variety of professional expertise to exercise 'undivided attention to supervision' and ensure an integrated approach to supervision of commercial banks, development finance institutions, non-banking finance companies, urban cooperatives banks and primary dealers. Certain amendments are being considered by the Parliament to enhance Reserve Bank's regulatory and supervisory powers.

Over the last few years, the several policy initiatives undertaken in the form of recapitalisation of the weak RRBs, deregulation of deposits and lending rates and relaxation to lend to nontarget groups, have improved their operational efficiency, governance and regulation and brought them almost at par with the rural branches of commercial banks.

The cooperative banks besides suffering from the problem of multiple supervisory authorities, also face the challenge of reconciling the democratic character with financial discipline and modernising systems and procedures. The Task Force on Cooperatives constituted by the Government (December 2004) has made several suggestions for the revival of the sector to be implemented in consultation with the State Governments. The Reserve Bank has adopted a cautious approach regarding granting licenses for new banks and branches of urban cooperative banks (UCBs), while focusing on consolidation within the sector through mergers and amalgamations. In addition, initiatives have been undertaken to gradually tighten the prudential norms for regulation and supervision of UCBs. As a prelude to revamping the sector, a vision document for UCBs has been released by the Reserve Bank, highlighting the importance of a differentiated regulatory regime for the sector.

The ongoing restructuring of AIFIs is evident in the recent conversion of Industrial Credit and Investment Corporation of India (ICICI) and Industrial Development Bank of India (IDBI) into banks. The Board of Directors of Industrial Finance Corporation of India (IFCI) Ltd. have approved, in principle, the merger with a bank.

In view of the deteriorating financial position of Industrial Investment Bank of India (IIBI) Ltd., the Government has undertaken a programme of restructuring its liabilities. Apart from Infrastructure Development Finance Company Ltd. (IDFC), there are three refinancing institutions *viz.*, National Bank of Agriculture and Rural Development (NABARD), Small Industries Development Bank of India (SIDBI) and National Housing Bank (NHB), and EXIM Bank. At the State level, the State Financial Corporations registered under the State Financial Corporations Act, 1951 and the State Industrial Development Corporations (SIDCs)-purvey credit to industries/sectors in different States. On balance, the development financial institution (DFI) model has become increasingly unsustainable and AIFIs are fast adopting the business model of a bank for long-term commercial viability.

Non-Banking Financial Companies (NBFCs) encompass an extremely heterogeneous group of intermediaries. The main area of concern has been the substantial growth in deposits of the Residuary Non-Banking Companies (RNBCs), with just two companies accounting for more than 80 per cent of the total deposits held by NBFCs. The Indian banking sector is gradually heading towards consolidation of core competencies of different financial intermediaries, which would engender greater economic efficiency in the form of lower transaction cost, and greater product sophistication.

Financial System: Current Status

There has been a notable reduction in the ratio of non-performing assets (NPAs) to advances in response to various initiatives, such as, improved risk management practices and greater recovery efforts driven, *inter alia,* by the recently enacted Securitisation and Reconstruction of Financial Assets and Enforcement of Security Interest (SARFAESI) Act, 2002. The financial performance of most of the PSBs has improved in recent times as reflected in their comfortable capital adequacy ratios and declining NPL ratios. The CRAR in respect of all categories of banks has improved. New private sector banks have displayed impressive performance particularly in terms of efficiency and customer service.

Financial Markets

A major objective of reforms in the financial sector was to develop various segments of the financial market as also eliminate segmentation across various markets in order to smoothen the process of transmission of impulses across markets, easing the liquidity management process and making resource allocation process more efficient across the economy. The strategy adopted for meeting these objectives involved removal of restrictions on pricing of assets, building the institutional structure and technological infrastructure, introduction of new instruments, and fine-tuning of the market microstructure.

The 1990s saw the significant development of various segments of the financial market. At the short end of the spectrum, the money market saw the emergence of a number of new instruments such as CP and CDs and derivative products including FRAs and IRS. Repo operations, which were introduced in the early 1990s and later refined into a Liquidity Adjustment Facility, allow the Reserve Bank to modulate liquidity and transmit interest rate signals to the market on a daily basis. The process of financial market development was buttressed by the evolution of an active government securities market after the Government borrowing programme was put through the auction process in 1992-93. The development of a market for Government paper enabled the Reserve Bank to modulate the monetisation of the fiscal deficit. The foreign exchange market deepened with the opening up of the economy and the institution of a market-based exchange rate regime in the early 1990s. Although there were occasional episodes of volatility in the foreign exchange market, these were swiftly controlled by appropriate policy measures. The capital market also underwent some metamorphic changes during the 1990s. The development of the financial markets was well supported by deregulation of balance sheet restrictions in respect of financial institutions, allowing them to operate across markets. This resulted in increased integration among the various segments of the financial markets.

Overview of Indian Capital Market

The Indian capital market is more than a century old. Its history goes back to 1875, when 22 brokers formed the Bombay Stock Exchange (BSE). Over the period, the Indian securities market has evolved continuously to become one of the most dynamic, modern, and efficient securities markets in Asia. Today, Indian market confirms to best international practices and standards both in terms of structure and in terms of operating efficiency.

Indian securities markets are mainly governed by

a) The Company's Act 1956,

b) the Securities Contracts (Regulation) Act 1956 (SCRA Act), and

c) the Securities and Exchange Board of India (SEBI) Act, 1992.

A brief background of these above regulations are given below:

a) The Companies Act 1956 deals with issue, allotment and transfer of securities and various aspects relating to company management. It provides norms for disclosures in the public issues, regulations for underwriting, and the issues pertaining to use of premium and discount on various issues.

b) SCRA provides regulations for direct and indirect control of stock exchanges with an aim to prevent undesirable transactions in securities. It provides regulatory jurisdiction to Central Government over stock exchanges, contracts in securities and listing of securities on stock exchanges.

c) The SEBI Act empowers SEBI to protect the interest of investors in the securities market, to promote the development of securities market and to regulate the security market.

The Indian securities market consists of primary (new issues) as well as secondary (stock) market in both equity and debt. The primary market provides the channel for sale of new securities, while the secondary market deals in trading of securities previously issued. The issuers of securities issue (create and sell) new securities in the primary market to raise funds for investment. They do so either through public issues or private placement. There are two major types of issuers who issue securities. The corporate entities issue mainly debt and equity instruments (shares, debentures, etc.), while the governments (central and state governments) issue debt securities (dated securities, treasury bills). The secondary market enables participants who hold securities to adjust their holdings in response to changes in their assessment of risk and return. A variant of secondary market is the forward market, where securities are traded for future delivery and payment in the form of futures and options. The futures and options can be on individual stocks or basket of stocks like index. Two exchanges, namely National Stock Exchange (NSE) and the Stock Exchange, Mumbai (BSE) provide trading of derivatives in single stock futures, index futures, single stock options and index options. Derivatives trading commenced in India in June 2000.

Major Reforms in the Indian Capital Market

The major reforms in the Indian capital market since the 1990s are presented below:

- As a first step to reform the capital market, the Securities and Exchange Board of India (SEBI), which was earlier set up in April 1988 as a nonstatutory body under an administrative arrangement, was given statutory powers in January 1992 through an enactment of the SEBI Act, 1992 for regulating the securities markets. Twin objectives mandated in the SEBI Act are investor protection and orderly development of the capital market.
- The most significant development in the primary capital market has been the introduction of free pricing. The issuers of securities are now allowed to raise the capital from the market without requiring any consent from any authority either for making the issue or for pricing it. However, the issue of capital has been brought under SEBI's purview in that issuers are required to meet the SEBI guidelines for Disclosure and Investor Protection, which, in general, cover the eligibility norms for making issues of capital (both public and rights) at par and at a premium by various types of companies, reservation in issues, *etc.*
- The abolition of capital issues control and the freeing of the pricing of issues led to unprecedented upsurge of activity in the primary capital market as the corporates mobilised huge resources. It, *inter alia*, exposed certain inadequacies of the regulations. Therefore, without seeking to control the freedom of the issuers to enter the market and freely price their issues, the SEBI further strengthened the norms for public issues in April 1996. Alongside, SEBI raised the standards of disclosure in public issues to enhance their transparency for improving the levels of investor protection. Issuers of capital are now required to disclose information on various aspects, such as, track record of profitability, risk factors, *etc.* Issuers now also have the option of raising resources through fixed price floatations or the book building process.
- Trading infrastructure in the stock exchanges has been modernised by replacing the open outcry system with on-line screen based electronic trading, unlike several of the developed

countries where the two systems still continue to exist on the same exchange. In all, 23 stock exchanges in India have approximately 8,000 trading terminals spread all over the country. This improved the liquidity of the Indian capital market and a better price discovery.

- The trading and settlement cycles were initially shortened from 14 days to 7 days. Subsequently, to further enhance the efficiency of the secondary market, rolling settlement was introduced on a T+5 basis. With effect from April 1, 2002, the settlement cycle was further shortened to T+3 for all listed securities. The settlement cycle is now T+2.
- All stock exchanges in the country have established clearing houses. Consequently, all transactions are settled through the clearing house only and not directly between members, as was practiced earlier.
- Several measures have been undertaken/strengthened to ensure the safety and integrity of the market. These are: margining system, intra-day trading limit, exposure limit and setting up of trade/settlement guarantee fund.
- Securities, which were earlier held in physical form, have been demateralised and their transfer is done through electronic book entry, which has eliminated some of the disadvantages of securities held in physical form. There are two depositories operating in the country.
- In India, all listed companies are now required to furnish to the stock exchanges and also publish unaudited financial results on a quarterly basis. To enhance the level of continuous disclosure by the listed companies, the SEBI decided to amend the Listing Agreement to incorporate the Segment Reporting, Accounting for Taxes on Income, Consolidated Financial Results, Consolidated Financial Statements, Related Party Disclosures and Compliance with Accounting Standards.
- The Indian capital market is also increasingly integrating with the international capital markets. One of the significant steps towards integrating Indian capital market with the international capital markets was the permission given to Foreign Institutional Investors (FIIs) such as, mutual funds, pension funds and country funds to operate in the Indian

markets. Indian firms have also been allowed to operate in the Indian markets. Indian firms have also been allowed to raise capital from international capital markets through issues of Global Depository Receipts (GDRs), American Depository Receipts (ADRs), Euro Convertible Bonds (ECBs), *etc.*

- Boards of various stock exchanges, which in the past included mainly brokers, have been broad-based in order to make them more widely representative so that they represent different interests and not just the interests of their members. Reconstituted Governing Boards have now broker and non-broker representation in the ratio of 50-50 apart from the Executive Director who has a seat on the Board and is required to be a non-broker professional. To remove the influence of brokers in the functioning of stock exchanges, the SEBI decided that no broker member of the stock exchange shall be an office bearer of an exchange or hold the position of President, Vice President, Treasurer, *etc.* Efforts are afoot to demutualise and corporatise the stock exchanges.
- Apart from stock exchanges, various intermediaries, such as mutual funds, stock brokers and sub-brokers merchant bankers, portfolio managers, registrars to an issue and share transfer agents, underwriters, debenture trustees, bankers to an issue, custodian of securities, venture capital funds and issuers have been brought under the SEBI's regulatory purview.
- There are now regulations in place governing substantial acquisition of shares and takeovers of companies. The Regulations are aimed at making the takeover process more transparent and to protect the interests of minority shareholders.
- Trading in derivative products, such as stock index future, stock index options and futures and options in individual stocks have also been introduced.

Foreign Institutional Investment in India

The liberalisation and consequent reform measures have drawn the attention of foreign investors leading to a rise in portfolio investment in the Indian capital market. Over the recent years, India has emerged as a major recipient of portfolio investment among the emerging market economies. Apart from such large inflows, reflecting the confidence of cross-border investors on the prospects of Indian securities market, except for one year, India received positive portfolio inflows in each year. The stability of portfolio flows towards India is in contrast with large volatility of portfolio flows in most emerging market economies.

The Indian capital market was opened up for foreign institutional investors (FIIs) in 1992. The FIIs started investing in Indian markets in January 1993. The Indian corporate sector has been allowed to tap international capital markets through American Depository Receipts (ADRs), Global Depository Receipts (GDRs), Foreign Currency Convertible Bonds (FCCBs) and External Commercial Borrowings (ECBs).

Similarly, non-resident Indians (NRIs) have been allowed to invest in Indian companies. FIIs have been permitted in all types of securities including Government securities and they enjoy full capital convertibility. Mutual funds have been allowed to open offshore funds to invest in equities abroad.

FII investment in India started in 1993, as FIIs were allowed to invest in the Indian debt and equity market in line with the recommendations of the High Level Committee on Balance of Payments. These investment inflows have since then been positive, with the exception of 1998-99, when capital flows to emerging market economies were affected by contagion from the East Asian crisis. These investments account for over 10 per cent of the total market capitalisation of the Indian stock market.

Limits on Foreign Institutional Investors

- Each FII (investing on its own) or sub-account cannot hold more than 10 per cent of the paid-up capital of a company. A sub-account under the foreign corporate/individual category cannot hold more than 5 per cent of the paid up capital of the company.
- The maximum permissible investment in the shares of a company, jointly by all FIIs together is 24 per cent of the paid-up capital of that company.

  The limit is 20 per cent of the paid-up capital in the case of public sector banks. The ceiling of 24 per cent for FII investment can be raised up to sectoral cap/statutory ceiling, subject to the approval of the board and the general body of the company passing a special resolution to that effect.

- A cap of US $1.75 billion is applicable to FII investment in dated Government securities and treasury bills under 100 per cent and the 70:30 route. Within this ceiling of US $1.75 billion, a sub-ceiling of US $200 million is applicable for the 70:30 route. (FIIs are required to allocate their investment between equity and debt instruments in the ratio of 70:30. However, it is also possible for an FII to declare itself a 100 per cent debt FII in which case it can make its entire investment in debt instruments.)
- A cumulative sub-ceiling of US $500 million outstanding has been fixed on FII investments in corporate debt and this is over and above the subceiling of US $1.75 billion for Government debt.

Growth of Indian Capital Market

The Indian equity market has developed tremendously since the 1990s. The market has grown exponentially in terms of resource mobilisation, number of listed stocks, market capitalisation, trading volumes, turnover and investors' base. Along with this growth, the profiles of the investors, issuers and intermediaries have changed significantly. The market has witnessed a fundamental institutional change resulting in drastic reduction in transaction costs and significant improvement in efficiency, transparency and safety. In the 1990s, reform measures initiated by the SEBI such as, market determined allocation of resources, rolling settlement, sophisticated risk management and derivatives trading have greatly improved the framework and efficiency of trading and settlement. Almost all equity settlements take place at two depositories. As a result, the Indian capital market has become qualitatively comparable to many developed markets. There are 23 stock exchanges in the country with 9413 listed companies as at end-December 2004. The market capitalization of BSE has grown over the period and is estimated at Rs.16,860 billion as at end-December 2004.

Latest Trends in Indian Stock Markets

Indian stock markets are currently trading at all-time high levels. The BSE Sensex (a BSE index comprising 30 large-cap companies with Base: 1978-79=100) closed at all-time high level of 7859.53 on August 17, 2005. On a point-to-point basis, the BSE Sensex has gained 21.05 per cent during the current financial year so far (up to August 17, 2005). The rally has been supported by strong investment by the

FIIs, satisfactory progress of monsoon, firm trends in the international markets and satisfactory financial results by the corporates for Q1 2005-06.

The market capitalization of BSE increased by 24.3 per cent to Rs.21,112 billion (60.7 per cent of GDP) as on August 17, 2005 over the level of March 31, 2005. The market capitalization as a percentage of GDP has increased from 43.5 per cent as at end-March 2004 to 54.6 per cent as at end-March 2005 due mainly to increase in the stock prices as well as listing of new securities. Despite unprecedented price levels, the price-earning ratio for Indian equities has remained attractive due to strong growth in corporate earnings. The P/E ratio of BSE Sensex, however, is marginally higher than that in the other emerging market economies, even though the ratio is much lower than that witnessed in earlier stock market rallies in India.

The gains in the stock markets in the financial year so far have been widespread among blue-chips as well as small and mid-cap stocks. The Indian stock markets have outperformed the other markets. On pointto-point basis, the BSE Sensex witnessed an increase of 21.05 per cent during current financial year so far (up to August 17, 2005) over end-March 2005, as compared with Hong Kong (14.3 per cent), Japan (5.2 per cent), UK (8.1 per cent), US (Dow Jones – 0.4 per cent), South Korea (15.3 per cent), Taiwan (3.9 per cent), Indonesia (3.1 per cent), and Malaysia (6.3 per cent).

Payment and Settlement System

In recent years, the endeavour of the Reserve Bank has been to improve the efficiency of the financial system by ensuring safe, secure and effective payment and settlement system. In the process, the Reserve Bank apart from performing the regulatory and oversight functions has also played an important role in promoting its functionality and modernisation on an on-going basis. The consolidation of the existing payment systems revolves around strengthening computerised cheque clearing, expanding the reach of Electronic Clearing Services (ECS) and Electronic Funds Transfer (EFT). The critical elements of the developmental strategy are opening of new clearing houses, interconnection of clearing houses through the Indian Financial Network (INFINET); development of Real Time Gross Settlement (RTGS) System, Centralised Funds Management System (CFMS), Negotiated Dealing System (NDS) and the Structured Financial Messaging System (SFMS). Similarly, integration of the various payment products with the systems of individual banks has been another thrust area. A Board for Regulation and Supervision of Payment and Settlement Systems (BPSS) has also been recently constituted to prescribe policies relating to the regulation and supervision of all types of payment and settlement systems, set standards for existing and future systems, authorise the payment and settlement systems and determine criteria for membership to these systems.

The Indian Financial Sector: Some Issues

The Indian financial system has undergone structural transformation over the past decade. The financial sector has acquired strength, efficiency and stability by the combined effect of competition, regulatory measures, and policy environment. While competition, consolidation and convergence have been recognised as the key drivers of the banking sector in the coming years, consolidation of the domestic banking system in both public and private sectors is being combined with gradual enhancement of the presence of foreign banks in a calibrated manner.

There has been improvement in banks' capital position and asset quality as reflected in the overall increase in their capital adequacy ratio and declining NPLs, respectively. Significant improvement in various parameters of efficiency, especially intermediation costs, suggest that competition in the banking industry has intensified. The efficiency of various segments of the financial system also increased.

The major challenges facing the banking sector are the judicious deployment of funds and the management of revenues and costs. Concurrently, the issues of corporate governance and appropriate disclosures for enhancing market discipline have received increased attention for ensuring transparency and greater accountability. Financial sector supervision is increasingly becoming risk based with the emphasis on quality of risk management and adequacy of risk containment.

Consolidation, competition and risk management are no doubt critical to the future of Indian banking, but governance and financial inclusion have also emerged as the key issues for the Indian financial system. The capital market in India has become efficient and modern over the years. It has also become much safer. However, some of the issues would need to be addressed. Corporate governance needs to be strengthened. Retail investors continue to remain away from the market. The private corporate debt market continues to lag behind the equity segment.

Role of Financial Institutions in India

The Financial Institutions in India mainly comprises of the Central Bank which is better known as the Reserve Bank of India, the commercial banks, the credit rating agencies, the securities and exchange board of India, insurance companies and the specialized financial institutions in India.

Reserve Bank of India

The Reserve Bank of India was established in the year 1935 with a view to organize the financial frame work and facilitate fiscal stability in India. The bank acts as the regulatory authority with regard to the functioning of the various commercial bank and the other financial institutions in India. The bank formulates different rates and policies for the overall improvement of the banking sector. It issue currency notes and offers aids to the central and institutions governments.

Commercial Banks in India

The commercial banks in India are categorized into foreign banks, private banks and the public sector banks. The commercial banks indulge in varied activities such as acceptance of deposits, acting as trustees, offering loans for the different purposes and are even allowed to collect taxes on behalf of the institutions and central government.

Credit Rating Agencies in India

The credit rating agencies in India were mainly formed to assess the condition of the financial sector and to find out avenues for more improvement. The credit rating agencies offer various services as:

- Operation Up gradation
- Training to Employees
- Scrutinize New Projects and find out the weak sections in it
- Rate different sectors.

The two most important credit rating agencies in India are:

- CRISIL
- ICRA.

Securities and Exchange Board of India

The securities and exchange board of India, also referred to as SEBI was founded in the year 1992 in order to protect the interests of the investors and to facilitate the functioning of the market intermediaries. They supervise market conditions, register institutions and indulge in risk management.

Insurance Companies in India

The insurance companies offer protection against losses. They deal in life insurance, marine insurance, vehicle insurance and so on. The insurance companies collect the little saving of the investors and then reinvest those savings in the market. The insurance companies are collaborating with different foreign insurance companies after the liberalization process. This step has been incorporated to expand the Indian Insurance market and make it competitive.

Specialized Financial Institutions in India

The specialized financial institutions in India are government undertakings that were set up to provide assistance to the different sectors and thereby cause overall development of the Indian economy. The significant institutions falling under this category includes:

- Board for Industrial & Financial Reconstruction
- Export-Import Bank Of India
- Small Industries Development Bank of India
- National Housing Bank.

Financial Services in India

In last few years, India has emerged as the one of the most rapidly growing economies in the world. India has been categorized with nations like Brazil, Russia and China (BRIC Nations) who are going to be the prime drivers of world economy in next few decades. Since the time, India first opened its gates to foreign investment (FDI & FII), there has been a complete turnaround. Now the traditional Hindu rate of growth is a thing of past and clocking 8%-9% GDP growth rate is the common norm. India along with other Asian powerhouse China makes for the fastest growing nations in the entire world. Even if we take the case of ongoing global recession, India has managed to perform far better than other nations. Right from banking system to financial regularities, the country has thrived on discipline and out-performance. The booming Indian economy resulted in widespread growth and arrival of new industries. The most sparkling phenomenon is in form of financial market of India.

Financial services in India has taken a giant leap from the days of standing in banks queue for several hours for opening a saving account or trying to get some fixed deposits (FD) done. The financial services have increased manifold and now people have the choice to choose the one that most suitably fits the bill.

There are several services like broking firms, investment services, financial consulting, evergreen national banks, numerous private banks, mutual funds, car and home loans, equity market and other banking services. Services are many and offered by blue chip names of the industry. Most of the companies in financial segment offer taxation services, project consultancy services and all the services of wide financial gamut.

Whether it's taking a car loan or booking your favourite house, going for pension plan or getting your child insured, numerous attractive financial services are available at affordable costs. Personal banking services have acquired an altogether new meaning. Now customers have multiple choices to choose from. One can find all the financial services on the internet that are just a call away.

With market sentiment turning positive due to the formation of a stable newly elected government, the ripple effect is likely to be felt across all the financial services in India. The sectors, including banking and insurance, and mutual funds are all beginning to reap the benefits of a good closure for 2008-09. The Indian economy is estimated to have grown by 6.7 per cent in 2008-09. According to the latest Central Statistical Organisation (CSO) data, financial services and real estate sector rose by 9.5 per cent in the first quarter of 2009-10.

The government has taken a number of steps in recent months to revive the economy, including slashing interest rates, lowering factory levies and more than doubling the limit on foreign investment in corporate bonds. The financial services space is a rapidly growing one in India. The country received US$ 45 billion in foreign currency remittances from non-resident Indians in 2008, the highest in the world. Foreign institutional investors' (FIIs) net investments in Indian equities crossed US$ 8 billion in calendar year 2009.

The mutual fund industry has seen an 8.7 per cent increase in the asset base for the month of August 2009, against an increase of 2.8 per cent in July 2009, largely due to significant inflows into debt schemes.

The average assets under management of the mutual fund industry stood at US$ 153.89 billion as at end August 2009, according to the data released by Association of Mutual Funds in India (AMFI).

With the capital market showing signs of revival, banks and financial companies that had put their mutual fund plans on hold are gearing up to enter the segment.

At present, nine players from the financial services sector are in various stages of entering the space. The list includes Bank of India, IDBI Bank, Axis Bank, Mahindra and Mahindra Financial Services (M&M Finance), SREI Infrastructure Finance, Bajaj Allianz, Indiabulls Financial Services, L&T Finance and Motilal Oswal.

India has increased its exposure to American debt securities by over three-fold to US$ 38.2 billion till March 2009 as against US$ 11.8 billion in March 2008, according to the data from the US Treasury Department.

The country's foreign exchange reserves rose by US$ 1.28 billion to touch US$ 277.64 billion for the week ended September 4, 2009, according to the figures released in the Reserve Bank of India's Weekly Statistical Supplement.

The World Bank and India have concluded negotiations for loans worth US$ 3.2 billion for recapitalising state-run banks and funding for the India Infrastructure Finance Company Ltd.

12

The Administration of Public Funds

The Importance of Proper Fiscal Administration has been Underestimated

Previous chapters have indicated that, during the first stages of the development of fiscal systems, the question of revenue was of greatest concern.

Gradually, consideration has been directed to the use to which the funds were put, until fiscal students have become much concerned about public expenditures. A third important phase of public funds-their administration-has been recognized only recently as being of any particular consequence.

It is true that in the very early development of fiscal systems much attention was given to methods for handling revenues and expenditures.

As the pressure for funds became more pronounced, however, attention became concentrated on sources of revenue, while little was thought or said concerning the management of the public funds. It is only recently that the importance of this aspect has again begun to receive due consideration.

Various factors have caused modern fiscal students to emphasize the importance of the proper administration of public funds. Expenditures, in numerous political divisions, have become so large that the burden of the revenue charge is felt keenly. Many political units have reached the limit of indebtedness, as well as the maximum tax rate, while a scarcity of funds still exists. Under such conditions the question naturally arises whether the revenues and expenditures have been properly handled. The increased emphasis which has been placed recently upon proper methods of accounting in private business enterprises, has no doubt stimulated interest in the handling of public funds.

A modern business firm keeps in close touch with revenues and expenditures through its skilled accountants, and because of this demand the importance of the accounting profession has increased many times. Since this close management has proved so beneficial to private enterprise, many have seen the need for a similar policy in handling public funds. The continual increase in the number of charges of graft and misappropriation of funds on the part of fiscal officials has no doubt been an important factor in leading citizens to demand a stricter account of the services which these officials render. It is the purpose of this chapter to indicate some of the deficiencies in methods that have been used in handling public funds, and to suggest some improvements.

The Administration of Public Funds Should Harmonize with Other Institutions

When the amount of funds which fiscal officials handled was small, the method in which they were administered was of little concern to others than the officials. As the amount of funds began to increase with the gradual extension of government activity, it became quite possible that the method of handling the funds would be of interest to others than the officials into whose hands the funds were placed.

Adam Smith's axiom that taxes should be paid at a time when it was most convenient is worthy of consideration. In the supply of capital there are seasons of scarcity and seasons of plenty. It is indicative of poor judgment on the part of the fiscal officials, if the collection of revenue is so arranged that the time for its payment comes when the contributor is least able to meet it-that is, at the season when money is already scarce. If such an arrangement exists, it will mean a still greater strain upon bank reserves than what would nominally occur, with a corresponding raise in the discount rate. If, on the other hand, fiscal officials so arrange that substantial payments by the government are made at times when money is already plentiful, the difficulties of a cheap money are increased by such action. In the formulation of fiscal plans, moreover, the possible effects on individual industries have not always been given due consideration.

Many illustrations of these difficulties have occurred in the revenues and expenditures of various political units. One of the outstanding examples, however, has been in the fiscal machinery of the Federal government. In the establishment of the first and second United States banks consideration was given to their ability to aid individual enterprise. President Jackson went to the extreme in using the government funds for the aid of general industry when he distributed them among the banks of his choice.

The resulting speculation, followed by the panic of 1837, led to the adoption of the independent treasury system. The system was not put into actual operation until 1847, and has since remained in some form.

The Independent Treasury-The original intention of the plan of the independent treasury was to keep all the funds of the government in this treasury or the sub-treasuries for which provision was made. The chief difficulty with this arrangement was that large sums of capital, which might otherwise have been used as the basis for bank credit, or for productive enterprise, were held in the vaults of the government until they were needed to meet some obligation.

These payments were of course at irregular intervals, and frequently had a noticeable effect on the money market. After some years the Secretary of the Treasury was authorized to make deposits, under certain conditions, with national banks. Such deposits were made at the discretion of the Secretary, and the opinions of all Secretaries were not the same, nor could a definite policy of any particular one be relied upon.

The result has been an element of uncertainty in the banking system and in the money market. It could not be foreseen just what policy would be followed by the

Secretary of the Treasury-Banks did not know whether to anticipate deposits or withdrawals. There was no law which regulated these activities, and the practice was so diverse that no definite action could be anticipated.

As there has been no uniformity in the receipts and disbursements of the government from year to year, or from month to month, so there has always been more or less uncertainty as to how banks and other industries would be affected by these variations in the operation of the treasury.

The result has been a constant speculation among banks as to what the action of the Secretary of the Treasury would be. The Secretary has been in no way connected with the banks or other industries, yet has had control over a factor which vitally affected their welfare-a situation under which it has been impossible to expect satisfactory cooperation.

The independent treasury system still exists, but it has sunk into insignificance to such an extent since the adoption of the Federal Reserve Banking System that its influence is scarcely felt.

The Expenditure of Federal Funds is Carefully Scrutinized

In the establishment of the Treasury Department there was a diversity of opinion as to what form it should take. Many felt that it would be unwise to intrust the handling of the nation's finances to any particular individual, and contended that the funds should be handled by a commission. Many considered that it would be impossible to secure a man who would be honest enough to intrust with so much responsibility.

After much debate the Treasury Department was established under one head, the Secretary of the Treasury. Unlike other departments, this department is independent of the control of the President, but is closely allied to Congress. To obtain information on financial matters, Congress may inquire directly of the Treasury Department, without the consent of the President.

Organization of Treasury Department-The internal organization of the Treasury Department was carefully worked out, and was designed to be a system of checks. At times it has proved rather cumbersome. Besides the Secretary there was to be appointed an assistant Secretary, a comptroller, an auditor, a treasurer, and a register.

As the business of the department expanded it became necessary to increase the number of some of these officers, and to assign particular funds to their jurisdiction. It is the duty of the comptroller to scrutinize the correctness of the accounts, and to countersign warrants drawn by the Secretary of the Treasury.

The register must preserve vouchers and bills, while the treasurer sees that no funds are improperly paid. The auditor must see that the accounts are properly kept. In order to secure funds from the

United States Treasury, it is first necessary that an appropriation be made by Congress, and that the warrant be signed by the Secretary, countersigned by the comptroller, and recorded by the register.

Later Modifications-As the business of the treasury expanded, the number of auditors and comptrollers was increased, and a portion of the accounts was distributed to the different branches. To use all the checks, however, which were first intended, began to prove too complex and cumbersome. In 1894 Congress modified the system by abolishing all the comptrollers except one. Such detailed revisions of accounts as had formerly been practiced were also modified.

There now are six auditors, whose duties are divided in the following manner: the first auditor takes care of the accounts of the Treasury Department; the second auditor handles the accounts of the War Department; the third auditor handles the accounts of the Department of Interior; the fourth auditor reviews the Navy Department accounts; the fifth auditor is concerned chiefly with the accounts of the State Department; while the sixth auditor looks after the accounts of the Post Office Department.

Under the present arrangement the work of the auditors is not reviewed by the comptroller, unless he has reason to question it, or unless some claimant makes an appeal which necessitates a review.

The comptroller keeps a record of congressional appropriations, and on the basis of these appropriations opens a credit account with the various departments of the amount of funds at their disposal. Warrants, when properly indorsed, are debited to these accounts, and it is one of the duties of the comptroller to see that warrants are not drawn in excess of the appropriations.

Claims against the government which the Treasury Department refuses to recognize may be reviewed in the Court of Claims, or carried from here to the Supreme Court. Recourse may also be had, of course, in petitioning Congress against any decision of the Treasury Department.

There has been little question as to the integrity of the Treasury Department, while the system of checks, cumbersome and time-consuming as it often is, has served the purpose for which it was intended. The funds of the government are closely guarded, and warrants are paid only to those who are expected to receive funds. It has not been deemed necessary, as in a number of countries, to have the accounts of the department audited by a legislative committee. Such an experiment was tried by the House of Representatives in the early years of the department, but was not continued.

The fact that the department officials may be called upon at any time to make a report to Congress, or may be subject at any time to an investigation of their affairs, has seemed to maintain the efficiency and integrity of the department at a comparatively high level. An avenue is left open to fraud, however, which would be difficult to detect under the present arrangement.

Revenues and Expenditures Should be Closely Correlated

The fact that some close relation should exist between a government's expenditures and revenues seems too obvious to mention. Yet fiscal officials have often lost sight of this first principle of sound financiering.

Funds have often been voted in excess of ordinary revenues, and without knowledge as to where revenue could be obtained. Revenues, on the other hand, have frequently exceeded the anticipated expenditures-a situation which usually leads to the squandering of public funds. The most common arrangement for a proper coordination of expenditures and revenues has been through the use of some form of a budget system.

Meaning of Budget-The term "budget" has no fixed general meaning. Its origin is probably from the Latin, bulga, meaning bag or purse. In the middle of the eighteenth century, when the Chancellor of the Exchequer in England made his speech on the finances, he took his accounts from a brugette (French for bag).

Thereafter the term budget was applied to this speech. A little later it was used in France to denote an estimate of receipts and expenditures. In some cases it is practically synonymous with revenue and appropriation legislation.

A comprehensive budget system, however, should include more than this. It should be a definte plan to include all the fiscal operations of a government for a specified time. It may involve different features, one logically following the other.

A comprehensive budget system, for example, might comprise, as an initial measure, a careful estimate of expenditure and revenues by some competent authority.

These estimates should be given the sanction of the legislative body through their incorporation into appropriation and revenue bills. Provision should be made for the execution of the plan under legal direction, while checks should be provided through proper auditing and accounting methods.

The fiscal, systems of some countries possess some of these features and omit others, while the officers to which the administration is given in different countries are likewise not always the same. For this reason mere reference to a budget system is unintelligible.

The citizenship of a state has a right to demand the most capable management of public funds. Government expenditures necessarily mean public burdens. The more the funds are squandered, the greater are the burdens upon the citizens in proportion to the rendition of the services for which the state was formed-that is, the things which can be done more efficiently by a collective organization than by individuals.

The use of a budget-a systematic administration of revenues and expenditures such as that outlined above-should, therefore, be demanded by every citizen in order to make his government susceptible to intelligent popular control and responsibility, and so that each taxpayer may know where and why he is paying.

13

Accounting and Organisational Cultures

Organisations have long been known to have distinct cultural properties. They create and sustain particular work customs. They establish norms for proper and improper behaviour and performance. They propagate stories and myths and are replete with rituals. Communities in organisations have particular codes of communication: behaviour, language, dress, presentation, design, architecture, ceremony...

The operation of work technologies in organisations is not a purely technical-rational affair. Rather it is embedded in a cultural system of ideas (beliefs, knowledges) and sentiments (values), in which actions and artifacts are vested with symbolic qualities of meaning. The appreciation of organisational dynamics requires a sensitivity to local frames of significance and interpretation. Accounting practices are a common feature of most work organisations.

Planning and budgeting activities, systems of hierarchical accountability, performance appraisal procedures, budgetary controls and remuneration arrangements, all rely to a greater or lesser extent on accounting practices.

Inevitably, therefore, accounting is likely to be implicated in organisations' cultural systems. But how and in what way? Drawing on the insights of Meyer & Rowan, Pfeffer & Salancik, DiMaggio & Powell, Scott, Zucker and others, one theme in the literature appeals to accounting's potential significance in the context of wider societal values and beliefs. Put crudely, organisations depend on a flow of resources for survival; society has beliefs in the efficacy of "rational" management practices; organisations which adopt such practices are more likely to be rewarded. Thus, recent empirically grounded studies have cast accounting as a culturally expressive symbol of rationality, particularly oriented towards powerful external constituencies, moderating environmental control. In this view, following especially Meyer & Rowan's discussion, accounting is often seen to be neutral in its effects within the organisation.

It is kept at arm's length, symbolically construed as necessary but irrelevant and, as it were, not taken seriously. It is purposefully uncoupled from organisations' core technological activities. All knowledges and practices can be reflexive, however. Accounting can reflect back on those institutions which adopt it. Hopwood, Hines, Miller & O'Leary and others have argued for its constitutive role in the construction of organisational life.

Finely crafted notions of costliness, efficiency, profitability, earnings-per-share and so forth, actively construct particular definitions of reality which privilege the financial and economic sphere. Rather than being kept at arm's length, uncoupled from organisations' core technological activities, these can permeate into organisational settings, leading to the creation of particular agendas (in the sense of objectives and priorities and the means for their achievement), stylized definitions of success and failure, the characterization of heroic performance and the mobilization of particular dynamics of change.

This suggests the possibility of a more intimate involvement of accounting in organisational cultures. In fact, evidence in the field suggests that accounting practices are not uniformly implicated in organisational activities. In some organisations, accounting is centrally involved in work rituals: financial achievement is celebrated; budgets are massaged, pored over and matter.

In others, accounting is incidental, perhaps existing as a practice, but with no particular significance. Similarly, entrepreneurial risk taking is sometimes valued for its own sake. Dynamic, decisive, action-oriented men and women who innovate are heroes, almost irrespective of the financial consequences.

In other organisations, risk taking is valued only if successful in financial terms. Arguably, the multi-faceted interplay of accounting with organisations' cultural and technical systems is under-researched.More empirically grounded research is needed to ascertain the way in which accounting is drawn upon by actors within organisations in the creation and maintenance of cultures.

Responding, with others, to appeals for field studies and for the study of accounting in its organisational and social context this paper reports a longitudinal study undertaken in one organisation to research this issue. The organisation is a railway company. The study focuses on its senior management ´elite: a group of approximately 120 people including head office executives, senior line management and people in senior staff positions (i.e. finance and engineering). Prior to the study, the dominant culture within this management group was well established and centred on engineering and production concerns. Accounting was incidental in this culture: it was necessary in the technical-rational sense of ensuring that revenues were accounted for and suppliers were paid, but it was not incorporated into the culture among the senior management ´elite in any significant way. Rituals, symbols and language celebrated the primacy of the engineering and production orientation. During the course of the study, a new culture emerged.

The previously dominant orientation was displaced by a new preoccupation with economic and accounting concerns. New accounts were crafted. Gradually, through action and interaction, they were coupled to organisational activities to reconstitute interpretations of organisational endeavour. Accounting actively shaped the dominant meanings given to organisational life, ultimately obtaining a remarkable significance in the senior management culture. A new set of symbols, rituals and language emerged to celebrate an economic rationale for organised activity. A new culture can be a major source of power, particularly if it gains ascendancy to become dominant, for it effectively alters the legitimacy of accepted criteria for action.

Culture

In recent years, a prolific literature has emerged to offer a wide array of perceptual, symbolic and processual characterizations of organisation. As a result, we are now used to conceptualizing organisations as bodies of thought, variously described as myths, causal schema, theories-of-action, interpretive schemes, ideologies, paradigms and so forth. The concept of culture, drawn from anthropology and ethnography, has entered the organisational literature as a framework for extending this ideational understanding of organisations.

Culture is an elusive concept. Here, drawing on Geertz' interpretive anthropology, it is defined to be the broad constellation of interpretive structures through which action and events are rendered meaningful in a community. Balinese cockfights, a sheep raid in Morocco, funeral rites in Java – or nearer home, the graduation ceremony, the distinguished lecture series, the publication of papers in prestigious journals – all have singular meanings in their respective communities (as does all social action). Culture is the "ordered clusters of significance", the shared "webs of significance" through which people appreciate the meaningfulness of their experience and are guided to action. Culture, as an ideational system, is produced and reproduced through action and interaction. But it is not just lodged in people's minds. Culture is public, the product of minds, between minds. Culturally significant events give public expression to the ideational system.

The appreciation of organisations as cultures brings the interpretive, experiential aspects of their activities to the foreground of analysis, emphasizing their expressive qualities. Looking at the railway, for example, the train is not seen as cold technology; the concourse is not just glass and marble; "Mr General Manager" is not an anybody; cost allocations are not mere calculations: everything is expressive.

Local knowledge, beliefs and values vest them with symbolic qualities of meaning. The train may be vested with a sacred quality (or not, as the case may be) quite beyond its technical properties; beliefs about the skills required to operate a railway and appropriate forms of organising may endow the General Manager with special status and privilege (or not). Cultural analysis attempts to uncover these meanings and to trace the underlying thematic relationships.

The objective is interpretation and "thick description": the production of rich contextually laden accounts conveying the symbolic content of social action. Meaning systems may differ within organisations, of course.

The train, the framing of the routing problem as a cost allocation issue and so on are likely to be interpreted differently by different groups.

Within the overarching concept of an organisation as a culture, it is sensible to recognize the possibility and likelihood of distinct subcultures existing among managerial teams, occupational groups, members of different social classes and so on; manyofwhichmaytranscend organisational boundaries.

As a limiting case, these subcultures may be isomorphic; more commonly, they may only partially overlap. Also, some maybe dominant-cultures and others counter-cultures, perhaps partially uncoupled from each other, or co-existing in an "uneasy symbiosis", or in contest with each other for dominance.

Moreover, cultures in organisations are not independent of their social context. They are interpenetrated by wider systems of thought, interacting with other organisations and social institutions, both importing and exporting values, beliefs and knowledge. Accounting is likely to be differentially implicated in these subcultures in organisations.

Accounting systems and information systems more generally, inevitably offer highly stylized views of the world. Any representation is partial, an interpretation through a particular framing of reality, rendering some aspects of events important and others unimportant; counter-interpretations are possible.

Accounting systems embody particular assumptions about organisation, rationality, authority, time and so forth. These may be more or less consonant with local subcultures in organisations. For example, to senior managers in some organisations accounting may symbolize efficiency, calculative rationality, order and so forth: "the name of the game is profit".

This may motivate the development of sophisticated accounting systems measuring economic performance this way and that. To others (nearer the ground?), accounting may symbolize confusion or irrelevance: "no one understands the business"; "when all else fails they resort to the numbers".

Similarly, meanings may differ across occupational groups. Commercial managers may appreciate accounting rather differently to engineers, for example. It is useful to think of societal cultures as emergent, unfolding through time and similarly with organisational cultures. That is not to say that given cultures do not survive for long periods, or that changes may be proactively managed: organisational cultures probably have inertial tendencies perhaps sometimes not even incorporating changes in wider patterns of social thought.

Rather, the implication is that culture is not programmed or static. The processes of cultural change in organisations are poorly understood, however. Perhaps cultural change is a political process: subcultures competing with one another for legitimacy and dominance. Perhaps cultural change is akin to the diffusion of organisational forms, whole fields of organisations rapidly adopting knowledge innovations in leading firms. Perhaps in a Kuhnian sense, cultural change is precipitated by crisis: the adoption of new cultural knowledge only being possible when faith is undermined, for example by the failure of strategies for subsistence. Maybe new cultures are autonomously crafted in organisations; or perhaps they are already there, "lying around" in counter-cultures, waiting to be discovered by others; alternatively, cultures may be imported from the environment through new actors.

Clearly, there are multiple modes and possibilities for cultural change. However, the point of importance for this paper is the conceptualization of cultural change as the uncoupling of organisational action from one culture and its recoupling to another.

It is a process of fundamental reinterpretation of organisational activities. Things cease to be what they were and become what they were not: a new reality, if you will. In the railway, for example, the sacred train could turn into cold steel, or the priest-like general manager could become an anybody.

Moreover, this process of uncoupling and recoupling is unlikely to be sudden, but emergent: the gradual disintegration of one coupling and the crystallization of another. This crystallization may be around an idea not fully understood, a kind of ill-articulated new knowledge, perhaps imported from the environment. In the railway, this idea was a new accounting.

Research Method

Arm's length analysis is clearly inappropriate for cultural analysis of the kind described here. Instead, it calls for closer engagement in the research setting and "interpretive" methodology.

Necessarily, this precludes the imposition of exteriorized accounts and radical critique. In part, the goal is "to grasp the native's point of view, his relation to life, to realise his vision of his world"; in part it is to reflect on the processes through which that vision comes to be and is sustained. This kind of research is necessarily qualitative. Data consist of descriptions and accounts provided by participants in the research site, together with the researcher's observations on activities and interactions and the context in which they take place. Data must be collected over an extended period of time so that processes can be recorded.

The researcher, in general, does not seek to test a prior hypothesis. Rather, he or she seeks to theorize through the data in an inductive manner. Analysis of the data is itself an emergent process. The researcher seeks gradually to develop an empathy with the data, to understand what they tell of participants' realities and the process through which they unfold. The researcher must constantly construct alternative interpretations until he or she is satisfied that the representation is a faithful account. Interpretations must be grounded in context and consistent with the chronological ordering of events and interactions. Finally, research results must be presented in such a way that the reader can independently judge their credibility, as far as is possible.

The study reported here was conducted over a period of two years, with follow up visits one year and two years later. It involved ongoing iterations between data collection and analysis. Access to the organisation was gained through various channels and contacts. The researcher was given freedom to interview anyone he wished. At no point in the data collection process did the researcher express opinions, save where it was necessary to prompt interviewees. Data were collected from staff within the organisation in several ways. The first source was a series of unstructured interviews. Approximately 30 managers were interviewed, sometimes twice or more times at the researcher's request. These included head office executives and their advisors or assistants, senior line management and people in senior staff positions (finance and engineering). Interviews averaged one and a half hours in length and were spread over the period of the research. They were tape-recorded and transcribed. Secondly, access was granted to various internal meetings. Debates were observed and dialogue noted. Activities in these meetings were subsequently written up in abbreviated form. Thirdly, data were collected through casual conversations and by simply "being around".

As the project progressed, the data were repeatedly analysed. At first, it seemed that there was a real probability of drowning in the data. Transcripts and notes were accumulating rapidly and the material appeared to be incoherent. This is apparently a common feature of the initial stages of cultural research. But different ways of making sense of it all were explored and gradually a pattern began to emerge. At each stage emerging appreciations were checked against the next round of data in an attempt to confirm the researcher's understanding of the situation. This continued until such time as the subsequent data became predictable.

It may be useful to indicate the precise way in which the data were found to give a coherent picture. Ultimately, the analysis hinged on three dimensions: role (function) and level of hierarchy of the subject and time. Firstly, the data were categorized according to content and underlying values. Opinions, sentiments, interpretations, confusions and so forth in each interview transcript were noted. This was done without reference to the identity of the person who had been interviewed. The data collected at any one time seemed to fall naturally into distinct constellations or clusters (in the sense that groups of people expressed similar views). Attaching identity to the data, it transpired that these constellations corresponded broadly to interviewees' roles and positions in the hierarchy. Among those performing similar roles (functions) at a similar level in the hierarchy, there was a marked similarity of perspective. Perspectives differed, however, across roles and at different levels of the hierarchy.

These data were set up on a two-dimensional space with role on one axis and hierarchy on the other. This exercise was repeated on data collected at different times and found to give similar results, in the sense that the data again fell into role-hierarchy clusters. The specific content of the data differed over time, however. So, the twodimensional spaces were set out in chronological order. In effect, a third dimension was added to the space, representing elapsed time.

Studying the content of the data as one moved through time, it transpired that the opinions, sentiments and interpretations of each group were in fact evolving in a systematic way. In this three-dimensional space was a story of unfolding meanings in the organisation. This was indicative of the existence of different cultures in the organisation and some systematic underlying trajectory in the emergence of those cultures. In fact, during the data collection process, it became clear that new interviewees' views were predictable, given a knowledge of (a) the role (function) of the participant, (b) his or her position in the hierarchy and (c) the time of the interview. At this point, the data were analysed from a different perspective. Specifically, the level of analysis shifted from content to process. The data were re-examined to see if the process through which the new meanings were emerging was observable. Some key turning points were obvious in the data. There was a series of events and interactions through which the emergence of the new meaning structure could be traced.

The Organisation

The research was undertaken in a major railway company. The company is referred to here as ER10 ("Euro Rail"). It is and has been for some while, in public sector ownership. It is large by any standards, employing approximately 160,000 people. It has a distinguished history.

History and Traditions

ER has its origins in the great private-sector railway companies set up in the middle decades of the last century. These each built and operated a main line out of the capital city, i.e. radial routes and associated branch lines. The companies are legendary. They raised capital to fund their projects on an unprecedented scale. Their railways were built by world-famous engineers who pioneered emerging industrial technology, designing magnificent steam locomotives and tracks and bridges which the world admired. The railways were and are, a visible celebration of Victorian accomplishment.

These companies enjoyed a monopoly in the nation's transport well into this century. They had good relationships with successive governments. They paid consistent dividends and their shares were blue-chip stocks.

This monopoly position and government patronage, coupled with a remarkable continuity in the underlying nature of their operations, rendered them highly bureaucratic: rules and procedures were well defined, there were clear chains of command and formalized systems for managing operations. Their managements were conservative, cultivating a belief in the uniqueness of railway management and the wisdom of practices built up over many decades. Importantly, though, while established as commercial concerns and earning their founders a handsome return, these companies also embraced a spirit of public service, for the railway network provided a transport infrastructure much needed for the pursuit of trade and manufacturing and for social mobility. This notion of public service was significant in the managements' interpretations of the railways: they took the rough with the smooth. They were run by "railway men": engineers and operators who took pride in the professional management of the railway and its public service.

The railway companies were nationalized in the late 1940s. In many respects, this was of limited significance.

The nationalized railway consolidated the old management structure: it was organised by region, each representing one of the radial routes out of the capital city; and each still managed by a General Manager (the same title as before). An Executive Committee was established to oversee policy decisions and to interface with government.

This committee comprised the regional General Managers together with the Chief Executive of ER and various engineering chiefs. Management practices of the former railways survived intact. Furthermore, nationalization reinforced the public service orientation, for this was the era of the Welfare State. Public-sector ownership established the railway as a social service. Its prime purpose was to provide a transport infrastructure. Profitability was secondary.

This interpretation of the railway remained dominant among senior managers for thirty years or more. Post-nationalization governments, faced with deficits and huge investment sums required for modernization, frequently sought to contain the costs of maintaining this infrastructure.

Following a fundamental review in the 1960s many branch lines were closed. Later, during the 1970s, the government imposed investment ceilings and set out expectations for the maximum level of its support.

But, although now tempered with a concern for thrift and the avoidance of waste, old traditions endured. Financial deficits continued. ER remained a bureaucratic organisation with a heritage of railway engineering and public service.

The railways were still run for practical purposes by regional General Managers, each one of these standing in a direct line of descent from a founding pioneer. They occupied the same grand offices. There were portraits of previous incumbents on their walls. They were, very consciously, carrying on a tradition of professional railway management.

This was the reality of the dominant "railway culture". The railway was a public service. The purpose of the railway was to run trains. In so doing profitability was secondary. The accepted professional concerns were to do with railway engineering and the logistical problems of operating trains. And although the "golden age" of steam had passed, new electrical and electronic technologies still offered scope for railway people to further their engineering heritage.

The Emergence of the Economic Perspective

In a profound sense, nationalization thirty years before had created a relationship of dependence for the railways, a dependence on government for sustenance. In the early 1980s the implications of this became clear.

Government policy became stringent. Social aims ceased to be a legitimate criterion for support. Government sought to impose harsh economic disciplines in all areas of public and private endeavour. Declaring a determination to "take on" the public services in particular, it orchestrated a campaign challenging the competence of publicsector management. For the railway, government "expectations" were translated into more specific financial "objectives". These were progressively tightened. Investment funds were withheld. Reporting escalating losses, ER found itself in a malign, resource constrained environment.

We need, for a moment, to backtrack. Apparently, in the late 1970s, the Chief Executive of the railway had set up a strategy think-tank to improve long-term planning.16 Embryonic ideas developed there and subsequently nurtured by a small group of executives, were now rolled out for more general consideration. Senior managers, by this time fully appreciative of the real hostility of government and the precarious position of the railway, fastened onto the ideas as a solution to the current problems.

The organisation, through the Executive Committee, created new management positions. For the first time, "Business Managers" were appointed. For analytical purposes (only), railway operations were broken down into market sectors: for example, long distance passenger traffic, short distance passenger traffic, freight, parcels and postal traffic.

Business Managers were assigned responsibility for developing strategies to enhance financial performance in each sector – in effect to manage the "bottom line(s)". These people were appointed outside the main line-management hierarchy of the railway. They were long-range planning people in staff positions at the Head Office, with no formal control or authority over railway operations. In fact, their initial responsibilities were thought to be confined to the identification of market-related initiatives. The Business Managers reported to the Chief Executive and joined the Executive Committee. But the regional management hierarchies remained intact. Regional General Managers, carrying on the old traditions, continued to run the railway.

The appointment of BusinessManagers was to have far reaching consequences, however, for it introduced a new "business" culture, a counter-culture. They brought a different interpretation of reality. For them the railway was a business, its purpose was to make profit. Engineering and logistical operations were essentially a means for extracting revenues from customers. Professional management was about making the railway profitable.

Business Managers were appointed without staff or support at the margins of the organisation. But during the course of the study, they gained influence at the expense of the regional General Managers. They persuaded many around them of their idea of a business railway. Gradually, people converted to the "business culture". Others left the organisation. The nature of dialogue and debate changed. Appeals to the old traditions of railway excellence and public service were repudiated. New kinds of policy decisions emerged, motivated by the business logic. Operational activities out in the regions began to be informed by the new rationale.

Now, the old world view, the preoccupation with engineering and logistics, the belief in the railway as a social service, the railway culture, has been substantially displaced by the business perspective, the belief that railways should be instrumental in making profit and managed to that end. The counter-culture has emerged to become the dominant-culture among the senior management. Traditions established over longer than a century were quickly overthrown.

Tracing the Dynamics of Change

The story is one of evolving interpretations, meanings and perceived possibilities. No one in the organisation foresaw the outcome at the start, not even the Business Managers. At first, their "business culture" was vague and indistinct, a kind of abstract generality. But as events unfolded, it became more specific. Possibilities for coupling their business reality to organisational action were perceived. Gradually, as people elaborated the new logic for organised activity, momentum was created. Capturing the emergent nature of these developments, one senior manager described the experience as "a voyage of discovery and development".

Firstly, it considers the context surrounding the appointment of Business Managers. Then it outlines the crafting of new accounting systems. Subsequently, it traces the process through which the new accounting was coupled to organisational activities and endowed with meaning. Finally, it gives an account of the regional General Managers' perspective in these events.

People and Context

The context of the Business Managers' appointments in ER is important in appreciating the trajectory of events. The railway was under acute threat. The competence of public-sector management was openly under challenge. The railway was charged with being "old fashioned". Governmental pressures for profitability were onerous and sanctions were being applied.

These threats were clearly appreciated by senior management. The railway has always prided itself on being modern in its technological activities. The charge of being "old-fashioned" in its management practice was deeply challenging. Moreover, there was some recognition that the old traditions were not, in themselves, proving sufficient to manage the threats away and needed to be supplemented in some way. The skills the Business Managers brought, marketing, long-term planning, "bottom line" management, had an image of modernity, enabling the railway to throw off the charge of being "old-fashioned" and were thought to be a useful supplementation of the railway traditions. Moreover, they were thought to be unintrusive, a "grafting-on" to the old traditions. The Business Managers had no operational authority. They were "back office" planning people. Their roles were defined through a remote accounting construct, the "bottom line", outside the prevailing mainstream understanding of railway activities. In bringing new knowledge to bear to cope with environmental pressures, theywere not expected to disrupt the railway or existing patterns of authority. Senior managers commented:

Everything has its time. You've got to realize the environment of the (transport) industry. We're now in the most competitive environment the railway has ever faced. And there were clear objectives emerging from the Government. These things made people think differently.... It's all in the market place in the end and how to exploit the market place. The traditional railway wasn't sensitive to the market place (Senior Executive).

We were weak in marketing and business issues generally. The government targets were stiff. We needed those skills (General Manager). Equally important are the personalities and backgrounds of the Business Managers. While they had all at some time worked in or with the railway, practically all had also worked outside. Thus, while they understood the railway culture and could talk railway talk, they also appreciated what they saw as wider business practice: "managing for profit". Furthermore, thesemen became evangelists, hungry people with a mission. They developed a zeal to convert the railway from a social service to a business enterprise.

In addition, the nature of their appointments was rather unusual (at least for a mechanistic organisation). There were no briefs or manuals. Ultimate intentions were not articulated. Business Managers were just told to see what they could do. We introduced it in an evolutionary way. We said: "Let's appoint Business Managers and then let it evolve. Be patient and let it evolve" (Senior Executive). When the Chief Executive introduced the Business Managers he didn't have any idea how to take the concept forward. I think he deliberately chose people who would win the day and left them to get on with it. It was up to each of us to build our influence. The regional General Managers had great centres of power: buildings and armies of people. They were the Gods on high, the last remnants of the Railway Companies. He wanted to stand back from it all and see what would happen (Business Manager).

They had, at best, a vague job description, one which they could legitimately expand. Subsequent events were not independent of changes in the social and political climate during the decade. It was one dominated by economic liberalism: deregulation in many spheres of activity, privatization of state owned enterprises and a sea change in attitudes towards the public services and the Welfare State.

These substantive effects were to come later, but there was already a clear "idealization" by government of private sector management practices and a belief that they could be introduced in the public sector. (Industrialists were rationalizing "old fashioned" work routines in the Civil Service, for example.) There was also a stated political agenda to subject the public services to "market disciplines" wherever possible.

Evolutionary Change and Organisational Acclimatization

The railway has long traditions and consensually accepted preoccupations. At first, the Business Managers could only see limited opportunities for coupling their concept to day-to-day activities. But as events unfolded, tentative new possibilities were perceived. Stage-by-stage, as if in episodes, their abstract notion of the business railway became more concrete.

The railway is a very formal organisation. People in it describe the management process in bureaucratic analogies, talking of "chains-of-command" and "good old soldiers falling into line". In meetings, people are often referred to through their official titles.

There is much deference to authority. The Business Managers recognized the significance of this formal management style in their quest to convert the railway.

In fact they worked through it. As their ideas evolved, in each episode they sought first to persuade the Chief Executive and his advisors.

These people were likely to be the most sympathetic to their economic rhetoric, for they interfaced with government and felt the external pressures most immediately. Carefully negotiating in principle a course of action, often after much private and closed debate, then, sure of their support, the Business Managers set out to convert a wider group.

Each episode involved a fairly small incremental step. None, in isolation, was especially threatening or difficult to accommodate in the old railway culture. Indeed, at first, even those who ultimately stood to lose influence and status appreciated the blending of the business perspective into the railway culture. As the organisation became acclimatized to each change, however, as each episode had a chance to "soak", so new possibilities were perceived. Repeatedly, new episodes were enacted.

Commenting on the way in which they operated, a Business Manager reflected: In the early days, there was nothing in writing, except that we had a responsibility for improving the bottom line. There were no organisation charts. This made life difficult. It was all about relationships.

We had to persuade everyone around us... As we did so, our ideas evolved. We became increasingly aware of the potential of the Businesses. Senior Executives recalled: Our ideas were constrained because we were... well I was going to say traditional railwaymen. We were coloured by the views of the complexity of running a railway. No one foresaw the present state as a possibility.

Our minds were opened. It takes time to change an organisation like the railways and to change attitudes. There's 150 years' history. You don't overturn that lightly. Nor would you want to, or the railways would cease to operate... The Business Managers recognized that. First, they convinced a small group, then gradually widened that group until everyone was aboard... They operated in stages... Incremental changes were easier to sell. It was easier to build commitment and minimize opposition from those who stood to lose... They took each stage to the limit.

Creating an Alternative Account

For the Business Managers the purpose of the railway was to make a profit. The significance of customers was revenues; the significance of operations, that is, trains, infrastructure and staff, was cost. Upon their appointment, however, there was no account of the railway's activities in each market sector consistent with their reality.

While profit or loss was measured for the organisation as a whole and was used in dealings with government, no such measures existed for component parts of the railway. In fact, during the 1970s, primarily for analytical purposes (rather than for responsibility accounting), the railway had moved towards a system of contribution accounting, matching directly traceable costs to revenues for various market segments. Common costs were not allocated to the segments. The railway is a remarkably integrated activity, with common staff, infrastructure and, to some extent, train-related activities, so these unallocated costs were very substantial. Senior accounting executives had long argued, both privately and publicly, that allocation was neither possible nor meaningful. Fundamental to the Business Managers' appointments, however, was not just a profit-contribution responsibility, but a "bottom line" responsibility and this called for the allocation of common costs. In a definite way, this "bottom line" responsibility had a normative symbolism – private sector managers were concerned with the "bottom line". But there was a more practical logic: this was to ensure that one or other of the Business Managers would be responsible for all costs and motivated, as events unfolded, to ask questions about the necessity and consequences of incurring cost. A Senior Executive commented:

You appoint a Business Manager and say: "We believe this is freight". The first thing he says is: "What's mine? What are the boundaries of my business?" Then he pursues questions such as: "How are costs being allocated to me? I want to know more about it. Let me analyse and fillet all the cost you are suggesting is mine"... Then he asks: "How do these costs relate to my revenues".

An individual within the accounting department was appointed to develop profit or loss measures by business sector. This person was in rather an invidious position.

Given senior finance officials' former public repudiation of the possibility of developing these measures, he had to tread carefully. He later recalled: At first I was not convinced that it was either sensible or feasible.

There's a whole history of avoiding cost allocations in the railway. But if the Business Managers were to take responsibility, they needed different Management Accounting. I was persuaded of this new way to run the railway. I wanted

Finance to play a fundamental part in supporting it. When was appointed I spent several months bouncing ideas offwalls – walls not people – because finance people didn't believe you could or should develop the information they needed. He became involved in intensive discussions with the Business Managers and with representatives of the Chief Executive's office. Different ways of apportioning costs were discussed and a firm of accountants consulted. The guiding principle was "cost exhaustion" – all costs incurred by the railway had somehow to be attributed to one or more of the businesses.

The precise details of the method of arriving at the profit or loss for each business are unimportant here. It suffices to say that it was founded on principles reflecting the primacy of use of resources and that the development of computer systems to operationalize the principle in full took some while. The significant point is that these measures were introduced, manually at first and that they were fundamental to the emergence of the new culture.

Business Managers were appointed without any operational authority. Their positions were an abstract economic construct. They were made meaningful through the new accounting constructs. Moreover, the accounting measures provided a means through which they could later couple debate on operational and physical concerns to an economic calculus. Reflecting on the penetration of the new account of organisational activities, one Business Manager observed: It's my impression that the engineers and after all we are an engineering company, had no real understanding of what they were doing in terms of the "bottom line"... Now the engineers know what a "bottom line" specification really is and they can respond to it. One regional General Manager commented: I always behaved with the "bottom line" inmind. But the Business Managers took it further. They challenge to a much greater extent. Making the railway profitable is the real meaning of the Business. And another: I didn't realize the extent to which budgets would be challenged and challenged so vehemently.

Coupling Railway Activities to the New Account

At the head of the railway is the office of Chief Executive. Attached to this are various staff functions – Finance, Engineering Directorates and so forth. Reporting to the Chief Executive in a line-management relationship are the General Managers of the regions. Underneath these are the railway operations. Overlaid on this management structure are formal planning and decision-making systems of various kinds. The BusinessManagers were appointed in staff positions outside the formal linemanagement structure of the railway organisation. They wished to explore their reality with others. But, there was, at first, no formal context for them to interact with others. Neither did they have the formal status they perceived necessary to influence others. In a sequence of moves, they sought, first, to institutionalize their status and then to secure bases for participating in an increasing range of dialogue and debate.

Securing status. First they lobbied the Chief Executive and his advisors for a change in reporting relationships. If he was serious about the idea of marketing and business planning in the railway, they argued, then they had to have comparable status to the regional General Managers. After some considerable debate, a new management structure was introduced. The Chief Executive appointed two Joint

Managing Directors, one taking a responsibility for the regions – the operations side of the railway, the regional General Managers; the other taking a responsibility for planning and marketing – in effect, the Business Managers. In a symbolic sense, although not at first in practice, this gave the Business Managers parity with the regional General Managers. It also stood for the Chief Executive's acknowledgement of the legitimacy of the "business" reality, the reality of the railways being managed for profit. Commenting on the significance of this, one Business Manager observed:

The General Managers used to report directly to the Chief Executive. The joint Managing Directors gave us parity. Creating contexts for interaction. Later, in subsequent episodes, they lobbied for successive changes in the formal planning and decision-making systems. Changes, they argued at each juncture, were necessary to provide a balance to the overbearing influence of the regional General Managers and engineers. Over the period of the study, three changeswere forthcoming. Each change secured opened up possibilities for perceiving the potential of the next. Firstly, the corporate planning system was revised.

This dealt with longer-term matters. Formerly, regional General Managers prepared plans and presented them to the Executive Committee for ratification. The change gave Business Managers a formal input into the preparation of plans. In fact, the planning process became "business-led", with these managers setting financial and other objectives for the regions, the regions being required to identify actions to achieve those objectives. Next, capital expenditure approval procedures were amended.

Formerly, regional General Managers and engineering chiefs had significant autonomy in the approval of capital expenditures. The new system required expenditure proposals to be underwritten by one or more Business Managers and effectively gave them a right to veto if they thought the proposals were uneconomic. Finally, budgeting systems were revised.

Budgets emanating from each region were analysed by market sector. Business Managers became involved in their review. The significance of these changes is that, in the context of ER's formal management style, formal systems and procedures imply rights to participate in and influence decisions and actions. The Business Managers' participation in the operation of these systems gave them a context to interact with others and question the rationale underlying railway decisions. In meetings, they could be seen translating operational and engineering concerns into the new profit calculus, feeding their financial vocabulary back into the stream of discourse. Appealing to the "ideal" of the profit-conscious customer-oriented private sector manager, they challenged and sometimes ridiculed beliefs.

Thus, participation in the planning procedures enabled them to reinterpret longer-run engineering and operational initiatives in business terms: what does it mean for the customer? Will it improve journey times and punctuality? What implications does it raise in terms of costs and revenues? Their sponsorship of capital investments enabled them to ask: will it improve train reliability, eliminating the need for back up resources? Can the businesses afford it? What are the investment options?

The redesign of the budgeting system gave them opportunities to challenge the cost effectiveness and profit implications of operational issues like train routing, train scheduling and the programming of maintenance.

Moving from the remote concerns of long-term planning, through capital investments, to immediate issues of train scheduling and maintenance programming, they recast management debate into a language of the "bottom line".

Others began to take up their vocabulary. Railway matters gradually came to be discussed as financial matters. Furthermore, planning and budgeting activities began to assume a new significance. Formerly, they were introverted acts of cost containment. Now they came to symbolize the search for profit-maximizing opportunities. Commenting on the importance of these changes in formal systems, a Business Manager observed:

We had responsibility for improving the profitability of the railway. But it wasn't clear who was in control – I think there was some diffidence in spelling that out with the utmost clarity. We lobbied to get control of the planning process. Clarity has emerged, now that we have taken responsibility for planning and budgeting. That's become our power base. Over time, these changes cumulatively extended the opportunity for Business Managers to interact with engineers and operators far beyond their original remit. Through this interaction, their ideas became more specific. But they were still located in the Head Office. Accordingly, in a later episode, they set about extending their influence into the regional organisations. They appealed to the Chief Executive for the appointment of individuals to represent their interests within the regions. These Regional BusinessManagers, once appointed, carried the economic perspective deep into the regional organisations, carving underneath the regional General Managers and giving Business Managers a direct line of influence to operational activities. One commented:

People in the regions are used to doing things without asking. They find themselves subject to our scrutiny. I can take things up in a big way, if necessary and howl for their blood.

And commenting on their influence, an operations manager in the regions observed:

Five years ago it would have been revolutionary to challenge what an engineer wanted to spend money on. Now it happens frequently. Consolidating the emerging reality through symbolic events. Through interaction in meetings and elsewhere, many in the organisation began to understand the Business Managers' emerging reality. Most also found it appealing. The continual attacks on the competence of public sector managers had worn morale down. To be business-like was "good", it gave them pride and made the railway modern. Increasingly people came to share the normative symbolism of the "bottom line". But to a large extent this was uncoupled from their concrete day-to-day activities. Meaningful symbols relating to everyday tasks, events and recollections through which people could connect the business reality to their ongoing decisions and actions, were absent.

As the situation unfolded, this changed, however. In parallel with the formal changes, a sequence of important events was enacted. The Business Managers staged "contests" with the regional General Managers, forcing collisions between the railway culture and the business culture. As before, they worked through the bureaucratic structure of the railway. Focusing, in each episode, on a specific issue demonstrative of their concerns, they sought first to persuade the Chief Executive and his advisors. Once sure of this group's support they set out to convert a wider group. Finally, they forced the issue for resolution. Again, each issue resolved opened up the possibility of the next. Three events stand out. They are reported in sequence.

The first concerned the disposition of locomotives and rolling stock. Over a period of time, one regional General Manager had been successful in acquiring resources to invest in high speed trains for passenger transport. These he zealously guarded against suggestions from other regional General Managers that they should be more widely dispersed on the railway network. The relevant Business Manager's analysis suggested that this situation was uneconomic. Profit could be improved by relocating some of these train sets to other regions. This Business Manager lobbied the Chief Executive and his advisors to have the location decision determined by economic criteria.

This was supported and the trains were moved. Commenting on this event, the relevant Business Manager observed: Regional prejudices had stopped the movement of high speed trains to the areas where they could earn the most money.

The General Managers were barons. You just didn't go into their territory. It was a sort of unwritten law. I got those trains moved early on, it was one of the first things I did.

A second event concerned capital investments. In this case, a major track was being upgraded to take faster trains. According to engineering precedent, it was usual to renew signalling equipment at the same time. The Business Manager's analysis indicated that this was neither necessary nor economic. Again, the Chief Executive was lobbied. The signalling was not renewed. As the Business Manager observed:

The main line was being electrified at significant expense. When wires are being strung over the track, it is customary to renew signalling equipment at the same time. We can't afford it. Anyway, the existing signalling will last another 15 years. All we needed to do was immunize the signals for electrification. The General Manager and his engineers were horrified. "This isn't the way to run a railway", they said. "It's a cash flow decision". A third decision concerned the scheduling of trains. Note that this is getting down to operational and logistical detail, by any standards the province of professional railway operators.

Traditionally, train schedules had been set to maximize operational convenience. For the sake of passenger convenience, a Business Manager wanted to alter the schedule on a route. This intervention was bitterly resented by the regional General Managers. Even in this case, the Business Manager's judgement was supported by the Chief Executive. Traditionally, timetables have been set for operational convenience. I was dissatisfied and wanted to change the frequency of trains on the route.

The General Manager was determined not to have it. I took it to the Chief Executive. I said to the General Manager half an hour before the meeting: "I've got to win and will win, the writing's on the wall whether you like or not. I like you, why are you putting your head in a noose? Why don't you back off?". But he didn't (Business Manager). All these events came to have a significance way beyond the decisions themselves. Each stood for a whole class of decisions, signifying the primacy of the business reality in relation to those kinds of decisions.

The high speed train issue redefined all decisions concerning the location of locomotives and rolling stock as economic decisions. The signalling decision redefined all investment decisions as economic decisions. The scheduling decision established the economic nature of detailed operational issues.

These events coupled the business culture to concrete railway activities. They were widely celebrated in the organisation, both in public documents and in internal discussions and are recalled in explanations of the emergence of the business rationale for railway management. Cumulatively, they embrace almost all aspects of the railway. People used them to attribute a new meaning to their everyday activities.

Not all decisions went in the Business Managers' favour, though. Secure in their conversion of the majority of the senior management ′elite, the Business Managers sought to explore their new reality with those within the organisation. As already noted, representatives were appointed in regional offices: Regional Business Managers. At first, these individuals reported formally to the regional General Managers and were on their payroll. The Business Managers wanted to pay their salaries from their own budgets to avoid them having divided loyalties. Regional General Managers found this unacceptable.

Apparently the Business Managers acted too soon; they lost. But the momentum they had already established was too great and they came back to win support some weeks later. A Business Manager explained:

There was a famous breakfast meeting where I soundly lost. The organisation was not ready. But of course, one rises again. Later, we were on firmer ground. I raised the matter again and I won the votes of everyone. In the regions, a similar process of change seems to be being enacted. These individuals appear to be following a similar strategy, gaining contexts for interaction, persuading others of their views and staging contests. The "bottom line" for each business is now decomposed into subsidiary "bottom line" accounts. In regional meetings, these managers reinterpret dialogue and debate through the subsidiary accounts. A sequence of new symbolic events is being enacted in each region. Commenting on his experiences, one Regional Business Manager observed: At first we had to stand out there in front battling on our own. But now it's like a tide coming in. Nobody can actually fight the tide. I'm coming in on a surfboard really.

The picture then, is one of sequencing, momentum and cumulation. The Business Managers started on their mission with a vague concept of a business railway. They secured increasing contexts for interaction. Their ideas gradually became more concrete and they persuaded others around them. In an episodic manner, moving from the general to the particular, they secured changes to reporting relationships and systems. Each episode was punctuated by a key event. These events became symbols of the business culture, endowing railway activities with a new meaning and provided a basis for continual and cumulative reinterpretations of railway operations.

Of course, there was tension. These decisions challenged the status of the regional General Managers and others who still subscribed to old beliefs. There was resentment and hostility. But the Business Managers let each step "soak" so the organisation could acclimatize, before embarking on the next episode and a majority of the senior management gradually converted to the "business culture". Appealing to another metaphor, a Senior Executive commented: We've lit a bonfire and it's burning like mad.

The Regional General Managers' perspective

Regional General Managers were steeped in tradition. They were the descendants of the railway pioneers, the bastions of the railway culture. The business culture struck at their values and beliefs. When asked why and how they had let these things happen, they responded:

It wasn't obvious at the time. The Business Managers were planners. We didn't expect the railway operations to change (General Manager). One quoted from a memo he had written to his staff immediately after the Executive Committee meeting which had approved the principle of the Business Managers' appointment:

The respective roles of Headquarters and the Regions will not change... Policies, as now will evolve from discussions. The Regions will participate... In fact, from the General Managers' perspective, the story is one of initial seduction, followed by surprise and ambivalence, defection and resignation. They were aware of external pressures for financial performance. Some thought it was a whim and would pass. But most perceived a need for a business perspective and supported the creation of the Business Managers' positions in the Executive Committee. When the Business Managers were appointed, most welcomed their influence. At an early stage, one General Manager commented:

This is good for us. I'm quite pleased at the way the culture is changing. You talk around now and nobody is in any doubt that the railway is business-led. And another, commenting on the decision to relocate the high speed trains: Why do we have fancy train sets? It's not for General Managers to play trains. It's to make the businesses more profitable. One joined the Senior Executives, representing the Business Managers. According to his critics, he is reputed to have seen "which way the wind was blowing", but he himself described it thus:

Initially I was opposed. But I saw the logic of the changes. I was converted. Thus, most found the abstract normative symbolism of the "bottom line" appealing. They thought it "good" to be more business-like. They aspired to "private sector practice". Few perceived the underlying momentum of events or their potential significance. Acting out the new rationale, they thought they need have no fear for the railway traditions. In fact, sitting in their grand offices with portraits and plaques around their walls and other symbols of former grandeur, it was inconceivable to them that the railway traditions could be undermined by anything.

As the significance of the economic reality emerged through subsequent events, however, the situation became less congenial for them. It threatened their pride as professional railway operators. Commenting on the resignalling decision noted earlier, a General Manager said:

We'll have to do it all again in 15 years' time. It's not a sensible longterm decision. Furthermore, the appointment of Regional Business Managers within their own organisations undermined their authority.

At this point, they protested vigorously. This prompted a report from the centre discussing the relationship between Businesses and the Regions. The report placated them with the soothing idea of Business Managers and regional General Managers as equals in a team-based organisation. Nevertheless, the business perspective continued to impinge on operational matters.

Many General Managers became unhappy. They thought the emerging decisions unprofessional and feared for the quality of the railway. By this time, however, their appeals fell on deaf ears. Most others among the senior management ´elite had converted to the business culture. The General Managers were characterized as reactionary, protective and old-fashioned. Towards the end of the study, most of them left the organisation or took "early retirement". One stayed in office a while longer. Shortly before his retirement he had this to say:

With the benefit of hindsight, I think the Chief Executive was right in allowing it through... But it's gone too far... While I've been in office, through good engineering management, I've just about managed to get rid of all the speed restrictions on the main line. Business Managers are taking a maintenance holiday [i.e. neglecting maintenance]. In five years someone will be faced with exactly the situation I inherited.

Former regional General Managers have been replaced with sympathetic men. They repudiate the old traditions. They are proud to subscribe to the business culture. A newly appointed General Manager had this to say: I personally feel that this new approach is right. I support the businesses.

I see it as my job to influence my current staff to accept the business managers. Far from being equals in a team, the regional General Managers are seen to be subservient to Business Managers.

"Business managers set policy and standards; regions implement". Career patterns have changed. To become a regional General Manager was the ultimate aspiration for a railway-man; by the end of the field research it was to become a Business Manager. There was open discussion of removing the regional General Managers from Railway Executive.

Accounting and Culture

Initially, there was a dominant "railway" culture. The Business Managers brought a counter "business" culture. This cascaded across the senior management ´elite to become dominant. The Business Managers had an abstract idea of a business railway. New accounts were crafted representing the railway as a series of businesses. The Business Managers gained contexts to interact with others. In these contexts, they recast dialogue and debate from a railway language of operations and engineering to their business language of markets and profit. Gradually the idea of a business railway became more specific. Moving from remote concerns to immediate issues, they persuaded others of their interpretations. There were contests over the definition of specific activities. The outcomes became symbols through which people attributed new meaning to railway operations. Momentum built up behind the business culture. People converted, others left. For senior managers, the abstract idea became a tangible, energizing reality, a source of pride. Now the railway culture is repudiated.

A broad range of theories can be brought to bear to interpret the pattern of these events. Fundamental to this account is the notion of culture as a system of ideas: beliefs, knowledges and values in which action and artifacts are vested with expressive qualities; and the idea that organisations have distinctive cultures. This is exemplified in the contrasting "railway" and "business" cultures described. Associated with this is the conceptualization of organisational change as a process of uncoupling and recoupling: exemplified in the railway by the uncoupling of activities from the railway culture and their recoupling to the business culture. We can also see 20 This characterization, of course, emphasizes change; and there is also a sense in which there is continuity. The railway still runs trains, it still provides a transport infrastructure (of sorts) and a theory of inertia in operation, change being precipitated by crisis.

The railway culture was remarkably resilient over many previous decades, despite several attacks; real threats only being perceived when the severity of the current onslaught on the public services became apparent. There are also traces of the "garbage can": the Business Management idea was developed independently of the crisis, only subsequently coupled to the threats facing the organisation.

Continuing, change was emergent. This was not a controlled process, relying on plans and rational analyses engineered by those standing outside, untainted as it were; the whole management group was bound up in the creation of the business culture. The process unfolded through tentative initiatives, buffeted by the timing of events, the ambition and (relative) political skills of the "champions" and other actors involved and their failures and successes. Nor were the vagaries of chance unimportant. Moreover, we see changes in systems (planning, capital investment, budgeting) interpenetrating the emergence and elaboration of the business culture.

It also is possible to appeal to the insights of institutional theory. Government, the railway's key environmental constituency, was intolerant of (what it saw as) managerial incompetence. The Business Management initiative could be interpreted as a symbol of the railway becoming more modern and business-like: the "bottom line" idea standing for the railway adopting private sector practices. Such solutions may have real and unintended internal consequences, however. One was the Business Managers amassing power and influence at the expense of the General Managers. Although a theoretically impoverished theory in this context, there is some link here with the strategic contingencies' perspective of intraorganisational power. Subsequent to the appointment of the Business Managers, the railway managed to persuade government to make funds available, on a one-off basis, for a major electrification project (giving rise to the signalling controversy discussed earlier). Apparently, approval was forthcoming as a result of the "rigourous business case" orchestrated by the relevant Business Manager.

The purpose here is not to discuss these theories further, however. It is to develop a cultural appreciation of accounting. The study shows that accounting was implicated differently in the two cultures described. At this point, it is appropriate to explicate its linkages to underlying knowledge, values and beliefs. A cultural system incorporates, among other things, knowledge about environments and strategies for extracting subsistence from them.

This knowledge is quite different in the two cultures. In the railway culture it revolved around the public service idea, later coupled to notions of thrift. Essentially, the knowledge was this: if the organisation provided the nation with a transport infrastructure (without undue waste), then sustenance would be forthcoming from government. This knowledge is not unique to the railway culture. The expectation that low-cost, generally available services will be rewarded by the state is common to many public service organisations in Europe, for example the health and education services. Given this knowledge, accounting was incidental in the railway culture: it was necessary to ensure that revenues were accounted for and suppliers paid and perhaps to contain waste, but that was the limit of its significance in the structures of meaning. The purpose of the railway was to run trains; operating the railway would be rewarded by government. In this knowledge, the train, therefore, was endowed with a special significance.

The business culture, revolving around the "bottom line", incorporates a quite different knowledge. Rather obviously, in view of events in ER, the bottom line constructs the notion of the railway as a profit-seeking enterprise. This is not just a matter of "cost efficiency", however, although that is important. More importantly, in ER it constructs the idea of looking to product markets, rather than to government, for sustenance. There is nothing somehow uniquely "public service" about the railway network in this construction. Rail transport is a product (or service), to be bought and sold like any other; in fact it is a series of products: intercity travel, freight, suburban commuting, etc. Revenues from these products, rather than government support, must cover costs; and, critically, revenues are earned in the market place. Survival depends on extracting resources from these markets, perhaps in competition with other firms. Hence the new-found concern for competition with other means of transport (road, air, buses), expressed by railway managers early in the account above, a concern which in the railway culture would have been probably inconsequential. Given this knowledge, accounting activities become hugely significant. The search for profit opportunities and the elimination of non-profit-making activities, is a quest for survival. It is now the customer, not the train, which has special importance.

No culture is completely coherent, of course. Each has ambiguities and contradictions. In ER, residues of the past create tensions. One is the partial incompatibility of the business culture with the restrictions placed on it by state ownership. ER is not allowed to borrow in financial markets to fund investment, for example and as government funds are tight, this means investments necessary for competitive purposes cannot always be made. It also has statutory obligations to keep certain branch lines open, even if they are unprofitable. Here it still looks to government for support (although a government conceptualized as a customer). Nevertheless, the underlying knowledge systems are quite different and constitute different realities.

This shift in knowledge which accounting helps to construct, the shift from looking to the state for subsistence to looking to markets, is fundamental and it interpenetrates the operation and management of ER's core technology with pervasive effects. For a start, it changes the appropriate form of organisation. In the old knowledge, the prime task was the operation of trains. The meaningful management structure was one which facilitated operations. The physical facilities of the railway are geographically laid out along the radial routes of the old prenationalization companies. Thus the appropriate management organisation was around these routes, i.e. the regional management structures. The regional General Managers and engineers, because of their acknowledged expertise in operating trains, were afforded substantial status and influence.

Now, in the new knowledge, this is "mere" production, subservient to markets. The prime task is serving markets. The meaningful form of management organisation is one which reflects and confronts markets. Since the long distance intercity travel market is not confined to one main line, for example, or the freight market confined to one region, the regional and business forms of organisation do not map perfectly onto one another. Hence the reorientation of management structures and systems around the Business Managers and their subsequent elaboration through the Business Manager's subordinates located in the regions.

Of course, there is still an operational task to be performed: trains, tracks, maintenance and so forth. But in this new knowledge it is Business Managers, with supposed expertise in markets and extracting resources from them, who attract status and influence. The changing knowledge also redefines the appropriate form of action. In the old knowledge, that of the celebration of the train, there were norms that made things intrinsically necessary.

"Of course" professional railwaymen renewed signaling equipment when they electrified the track, for example; it was inconceivable not to do so. The train needs to be taken care of and nurtured. The interest in thrift, the avoidance of waste, also meant the elimination of activities not strictly necessary for the operation of trains: training staff to smile at customers, for example.

In the new knowledge, activities are neither intrinsically necessary, nor intrinsically wasteful. Rather they are judged for their consequences in the market. Through the "bottom line", activities become desirable to the extent that they add more "value" than they cost. This is not simply cost minimization: the avoidance of unnecessary gold-plating. The "bottom line engineering specification", mentioned earlier, means designing for the market, as it were: adding comfort, reliability, speed, customer service where its returns outweigh its cost. Attractive concourse design is not wasteful extravagance, it is reinterpreted as a "good" thing which brings in custom.

Action is also judged against a different concept of time. In the old knowledge, time was practically infinite. The railways were built to last for decades, for centuries. The nation would always need a transport infrastructure. Professional standards were oriented towards doing a long-lasting thorough job. Government would reward the railway for maintaining the viability of the network into the future. In the new knowledge, the concept of time is much shorter. Survival is a day-to-day affair. Markets are ephemeral. Don't spend money now on activities that you can put off until the future. Take "maintenance holidays" where you can: deterioration of the infrastructure can be remedied later.

The point being made here is that accounting can play a significant role in constructing specific knowledges. Accounting systems embody particular assumptions about rationality, organisation, authority, time and so forth. If these permeate into underlying values, knowledges and beliefs they can have very real consequences. Above we see accounting coming in to the organisation to construct a new theory of subsistence, which in turn implies particular modes of organising, patterns of influence and authority, criteria for action and a new concept of time.

The cultural knowledge described here was not discovered completely formed. Nor was it coupled to the railway's management structures (or to action) in an instant. Rather the meaning of the bottom line gradually crystallized around the initial accounts and the coupling had to be actively crafted. The business culture unfolded in episodes: bursts of exhausting creativity, each building on what had previously been accomplished and punctuated by a concluding event; followed by a pause for consolidation, recovery and imagination before the next. Successive episodes moved from the abstract realm to the particular; from long-term issues to immediate issues. In each, senior management struggled to reconceptualize a class of activities; then it was uncoupled, or perhaps one should say wrenched, from the railway culture and recoupled to the business culture. Again and again these episodes continued, until cumulatively practically all classes of railway activity were redefined. Later, in the regions, a similar process of episodic uncoupling and recoupling was enacted. In the process, linkages to the railway culture were only bit-by-bit ruptured.

The general point arising is that organisations have different classes of activity. Cultural change is not simply uncoupling and recoupling, or even reconceptualization. Each class of activity may need to be separately uncoupled and recoupled. During the process, different classes of activity may be informed by different rationales and knowledge. In ER, this led to a strange schizophrenia in the organisation (and difficulties in making sense of the data), in which some activities were railway-culture issues and some business-culture issues. It also led to strange disjunctures between the interpretive schemes brought to bear in the head office and in the regions. Only towards the end of the research did this schizophrenia begin to be resolved.

This process, however, needs to be enveloped in an awareness of the conditions for its possibility, conditions for the emergence of the particular culture described. In some ways, perhaps, the business culture in ER may be seen to be inevitable. Today, the belief in markets (as an optimal form of organisation) seems to be firmly entrenched in Anglo-American political cultures and in those of some continental-European states. Governmental pressures, inevitably, in this view, led to investment in financial calculation and the construction of the railway as a business enterprise. Support for this "theory of inevitability" might be sought by retrospective application of the present political determination to privatize ER, or at least some of its businesses.

As Fligstein notes, in a rather different critique, such an interpretation relies on understandings of the present to construct appreciations of the past: interpreting the past through the present, rather than the present through the past. ER had a remarkably strong heritage which survived previous attacks.

In the early 1980s, its privatization was not just undiscussed, it was inconceivable. Arguably, the business culture in ER, the reconstruction of the railway through the "bottom line(s)" as a series of businesses, actually created preconditions for the discussion of privatization, not vice versa.

For sure, the early 1980s witnessed the beginnings of the sea change in attitudes towards the public services that swept across the political culture later in the decade. Through influential right-wing think-tanks the idea of subjecting public services to an entrepreneurial principle was then emerging, later to be manifested in the "rolling back" of the public sector through the privatization of many public utilities and attempts to introduce market mechanisms in others. Associated with this was the emerging idea of the "dependence" culture and its repudiation; to be replaced by an "enterprise" culture. Individuals and organisations, were expected to take a responsibility for their own destiny.

However, the initiative for business management in ER, conceived in the late 1970s, preceded these political developments and appears to have been a substantially autonomous development in a separate arena: as one of the initiators in the senior management group explained, it was "the product of thinking railwaymen". But such evidence as is available supports the view that the initiative was developed largely independently of political ideas, its private sector leanings probably owing more to the advice of a few business consultants than to any political agenda.Certainly it was not government-inspired; indeed government was initially sceptical, only later endorsing the ideas (and applying them to its own ends).

That said, the initiative was congruent with the ideas emerging outside and its subsequent elaboration into the business culture undoubtedly owes much to their development. Even here, though, due importance must be attached to the specific circumstances within the organisation.

Public sector management was under challenge, morale was low.Many in the senior management group were receptive to the new ideas. Business Management was seen as a home-grown solution to governmental attack.

It expressed some kind of empowerment, a potential freedom from the yoke of government restriction and an opportunity for managers to show their entrepreneurial capabilities.

Bibliography

Alexander, D. and Nobes, C.: *Financial Accounting: An International Introduction,* Financial Times/Prentice Hall, Harlow, 2001.

Ansoff, H. I.: *The New Corporate Strategy,* JohnWiley & Sons, NewYork, 1988.

Anthony, R. N.: *Planning and Control Systems: A Framework for Analysis,* Harvard Business School Press, Boston, MA, 1965.

Bardsley, N., Cubitt: *Assessing Experimental Economics,* Princeton University Press, Princeton, 2009.

Beaver, W. H.: *Financial Reporting: An Accounting Revolution,* Prentice Hall, Englewood Cliffs, 1981.

Beaver, W. H.: *Financial Reporting: An Accounting Revolution,* Prentice Hall, Englewood Cliffs, 1981.

Caplin, A. and Schotter, A.: *The Foundations of Positive and Normative Economics,* Oxford University Press, New York, 2008.

Carpenter, P.: *Ebrands: Building an Internet Business at Breakneck Speed,* Harvard Business School Press, UK, 2000.

Carr, N. G., Editor: *Digital Enterprise: How to Reshape Your Business For a Connected World,* Harvard Business School Press, 2001.

Dalton, John M.: *How The Stock Market Works,* Prentice Hall Press, New York Institute of Finance, 1988.

Dimson, Elroy: *Stock Market Anomalies,* Cambridge University Press, Cambridge, 1988.

Downs, A.: *Inside Bureaucracy,* Little, Brown and Company, Boston, MA, 1966.

Emmanuel, C., Otley, D. and Merchant, K.: *Accounting for Management Control,* Chapman & Hall, London, 1990.

Farmer, Mayuri J.: *An Accounting Evaluation of Performance of Indian Public Sector Banks,* Shanti Prakashan, Delhi, 2003.

Friedman, M.: *Capitalism and Freedom*, University of Chicago Press, Chicago, 1982.

Galbraith, J. R. and Nathanson, D. A.: *Strategy Implementation: The Role of Structure and Process*, West Publishing Company, St Paul, MN, 1976.

Goodman, Rae Jean B.: *An Assessment of Recent Changes and Proposals in S&L Taxation*, Federal Home Loan Bank Board, Washington, DC, 1983.

Hammer, M. and Champy, J.: *Reengineering the Corporation: A Manifesto for Business Revolution*, Nicholas Brealey Publishing, London, 1993.

Hobsbawm, E.: *The Age of Revolution: Europe 1789–1848*, Phoenix Press, London, 1962.

Jain, Sugan C.: *Accounting Reforms*, RBSA Pub, Delhi, 2006.

Jaiswal, Kripa S.: *Challenges of Accounting*, Adhyayan, Delhi, 2008.

Kane, Edward J.: *The Gathering Crisis in Federal Deposit Insurance,* The MIT Press, Cambridge, 1985.

Kumar, Ashvine and Shafali Sharma: *Book of Accounting Terms*, Vista International, Delhi, 2007.

Luca, Cornelius: *Trading in the Global Currency Markets,* Institute of Finance/ Prentice Hall Press, New York, 2000.

Nelson, Judy A.: *Feminism, Objectivity and Economics,* Routledge, London and New York, 1996.

Raj, Karan: *Advance Dictionary of Accounting*, Ivy Pub, Delhi, 2008.

Sarker, J.B.: *Accounting and Finance: Contemporary Issues,* Deep and Deep, Delhi, 2001.

Tan, Pearl and Peter Lee: *Advanced Financial Accounting*, Tata McGraw-Hill, Delhi, 2011.

Vatter, W. J.: *Managerial Accounting*, Prentice Hall, New York, NY, 1950.

Watts, R.L. and Zimmerman, J.L.: *Positive Accounting Theory,* Prentice Hall, Englewoods Cliffs, NJ, 1986.

Index

K

M

O

P

R

S

T

U

V

W

❑❑❑